W9-BVT-637

Critical Acclaim for Books by Gen and Kelly Tanabe

Authors of *Get Free Cash for College, The Ultimate Scholarship Book* and *How to Write a Winning Scholarship Essay*

"Upbeat, well-organized and engaging, this comprehensive tool is an exceptional investment for the college-bound."
—*Publishers Weekly*

"A present for anxious parents."
—Mary Kaye Ritz, *The Honolulu Advertiser*

"Helpful, well-organized guide, with copies of actual letters and essays and practical tips. A good resource for all students."
—*KLIATT*

"Upbeat tone and clear, practical advice."
—*Book News*

"Unlike other authors, the Tanabes use their experiences and those of other students to guide high school and college students and their parents through the scholarship and financial aid process."
—*Palo Alto Daily News*

"What's even better than all the top-notch tips is that the book is written in a cool, conversational way."
—*College Bound Magazine*

"A 'must' for any prospective college student."
—*Midwest Book Review*

"Invaluable information ranging from the elimination of admission myths to successfully tapping into scholarship funds."
—Leonard Banks, *The Journal Press*

"The Tanabes literally wrote the book on the topic."
—*Bull & Bear Financial Report*

"Offers advice on writing a good entrance essay, taking exams and applying for scholarships and other information on the college experience—start to finish."
—*Town & Country Magazine*

"Tanabe, an expert on the application process, can discuss such topics as how to get into the college of your choice, ways to finance your college education, applying online and what universities are looking for in a student."
—*Asbury Park Press*

"Filled with student-tested strategies."
—Pam Costa, *Santa Clara Vision*

"The first book to feature the strategies and stories of real students."
—*New Jersey Spectator Leader*

1001 Ways to Pay for College

Eighth Edition

Gen and Kelly Tanabe

Harvard graduates and award-winning authors of
*Get Free Cash for College, The Ultimate Scholarship
Book* and *How to Write a Winning Scholarship Essay*

1001 Ways to Pay for College (Seventh Edition)
By Gen and Kelly Tanabe
Published by SuperCollege, LLC
2713 Newlands Avenue, Belmont, CA 94002
650-618-2221
www.supercollege.com

Copyright © 2017 by SuperCollege, LLC. Previous editions © 2003, 2005, 2007, 2009, 2011, 2013, 2015.

All rights reserved. No part of this book may be reproduced, stored in a retrieval system or transmitted, in any form or by any means, electronic, mechanical, photocopying, recording or otherwise, without the written permission of SuperCollege. This book is protected under International and Pan-American Copyright Conventions.

Credits: Cover design by TLC Graphics, www.TLCGraphics.com. Design: Monica Thomas. Cover image © istockphoto.com/Alex Slobodkin. Illustrations by Terry Smith (www.t-smith. org). Back cover photograph by Alvin Gee (www.alvingee.com).

Trademarks: All brand names, product names and services used in this book are trademarks, registered trademarks or tradenames of their respective holders. SuperCollege is not associated with any college, university, product or vendor.

Disclaimers: The authors and publisher have used their best efforts in preparing this book. It is sold with the understanding that the authors and publisher are not rendering legal, accounting, investment, tax or other professional advice. The reader must seek the services of a qualified professional for such advice. The authors and publisher cannot be held responsible for any loss incurred as a result of specific financial, tax or investment planning decisions made by the reader. The authors and publisher make no representations or warranties with respect to the accuracy or completeness of the contents of the book and specifically disclaim any implied warranties or merchantability or fitness for a particular purpose. The accuracy and completeness of the information provided herein and the opinions stated herein are not guaranteed or warranted to produce any particular results. The authors and publisher specifically disclaim any responsibility for any liability, loss or risk, personal or otherwise, which is incurred as a consequence, directly or indirectly, of the use and application of any of the contents of this book.

ISBN 13: 978-1-61760-125-5

Manufactured in the United States of America
10 9 8 7 6 5 4 3 2 1

Library of Congress Cataloging-in-Publication Data
Tanabe, Gen S.
  1001 ways to pay for college : strategies to maximize financial aid, scholarships and grants / Gen Tanabe, Kelly Tanabe. -- Eighth edition.
      pages cm
  Summary: "A resource for collegebound students and their parents on college financial aid, scholarships, loans, and grants. Provides strategies for finding and winning scholarships, tax credits, asking for more financial aid, saving, student loan forgiveness, financial aid applications, state financial aid, military service, adult students, graduate students, and internships"-- Provided by publisher.
  ISBN 978-1-61760-125-5 (paperback)
  1. College costs--United States. 2. Student aid--United States. 3. Scholarships--United States. 4. Student loans--United States. I. Tanabe, Kelly Y. II. Title. III. Title: One thousand one ways to pay for college. IV. Title: One thousand and one ways to pay for college.
  LB2337.4.T357 2017
  378.3'80973--dc23
                              2014043186

CONTENTS AT A GLANCE

TABLE OF CONTENTS

Chapter 16: Make Your College Cheaper / 355

Chapter 17: Be a Dorm Room Entrepreneur / 373

This book is the culmination of more than 11 years of research and work. It has benefited from countless students, parents, financial aid officers and scholarship judges that we have met. Their insight and knowledge were invaluable.

We would like to dedicate this book to these people. And to you, our dear reader, we hope you will use the lessons in this book to make your college dreams possible.

ONE

The Many Ways To Pay For College

There's More Than One Way To Pay For College

The acceptance letter that you've been waiting for finally arrives. You tear it open and jump up and down with excitement—you've been accepted! All those months of hard work filling out applications and writing essays have paid off. You're ready to pack your bags and head for your future. There's just one thing stopping you.

The tuition bill.

When we got into college, we thought the only way to pay for it was from our (and our parents') own wallets. Unfortunately, we learned that these wallets weren't as fat as we imagined and so we were forced to look elsewhere. What we found amazed us. It turned out there were a lot of ways to pay for college besides from our own pocket.

We focused most of our energies on finding and winning scholarships. Together we won over $100,000 in scholarships, which went a long way toward paying for Harvard. Unfortunately, even that amount of money only covered half of what it would cost for four years of college. In addition to scholarships, we also turned to campus jobs, summer internships, tax breaks, asking the college for more money, creative

savings strategies and careful budgeting. It was through a combination of these efforts that we were able to ultimately graduate from Harvard debt-free.

Our experience was just one of 1,000 possible ways that enterprising students pay for college. From lucrative dorm room enterprises to taking advantage of loan repayment programs to volunteer work that pays for college, there are literally thousands of ways that you can make college affordable.

In this book we present what we consider to be the top 1001 ways to pay for college. In our experience, the reason most families feel so stressed about paying for school is not so much a lack of money but rather a lack of knowledge of the resources available. So in the following pages we present the best ways to pay for school. Some of the ways you may have heard of but never really understood, while others may be totally new.

We know that you'll learn a lot in this book, but we also hope that you'll be inspired by the options you discover. We want this book to jump-start your thinking and get you excited about taking advantage of the many opportunities that exist.

The majority of the strategies in this book are appropriate for all students. It doesn't matter if you're a high school student starting college, a college or graduate school student halfway done or an adult going back to school–you'll find strategies and ideas to help you pay for college. Of course, if you're a parent of a student and your wallet isn't as fat as your child imagines, then this book is for you, too.

Here are just a few examples of what you'll find inside. You'll learn how to:

- Find the best scholarships **#1**
- Double your scholarship dollars **#234**
- Win money from contests only open to students **#333**
- Find guaranteed scholarships **#380**
- Pay in-state tuition even if you are an out-of-state student **#384**
- Get rebates for college every time you shop **#386**
- Grow your money with a Coverdell Education Savings Account **#389**
- Maximize your 529 Savings Plan **#404**
- Prepay your education at today's prices with a pre-paid tuition plan **#408**
- Double your college savings with an Individual Development Account **#467**
- Invest strategically for college **#470**
- Claim your $2,500 American Opportunity tax credit **#482**
- Take advantage of your $2,000 Lifetime Learning credit **#484**

- Deduct student loan interest from your taxes #489
- Get the most financial aid you deserve #495
- Ask for more financial aid #539
- Safeguard your money from financial aid scams #546
- Get the state to pay for your education #557
- Select the best student loan #624
- Put your loan payments on hold #628
- Have your student loan forgiven #642
- Have the military pay for your education #705
- Save the money you already have #755
- Make your college cheaper #788
- Attend a tuition-free college #795
- Earn credit for life experiences #810
- Find two-for-one tuition deals #818
- Get tuition discounts with an alumni referral #821
- Launch your own dorm room enterprise #824
- Locate the most lucrative internships and campus jobs #866
- Go to school part-time #900

And much, much more!

The Right Psychology

The great Green Bay Packers football coach Vince Lombardi once said, "The difference between a successful person and others is not a lack of strength, not a lack of knowledge, but rather a lack of will."

We can arm you with all of the resources and knowledge that you need to pay for college. But we cannot provide you with the motivation to make it happen. Few people talk about the psychology that you need to pay for college. In interviewing thousands of students, we have noticed that along with the knowledge there is also a mental aspect. Paying for college is not easy but neither is anything else that is worth having. So to stay in the game you need to have the right frame of mind. Here are the characteristics that we found to be shared by the students who were able to successfully find ways to pay for college even though they had little or no money of their own:

Persistence. This is a key trait. You need to continue despite any setbacks that you may face. We applied to many scholarships that we didn't win, but we never let that prevent us from applying to the next one.

Creativity. Some of the most successful students we met adapted methods to pay for college to their own situation. In this book you'll learn all of the ways that you can pay for college. However, for your specific case you may need to be creative about how you apply a specific example to yourself.

Long-term vision. The struggle to pay for school is a marathon, not a sprint. It involves adding up little victories here and there throughout the time you are in college. Break down your challenge into smaller pieces, and take it one step at a time. Just like putting money in the bank, to reach your goal you need to start with one penny and then add another and another.

Faith. You need a little faith to play this game. This is not the lottery, and there are no immediate results. Filling out the FAFSA form to apply for financial aid is a lot of work, and the outcome is far from guaranteed. Have faith that what you are doing will pay off in the long run.

Just as we did, in your quest for money for college you'll have your fair share of successes and failures. Having the right mindset is what propels you forward toward your goal. Keep these psychological pointers in mind as you read through this book and especially when you start to put these ideas into action.

Whether you just need a few extra dollars or to foot your entire tuition bill, we're confident that the ideas that follow will inspire you to find ways to pay for your education. Your education is the most important investment that you'll make in yourself. It will set you up for a lifetime of success. Now let's look at the many ways that you can make this investment affordable.

Win A Scholarship

How To Find A Scholarship

The best money is free money, and there is no better free cash for college than scholarships. We personally used scholarships to pay for a significant part of our education. We started during our junior year in high school and didn't stop until we had graduated from college. In total, we won over $100,000 in scholarships. While this may seem like a lot we've met students who have won much more.

One student we know won over $2 million in scholarships. Of course, she couldn't use all of this money since it was more than the entire cost of her college. But what a problem to have! Too much free money! Another student we met was a senior in high school when he started applying for scholarships. By graduation he had applied to 95 scholarships. Of these he only won seven. However, these seven totaled more than $48,000. Not too shabby for only one year of work. And he can't wait to continue applying for scholarships once in college!

There are two important steps to finding a scholarship:

Step 1: Become an expert on what scholarships are available. How can you find something if you don't know what you're looking for? That's the situation many students find themselves in when starting their scholarship search. For example, did you know that many unions give scholarships to the children of members? If you didn't then you probably would never even think to ask your parents if they are members of a union. Or how about this one: Did you know that professional sports teams award scholarships that have nothing to do with athletics? If you didn't then you might have totally ignored looking for scholarships from your hometown major league baseball team.

The best way to learn what scholarships are available is to expose yourself to as many scholarships as possible—even if they are not ones you will apply to win. By doing this you will get a better idea of what is out there and it will jumpstart your thinking about where to look. We recommend that besides

---

> ## Finding the right scholarship is like ... looking for the perfect pair of pants
>
> Here's an analogy to help you see why choosing the right scholarships is critical to actually winning a scholarship. Imagine that you are looking for the perfect pair of jeans at an outlet store. If you run in and grab the first pair on the rack, chances are it won't fit. It will probably pinch or sag in all the wrong places. But if take spend your time to dig through the piles of clothes, search out the racks in the back of the store and try everything on before you buy you'll leave with the perfect pair.
>
> Finding a scholarship is no different. You need to know where to look and give yourself enough time to pick and choose from what you find. If you make sure that a scholarship fits your unique background, talents or achievements, you insure that you don't waste your time on scholarships you won't win. Just like pants, make sure the scholarship fits before you apply.

reading this chapter you also pick up a good scholarship directory such as our book, *The Ultimate Scholarship Book*, and start flipping through the pages. Even though there will be awards that you won't be eligible for, by exposing yourself to what is available you will start to make connections between your background, interests and future goals and various sources for free money.

Step 2: Search everywhere for scholarships that fit you. Too many students begin and end their scholarship search on the Internet. Then, after finding a bunch of awards they blindly fire off applications. What a terrible way to try to win. It will only result in a pile of rejection letters and even more frustration.

To maximize your chances of winning a scholarship you need to look everywhere—and that means getting out of your chair and looking beyond the Internet. Some of the best scholarships are found far from the beaten path. It takes more time and effort to find these scholarships but if you are willing to do some detective work you will be rewarded with a ton of scholarship opportunities.

The Golden Rule Of Searching For Scholarships

In this chapter we'll show you all of the places where you can find scholarships. As you start your own search, you'll undoubtedly turn up all kinds of awards—probably more than you'll ever have time to apply to. But don't stop looking. If there is one golden rule for finding a scholarship it is to never stop looking. You simply never know where you might discover the perfect award.

I (Kelly) actually found a scholarship as the result of having a headache. I was taking a Tylenol and while looking at the little bottle noticed that Tylenol (http://www.tylenol.com/news/scholarship) offered a scholarship. That headache turned out to be worth $1,500. It was the most lucrative headache I have ever had!

So put on your detective cap, and let's look at the best places to find scholarships. We will begin in a place that is just outside of your door: your own backyard.

Scholarship Gold Buried In Your Own Backyard

The most obvious place to find a scholarship is often the last place students look: in their own communities. While the prizes for backyard scholarships may not be as large as the more widely publicized national awards, they often have significantly less competition. This means you are much more likely to win. Think about it. Would you rather lose a $10,000 nationwide scholarship competition or win a $1,000 scholarship from your community?

Winning several backyard scholarships adds up quickly. Our own experience is proof. When we tell people that we won over $100,000 in awards, they oftentimes assume that we won one or two jackpots. Nothing is farther from the truth. We were able to accumulate this money by winning lots of little scholarships, many from our own community. As long as the scholarship fits you should apply no matter how much (or little) it's worth.

With this in mind, let's explore your own backyard and see what kind of scholarship gold we can uncover.

1.

Avoid reinventing the wheel by visiting your counselor

We have never met a college or career counselor (and we have met thousands) who does not keep a list of local scholarships. Whether your counselor posts these scholarships on a bulletin board, lists them in a newsletter or updates them online, take the initiative to find out what they know. Whenever a new scholarship is created the organization will usually send a notice to counselors at nearby schools. Over the years counselors become familiar with dozens of local awards. Most can tell you what scholarships are offered by the clubs and organizations in your community. They can give you leads on tracking down scholarships offered by local businesses and even awards sponsored by alumni. Take advantage of the knowledge your counselors already have. It will save you valuable time that you can spend applying to more scholarships.

2.

Service clubs are there to serve you

Remember that breakfast sponsored by the Lions Club that your parents dragged you to on Saturday morning? Ever wonder why these community clubs have such fundraisers? It's to help students like you, silly! Service organizations like the Lions Club (as well as dozens of others) raise money to provide scholarships to students in their communities. Look online and make a list of the service clubs in your community. While you're at it, why not dial the number and ask if they offer a scholarship?

Keep in mind that most service clubs also belong to a national organization. Both the local and the national organization may offer their own scholarships. The Kiwanis International Foundation offers scholarships for Key Club members as well as oratorical and talent contests.

In addition to looking online, visit your community center. The people who work there should know the names of most of the service clubs in your community. Your local public librarian can also help you find these organizations. To get you started here are a few of the most common service clubs. The websites provided are for the national organization. On the national website you can not only find out if they offer a scholarship but also find the contact information of local chapters.

While the following service organizations may offer awards at the national level, some only offer scholarships through their local chapters. If you don't find information about awards through the national organization, you can still use their website to locate your local chapter.

3. Altrusa
http://www.altrusa.com
This international service organization proves that business is not all about the bottom line. Its members are business and professional leaders who are committed to community improvement through volunteerism. Your best bet is to contact your local chapter to see what scholarships are available.

4. American Legion and American Legion Auxiliary
http://www.legion.org and http://www.legion-aux.org
This community service organization has almost 3 million members who are all veterans. Almost every city and town in

---

What is the purpose of the scholarship essay?

There are two main reasons that you are asked to submit an essay with your scholarship application.

The first is to show the scholarship judges why you deserve to win the scholarship. This does not mean that you should overtly campaign for your victory, composing a top 10 list of why you should be the winner, but you want to point out your achievements and be proud of your accomplishments.

The second reason why you are asked to write an essay is to share something about yourself that is not conveyed in your application. Scholarship committees view essays as a way to learn more about you and to gain insight into who you really are. Don't just list off accomplishments that are also found in your application. Use your essay to help the scholarship judges get to know you better.

America has an American Legion post. With such a membership, you might expect that you'd need some connection to the military to win a scholarship. In truth what is most important is that you can demonstrate your contribution to your community. Military service is not required. Both the American Legion and its sister organization, the American Legion Auxiliary, place a high value on community service that is reflected in their scholarships. On the national level ask about the *Eagle Scout Award, Oratorical Contest, Nursing Scholarship, Girl Scout Achievement Award, National President Scholarship, Samsung Scholarship, Non-Traditional Student Scholarship* and *Spirit of Youth Scholarship.*

5. The American Red Cross
http://www.redcross.org
Through its many local chapters the Red Cross provides a variety of services particularly during times of national disasters. The Red Cross also sponsors the Junior Red Cross. If you have volunteered with the organization, ask about the *Navin Narayan Scholarship.*

6. The Association of Junior Leagues International
http://www.ajli.org
This women's organization is committed to promoting volunteerism, developing the potential of women and improving communities. Contact your local chapter to see what scholarships may be available.

7. Boys and Girls Clubs
http://www.bgca.org
Each club provides programs that promote and enhance the development of children as well as give them a safe place to go after school. Most of their scholarships are club-based, which means you need to find and apply through your local club.

8. Campus Outreach Community League (COOL)
http://www.cool2serve.org
Student activists, volunteers and community leaders are all welcome to become members of this club. This non-profit group seeks to mobilize college students to get involved with their communities by supporting campus-based community service programs. Check with your campus COOL club to see what scholarship opportunities may be available.

9. Circle K

http://www.circlek.org

This is the college version of Kiwanis International and is dedicated to helping students become responsible leaders and citizens. On the national level ask about the *Past International Presidents' Scholarship, Himmel Scholarship, J. Walker Field Endowed Scholarship* and the *Cunat Visionary Scholarship*.

10. Civitan

http://www.civitan.org

Counting Thomas Edison as one of its members, Civitan is a volunteer organization that serves individual and community needs with an emphasis on helping people with developmental disabilities. On the national level ask about the *Shropshire Scholarship*.

11. The Elks Club

http://www.elks.org

If you think that you are one of the top 500 high school students in the country, consider the *Most Valuable Student Scholarship* program from the Elks, which awards up to $15,000 per year. The Elks Club is a fraternal organization dedicated to charitable works and has more than 2,100 lodges and over 1.1 million members. On the national level ask about the *Most Valuable Student Scholarship, Eagle Scout Award, Emergency Educational Fund Grants, Gold Award* and *Legacy Awards*. Many lodges also give scholarships to students in the community.

12. Fraternal Order of Eagles

http://www.foe.com

Their slogan is "People Helping People." To make this a reality the Eagles build training centers around the world, raise money to combat heart disease and cancer and help those with disabilities and seniors. If you are a member ask about the *Eagles Memorial Fund*. Also, check your local club to see what scholarships they offer.

13. Friends of the Library

http://www.folusa.org

The Friends do a lot more than run the best used book fairs. They are instrumental in supporting and fundraising for your local public libraries. Both Friends of the Library as well as the your local library may offer community scholarships.

14. Kiwanis International

http://www.kiwanis.org

This is a worldwide club for service and community-minded individuals. Kiwanis perform all kinds of community-based service projects. You can get an early start in the organization in high school in the Key Club and an even earlier start in junior high school in the Builders Club. On the national level ask about the *Presidential Freedom Scholarships* and the *Kiwanis International Foundation Scholarships*. Be sure to also find your local club and inquire about their scholarship opportunities.

15. Knights of Columbus

http://www.kofc.org

The Knights of Columbus is the largest lay organization in the Catholic Church and supports a variety of community and charitable programs. While the local councils establish their own scholarships, on the national level the *Father Michael J. McGivney Vocations Scholarship* and the *Bishop Thomas V. Daily Vocations Scholarship* are available to help students who are in theology programs.

16. Lions Club International

http://www.lionsclubs.org

The International Association of Lions is the largest service organization in the world with more than 1.4 million members. Lions members are dedicated to community service and other charitable goals. Almost all scholarships are awarded by local chapters including the Leo Club, which is the youth version of the Lions Club. You don't have to be a Lions member to win.

17. The National Exchange Club

http://www.nationalexchangeclub.com

This all-volunteer service organization is committed to serving the community and igniting the spirit of community service throughout the country. The group is a strong advocate of youth programs and sponsors several recognition programs for students. On the national level ask about the *Youth of the Month Awards*.

18. The National Grange

http://www.nationalgrange.org

Members of this organization share a common interest in community involvement and agricultural and rural issues. Check with your state Grange association for specific scholarships.

19. NeighborWorks

http://www.nw.org

This group is dedicated to revitalizing neighborhoods through innovative local partnerships of residents, businesses and government. Contact your local NeighborWorks program to see if they offer a scholarship in your area.

20. Optimist International

http://www.optimist.org

If you're a strong writer or communicator, Optimist International offers several scholarships for you. Meeting the needs of young people in communities worldwide, Optimist International volunteers lead service projects to assist and empower youth. On the national level ask about the *International Communications Contest, International Essay Contest* and *International Oratorical Contest.*

21. Performing arts center

http://www.performingarts.net

You may think that your local performing arts center is just a place to watch singers and dancers. However, if you are a performer yourself, your local center may not only enhance you culturally but also financially. Often these non-profit organizations sponsor scholarship competitions in the arts.

22. Rotaract and Interact

http://www.rotaract.org

Affiliated with Rotary Clubs, Rotaract and Interact Clubs are aimed at students and young adults. The groups promote leadership and responsible citizenship, high ethical standards in business, international understanding and peace. On the local level inquire about the *District Scholarships.*

23. Rotary Club

http://www.rotary.org

If you dream of living or working abroad, the Rotary Club can help fulfill your dream through their *Ambassadorial Scholarship*. This club brings together business and professional leaders to provide humanitarian service, encourage high ethical standards and help build goodwill and peace in the world. On the national level ask about the *Ambassadorial Scholarships* and the *Cultural Ambassadorial Scholarships*. Many local clubs also sponsor scholarships in their communities.

24. Ruritan

http://www.ruritan.org

Don't think that you will miss out on scholarships just because you don't live in a major metropolitan area. Ruritan, a civic organization made up of local clubs in small towns and rural communities, offers several awards for students. Ask your local club about the *Student Scholarship Program* and if they participate in the *Double Your Dollar Educational Grant Program*.

25. Salvation Army

http://www.salvationarmyusa.org

The Salvation Army is dedicated to caring for the poor and feeding the hungry. It also sponsors and supports many youth programs. Check your local organization to see if they offer college scholarships.

26. Sertoma International

http://www.sertoma.org

Their name stands for "SERvice TO MAnkind." This volunteer organization is dedicated to helping people with speech, hearing and language disorders. On the national level ask about the *Hearing Impaired Scholarships* and the *Communicative Disorders Scholarship Program*.

27. Soroptimist International of the Americas (SIA)

http://www.soroptimist.org

Your efforts may be rewarded with a scholarship if you're a young woman who volunteers, especially if your work benefits girls or women. Soroptimist members include women of all professions who believe in the importance of awareness, advocacy and action in the service of community and society. On the national level ask about the *Violet Richardson Award* and the *Woman's Opportunity Awards Program.*

28. U.S. Jaycees
http://www.usjaycees.org
The U.S. Junior Chamber (Jaycees) provides its members with an opportunity to develop as leaders in their communities by getting involved with civic affairs. On the national level ask about the *War Memorial Fund Scholarship, Thomas Wood Baldridge Scholarship* and *Charles R. Ford Scholarship.* Membership is not required for many of the awards.

29. Veterans of Foreign Wars (VFW)
http://www.vfw.org
This advocacy group for veterans is also committed to promoting volunteerism and community service. The VFW and its Ladies Auxiliary sponsor on the national level the *Voice of Democracy Audio Essay Contest, Patriot's Pen Youth Essay Contest, Teacher of the Year Award, Outstanding Scouts Award* and the *Hero's Recognition Program.* Don't forget to check with your local VFW post to find any specific scholarships aimed at students in your community.

30. White House Office of Social Innovation and Civic Participation
http://www.whitehouse.gov/administration/eop/sicp
This national effort to encourage volunteerism is coordinated at the White House. Its mission is to strengthen our culture of service and help find opportunities for every American to volunteer. Look at the prizes and challenges under the office's initiatives.

31. YMCA/YWCA
http://www.ymca.net
When you think of the YMCA, you might envision summer camp. But what you should think of is scholarships. With more than 2,400 branches this organization provides a host of health and social services to the community. Contact your local Y to find out about scholarship opportunities.

> ### When should I start applying for scholarships?
> ### When is it too late to apply for scholarships?
>
> Our mantra is simple: It's never too early or too late to apply for scholarships. If you can believe it, there are scholarships that you can win as early as seventh grade!
>
> On the other hand, you also don't want to stop applying for scholarships just because you graduated from high school. You can continue to apply for scholarships throughout your time in college or graduate school.

32. Zonta International
http://www.zonta.org
This organization of business executives and professionals is dedicated to the improvement of the status of women worldwide. On the national level ask about the *Amelia Earhart Fellowship Fund, Jane M. Klausman Women in Business Scholarship Fund* and the *Young Women in Public Affairs Fund.*

33.

Scholarships from religious organizations
If you are a member of an organized religion ask your minister, pastor, reverend, rabbi, priest or monk if the church sponsors a scholarship. Many religious organizations offer awards to members of their congregation. If they don't, politely suggest that they should.

Make sure you also check out the national or international organization of the church. In addition to any scholarships that the local church awards, the national office of the Presbyterian Church, for example, also awards scholarships nationally. Below is just a sample of the organized religions that offer scholarships to their members.

34. Assemblies of God
http://www.ag.org
On the national level the church offers a variety of scholarships including the *National Youth Scholarship* and the *Touch With Hope*

Scholarship for single mothers. The website also has a special section on college planning for Assemblies of God members at http://colleges.ag.org.

35. Baptist Church
http://www.abc-usa.org
The American Baptist Churches support American Baptist undergraduate, graduate and seminary students. To support growth in ministry skills, the church also assists pastors and those in other church vocations. All applicants must be members of an American Baptist church for at least one year before applying.

36. Catholic Church
https://www.catholicunitedfinancial.org
Catholic United Financial provides educational support through the *College Tuition Scholarship*. If you are a member of the First Catholic Slovak Ladies Association (http://www.catholicworkman.org) you may also qualify for their scholarship program.

37. Church of Jesus Christ of Latter-Day Saints
http://www.byu.edu
If you plan to attend Brigham Young University, check out the website and visit the department in which you plan to major. Most have a list of scholarships available to students within the major and some are designated for Mormons.

38. Evangelical Lutheran Church
http://www.elca.org
Begin your search at the website of the Evangelical Lutheran Church in America. You can search the site for specific scholarships as well as find links to related organizations such as the Women of the Evangelical Lutheran Church in America. This group in particular offers a number of scholarships including the *Opportunity Scholarships for Lutheran Laywomen.*

39. Judaism
http://www.hillel.org
There are a variety of scholarships for Jewish students. A good starting point is the Hillel, which sponsors several grant and scholarship competitions as well as produces several useful

guides for Jewish students. Another useful resource is the Bureau of Jewish Education, which has branches in most major cities. You can use the telephone book or a search engine like Google or Yahoo to find the one nearest you. Once you locate your bureau you'll find that it often has a list of scholarships for local Jewish students. The website for the bureau in San Francisco (http://www.jewishlearningworks.org), for example, has a page that lists most of the scholarships for Jewish students in Northern California.

40. Methodist Church
http://www.umc.org
The church sponsors several scholarship programs including the *Foundation Scholarship Program*, which awards $1,000 scholarships to more than 400 students. The church also has *Ethnic Minority Scholarships* and *General Scholarships* for older students and students who demonstrate leadership. The General Commission on Archives and History (http://www.gcah.org) also offers several research and writing grants for students interested in studying the history of the church.

41. Presbyterian Church
http://www.pcusa.org
The church offers a variety of awards to members who are enrolled in college. High school seniors can apply for the *National Presbyterian College Scholarship*, graduate students can apply for the *Continuing Education Grant* and medical students can apply for the *Grant Program for Medical Studies.*

42. Seventh-Day Adventist
http://www.adventist.org
Visit the church's website to find scholarship programs sponsored by individual churches. On the national level there is also the *General Conference Women's Ministries Scholarship Program* (http://wm.gc.adventist.org), which has awarded more than 550 scholarships since 1994. The scholarships are for women who plan to attend a Seventh-Day Adventist college and who otherwise would be unable to afford a Christian education.

43. Society of Friends (Quakers)
http://www.fum.org

The United Society of Friends Women International adminis-ters the *John Sarrin Scholarship*. This award provides money for students preparing for ministry.

44. United Church of Christ
http://www.ucc.org
The church offers the *UCC Seminarian Scholarship* for students preparing for ministry. Certain colleges have also designated funds for students who are members of the United Church of Christ. Currently the colleges with special scholarships for UCC students include Catawba College, Cedar Crest College, Dillard University, Doane College, Drury University, Elmhurst College, Elon College, Heidelberg College, Hood College, Lakeland College, Olivet College, Pacific University, Ripon College and Talladega College. You can check the national website for any additions to this list. In addition, the national offices of the United Church of Christ offer a limited number of awards from individual donors.

45.

Money from your parents' worker's union
If your parents or even grandparents belong to a union or if you plan to enter a field that has a union, check the union for scholarships. The Teamsters, for example, offer the *James R. Hoffa Memorial Scholarship Fund* for the children of its members. The union gives 75 scholarships a year of $1,000 to $10,000 per award. You can learn more at http://www.teamster.org.

For some scholarships, you must have a family member who is a member of the organization. For others, you don't have to be a member but must plan to enter a related career field. Contact the unions through either the address listed below or their website. Even better, have Mom or Dad ask their union directly. The following list of unions offer scholarship programs for their members, for the children of their members or for students entering related career fields.

46. Air Line Pilots Association
Undergraduate College Scholarship
1625 Massachusetts Avenue, NW

Chapter 2: Win a Scholarship • 35

Washington, DC 20036
http://www.alpa.org

47. American Federation of School Administrators
AFSA Scholarship Awards
1101 17th Street, NW, Suite 408
Washington, DC 20036
http://www.afsaadmin.org

48. American Federation of State, County and Municipal Employees
AFSCME Family Scholarship
1625 L Street, NW
Washington, DC 20036
http://www.afscme.org

49. American Federation of Teachers
Robert G. Porter Scholars Program
555 New Jersey Avenue, NW
Washington, DC 20001
http://www.aft.org

50. American Federation of Television and Radio Artists
Scholarships of the AFTRA Heller Memorial Foundation
5757 Wilshire Boulevard, 7th Floor
Los Angeles, CA 90036
http://www.sagaftra.org

51. Asbestos Workers International Union
Asbestos Workers International Union Scholarship
9602 M.L. King Jr. Highway
Lanham, MD 20706
http://www.insulators.org

52. Association of Flight Attendants-CWA
Association of Flight Attendants Annual Scholarship
501 Third Street NW
Washington, DC 20001
http://www.afacwa.org

How do I write a winning scholarship essay?

When it comes to winning a scholarship you often need to write a powerful essay. Your essay is critical to convincing the judges to give you their money. When you are writing your scholarship essay, don't make any of the following mistakes:

Missing the question. It seems obvious, but enough students make this mistake that it needs to be emphasized: Be sure your essay answers the question.

Not having a point. If you cannot summarize the point of your essay in a single sentence, you may not have one.

Topic is too broad. Don't try to cover too much in the limited space of the essay.

Mechanical errors. Spelling and grammatical errors signal carelessness.

Not revealing something about you. Regardless of what the essay is about, it needs to reveal something about who you are, what motivates you or what is important to you.

Being ordinary. For your essay to stand out from the pile of other applicants, either the topic needs to be unique or the approach original.

If you want to learn more about writing a winning essay as well as read examples of 30 successful scholarship essays, take a look at our book, *How to Write a Winning Scholarship Essay*.

53. Bakery, Confectionery, Tobacco Workers and Grain Millers International Union
BCTGM Scholarship and *Vaughn Ball Memorial Scholarship*
10401 Connecticut Avenue, Floor 4
Kensington, MD 20895
http://www.bctgm.org

54. Boilermakers, Iron Ship Builders, Blacksmiths, Forgers and Helpers (IBB)
IBB Scholarship Program

753 State Avenue, Suite 570
Kansas City, KS 66101
http://www.boilermakers.org

55. Bricklayers and Allied Craftworkers (BAC)
Harry C. Bates Merit Scholarship
620 F Street, NW
Washington, DC 20004
http://www.bacweb.org

56. Brotherhood of Locomotive Engineers
International Western Convention (IWC) and *GIA Scholarship*
7061 East Pleasant Valley Road
Independence, OH 44131
http://www.ble.org

57. Chemical Workers Union Council, (UFCW)
Walter L. Mitchell Memorial Scholarship
1655 West Market Street, 6th Floor
Akron, OH 44313
http://www.icwuc.net

58. Communications Workers of America
CWA Joe Beirne Foundation Scholarship
501 Third Street, NW
Washington, DC 20001
http://www.cwa-union.org

59. Glass, Molders, Pottery, Plastics and Allied Workers International Union
Memorial Scholarship
608 East Baltimore Pike
Media, PA 19063
http://www.gmpiu.org

60. Graphic Communications International Union
Anthony J. DeAndrade Scholarship
25 Louisiana Avenue, NW
Washington, DC 20001
http://www.teamster.org/divisions/graphic-communications

61. International Alliance of Theatrical Stage Employees, Artists and Allied Crafts of the U.S.

Richard F. Walsh Award, Alfred W. DiTolla Award and *Harold P. Spivak Foundation Award*
207 W. 25th Street, 4th Floor
New York, NY 10001
http://www.iatse.net

62. International Association of Machinists and Aerospace Workers

International Association of Machinists and Aerospace Workers Scholarship for Members and *International Association of Machinists and Aerospace Workers Scholarship for Members' Children*
9000 Machinists Place, Room 117
Upper Marlboro, MD 20772
http://www.goiam.org

63. International Organization of Masters, Mates and Pilots

International Organization of Masters, Mates and Pilots Scholarship
700 Maritime Boulevard, Suite B
Linthicum Heights, MD 21090
http://www.bridgedeck.org

64. International Union of Electronic, Electrical, Salaried, Machine and Furniture Workers-Communications Workers of America (IUE-CWA)

The IUE-CWA International Paul Jennings Scholarship
2701 Dryden Road
Dayton, OH 45439
http://www.iue-cwa.org

65. International Union of Painters and Allied Trades of the United States and Canada

S. Frank Bud Raftery Scholarship
7234 Parkway Drive
Hanover, MD 21076
http://www.iupat.org

66. Iron Workers, International Association of Bridge, Structural, Ornamental and Reinforcing
John H. Lyons, Sr., Scholarship Program
1750 New York Avenue, NW, Suite 400
Washington, DC 20006
http://www.ironworkers.org

67. National Alliance of Postal and Federal Employees
Ashby B. Carter Memorial Scholarship
1640 11th Street, NW
Washington, DC 20001
http://www.napfe.com

68. National Association of Letter Carriers
Ashby B. Carter Memorial Scholarship
20547 Waverly Court
Ashburn, VA 20149
http://www.nalc.org

69. Office and Professional Employees International Union
Howard Coughlin Memorial Scholarship and *John Kelly Labor Studies Scholarship*
80 Eighth Avenue
New York, NY 10011
http://www.opeiu.org

70. Professional and Technical Engineers, International Federation
Professional and Technical Engineers, International Federation Scholarship
501 3rd Street, NW, Suite 701
Washington, DC 20001
http://www.ifpte.org

71. Retail, Wholesale and Department Store Union District Council (RWDSU)
Alvin E. Heaps Memorial Scholarship
370 Seventh Avenue, Suite 501
New York, NY 10001
http://www.rwdsu.info

Is it worth it to apply for a scholarship even though I'm not guaranteed to win?

In our case it certainly was. We earned more money per hour applying for scholarships than we could have at any part-time job. But was our experience unique?

When we wrote *How to Write a Winning Scholarship Essay*, we interviewed hundreds of students who won scholarships. We selected 30 to feature in the book and asked them to estimate how many hours they spent in total applying for scholarships. This includes searching for awards and completing the applications—both for awards they won and lost. Then we took the total amount of money that they won and divided it into the total hours.

The result was that on average these students were making $300 per hour from their scholarship efforts. Now if you can find a part-time job that pays more than $300 an hour then take the job and forget about scholarships. If you can't, then we strongly recommend that you consider applying.

Sure there is no guarantee that you will win every scholarship. We certainly lost more than we won. But of the scholarships that you do win, you will find that the amount will more than make up for all of your hard work and time.

72. Screen Actors Guild
John L. Dales Scholarship
5757 Wilshire Boulevard, 7th Floor
Los Angeles, CA 90036
http://www.sagaftra.org

73. Seafarers International Union of North America
Charlie Logan Scholarship Program for Dependents
5201 Auth Way
Camp Springs, MD 20746
http://www.seafarers.org

74. Service Employees International Union
SEIU-Jesse Jackson Scholarship, Service Employees International Union

Scholarship and *Union Women Summer School Scholarship*
c/o Scholarship Program Administrators Inc.
1800 Massachusetts Avenue, NW
Washington, DC 20036
http://www.seiu.org

75. Sheet Metal Workers' International Association

Sheet Metal Workers' International Scholarship Fund
1750 New York Avenue, NW, 6th Floor
Washington, DC 20006
http://www.smart-union.org/sheet-metal/

76. Transport Workers Union of America

The Michael J. Quill Scholarship Fund
501 3rd Street, NW 9th Floor
Washington, DC 20001
http://www.twu.org

77. Union Plus

Union Plus Scholarship Program
1100 1st Street, NE Suite 850
Washington, DC 20002
http://www.unionplus.org

78. United Food and Commercial Workers Union

UFCW Suffridge Scholarship
1775 K Street, NW
Washington, DC 20006
http://www.ufcw.org

79. United Mine Workers of America

Lorin E. Kerr Scholarship Fund and *UMWA/BCOA Training and Education Fund*
18354 Quantico Gateway Drive, Suite 200
Triangle, VA 22172
http://www.umwa.org

80. United Transportation Union

United Transportation Union Scholarship
1750 New York Avenue NW, Sixth Floor

Washington, DC 20006
http://www.smart-union.org/td/

81. Utility Workers Union of America
Utility Workers Union of America Scholarship
1300 L Street, NW #1200
Washington, DC 20005
http://www.uwua.net

82.

Have your parents talk to their employer

Besides the annual company picnic, many employers offer scholarships as a benefit to employees. Have your parents check with their human resources (HR) department or manager to see if their company offers a scholarship program.

The children of Wal-Mart employees, for example, are eligible to compete for the *Walton Family Foundation Scholarship*, which is worth $8,000. Wal-Mart gives out 120 of these scholarships per year. Find out more at http://foundation.walmart.com.

You may be surprised to find that your parents' employers, whether international conglomerates or local businesses, offer awards.

83.

Win a scholarship for your parents' or grandparents' military service

If your parents or grandparents served in the U.S. Armed Forces you may qualify for a scholarship from a military association. Each branch of the service and even specific divisions within each branch have associations.

The 25th Infantry Division Association (http://www.25thida.com), for example, sponsors the *25th Infantry Division Association Scholarship* that aids the children and grandchildren of active and former members. The American Legion Auxiliary (http://www.legion-aux.org) offers the *National President Scholarship* for children of veterans. Speak with your parents and grandparents about their military service and ask if they belong to or know of any of the military associations. Also, see Chapter 14 for more military awards.

84.

Hit up your employer

Flipping burgers may have an upside. Even if you work only part-time you may qualify for an educational scholarship given by your employer. Speaking of burgers, McDonald's offers the *National Employee Scholarship* to reward the accomplishments of its student-employees. Every year, McDonald's selects one outstanding student-employee from each state to receive a $1,000 scholarship. In addition, the employee who demonstrates the highest commitment to school, work and community service is named *McScholar of the Year* and receives a $5,000 scholarship. Now that is something to flip for! Get more details at http://www.mcdonalds.com/usa/good/community.html. So, if you have a full- or part-time job, be sure to ask your employer about a scholarship.

85.

Get cash from your hometown professional sports team

Is your city the home of a professional sports team? If so contact the front office to see if they offer scholarships. In our area the Major League Baseball team the San Francisco Giants sponsors the *Junior Giants Scholarship*. Each year the Giants select 10 eighth grade scholars to receive a $2,500 scholarship if they successfully complete high school and go to college. Visit the Giants' website at http://sanfrancisco.giants.mlb.com and click on the "community" link.

Visit the official website of your hometown professional teams (see the addressed listed below) and look for a "community," "foundation" or "player's foundation" link. If you don't find information about scholarships, contact the team directly since sometimes their awards are not well publicized on their websites.

86. Major League Baseball
http://www.mlb.com

87. National Basketball Association
http://www.nba.com

88. National Football League
http://www.nfl.com

89. National Hockey League
http://www.nhl.com

90. Professional Golf Association Foundation
http://www.pgafoundation.com

91. Women's National Basketball Association
http://www.wnba.com

92.

Don't ignore businesses big and small

As a way to say "thank you" to customers, many businesses offer scholarships for students who live in their community. If your city is the home of a large company then you can almost bet that they offer a scholarship.

As an example, the Bill and Melinda Gates Foundation (http://www.gatesfoundation.org) offers scholarships for students who attend selected schools in the state of Washington, where Microsoft is based.

To find businesses in your area, check with your local chamber of commerce. You can visit the national chamber of commerce online at http://www.uschamber.com and from there you can find your local chamber. Most chambers maintain a directory of member companies that you can view.

While you are searching don't ignore the more successful mom and pop businesses either. In communities across America countless grocery stores, restaurants and even pet shops fund scholarships for students in their areas.

93.

Scholarships from your extracurricular activities

Besides doing what you enjoy, an added benefit of being involved in an extracurricular activity is that you may qualify for a scholarship. Ask your activity advisor if your group offers a scholarship for members. Also, if your club is part of a national organization, check with the national office to see if they sponsor a scholarship. The National Honor Society (https://www.nhs.us), for example, gives scholarships through both the local school chapters and through the national organization. Some scholarships offered by the national organization may require nomination by your local club. Don't let that stop you. Just ask your advisor to nominate you!

The following are some of the more popular extracurricular activities that have national affiliations. Remember to check with both your local and national parent chapter.

94. American Mensa Society
http://www.us.mensa.org

95. Amnesty International
http://www.amnesty.org

96. BETA Club
http://www.betaclub.org

97. Boy Scouts
http://www.scouting.org

98. Boys and Girls Club of America
http://www.bgca.org

99. DECA
http://www.deca.org

100. Educational Theatre Association
http://www.edta.org

101. Family, Career and Community Leaders of America
http://www.fhahero.org

102. 4-H Clubs
http://www.fourhcouncil.edu

103. Fraternity or sorority
Contact your national chapter to learn what awards may be available to members.

104. Future Business Leaders of America
http://www.fbla-pbl.org

105. Future Farmers of America
http://www.ffa.org

106. Girl Scouts
http://www.girlscouts.org

107. Interact Club
http://www.rotary.org

108. Junior Achievement
http://www.ja.org

109. Key Club
http://www.keyclub.org

110. Leo Club
http://www.lionsclubs.org

111. Model United Nations
http://www.nmun.org

112. Mu Alpha Theta
http://www.mualphatheta.org

113. National Forensic League
http://nflonline.org

114. National Foundation for Teaching Entrepreneurship
http://www.nfte.com

115. The National Honor Society
https://www.nhs.us

116. National Rifle Association
http://www.nrahq.org

117. Quill and Scroll
http://www.quillandscroll.org

118. S.A.D.D.
http://www.saddonline.com

Are there weird scholarships like ones for left-handed students?

If you think that winning a scholarship based on your last name or your ability with duct tape is weird, well then the answer is yes, it is true that there are weird scholarships. These awards exist because wealthy alumni or donors with peculiar traits they want to promote make donations to colleges. Of course, the college is not going to turn down free money for its students. That's how many of these strange scholarships are started. At the end of this chapter we highlight a few of the more off beat scholarships. As you search for scholarships you too will encounter some truly outrageous ones.

119. Skills USA
http://www.skillsusa.org

120. Students in Free Enterprise
http://www.sife.org

121.

Your college financial aid office is a gold mine

You might think of the financial aid office as only helping students with need-based financial aid. It's true that this is the first place that you should go if you have financial need. But even if you don't, this office can still be helpful. If you are already in college (or even if you just live near one) pay a visit to the financial aid office. This office serves as a clearinghouse for any scholarship opportunities at your school and within your community. Like high school counselors, many financial aid offices also maintain a list of scholarship opportunities. Even if you are not receiving financial aid you can still make an appointment to speak with a financial aid counselor about the various scholarship opportunities at your college.

122.

Career service offices offer more than job resources

When you are a college senior and looking for a job, the career service office will become your second home. However, many career service offices also keep lists of scholarships and in particular those that might help you get a summer internship or even pay for you to study abroad. Don't wait until your last year in college to see what the career service office has to offer.

123.

Visit your department's administrative assistant

One of the most valuable people at your college is not the president or the dean or even your favorite professor, it's the administrative assistant of your department. This one person knows more about what happens in your major than any other person. They have probably been in the department the longest. Take some time to talk to the department administrative assistant. Ask him or her about what kind of scholarship opportunities and competitions are available to students with your major.

When I (Gen) was a history major at Harvard I asked the department assistant what kind of scholarships were available. She reached under her desk and pulled out a thick binder filled with scholarships. "You are the first person to ask to see the binder this year," she said as she handed it over. It was a gold mine of scholarships and all I had to do was ask.

Here are just a few examples of what you might find. The University of Massachusetts at Amherst has such scholarships as the *Philip Weiss Memorial Scholarship* for students majoring in Judaic Studies, the *Butterworth Scholarship* for juniors and seniors studying floriculture or ornamental horticulture and the *Stephen R. Kellogg Scholarship* for sophomores in the civil and environmental engineering department. Just asking around within your own major will turn up a lot of possibilities.

124.

Take money from your local politicians for a change

Even if you didn't vote for them or if you aren't old enough to vote, you may get some help from your local politicians. Many establish scholarships for students who live in their district as way of saying "thank you" to their constituents. Contact your local politicians' offices to find out more.

125.

Search your community newspaper for past winners

Your local newspaper is a treasure map to finding local scholarships. In the fall and spring scholarship organizations announce their winners, and your community newspaper often prints their names. Go through back issues or search the newspaper articles online (search for the words "scholarship" and "scholarship winner") to find announcements of last year's winners. Note who gave the scholarship and find out if you can apply for the same award this year.

Flipping through our local newspaper recently we found an announcement of a student who won a scholarship sponsored by a group that promoted vegetarianism. If you are a vegetarian then you too may apply for this award at http://www.vrg.org. You just never know what you'll find in your community newspaper.

Searching Beyond Your Backyard

At some point you will exhaust your local resources. You will have knocked on the doors of the local businesses, pored through the back issues of the community newspaper and practically camped out in your financial aid office. When you get to this point, it's time to move on. We're talking about the big leagues–the national scholarships. There are scholarships from large businesses, professional associations and philanthropic and charitable organizations. There are awards based on academic interest, talent, future career goals, race and ethnicity and more. What ties all of these scholarships together is that they are open to students from across the country.

In general, scholarships offered outside your community give larger prizes. Unfortunately, they also attract more competition, but don't let that scare you. We have met hundreds of students who have won scholarships, and every single one who won a national level competition told us that they never expected it. Most even wondered beforehand if they should even spend the time to apply. If they had listened to their inner doubts they never would have won. It might sound trite, but it's true: You can't win if you don't apply.

Let's make the world our scholarship hunting ground and look for awards both far and wide.

126.

Unleash the power of the Internet

The Internet puts the world's biggest library at your fingertips and allows you access to an unprecedented amount of information. It can also be truly frustrating. The problem with searching for scholarships online is that there is no filtering. Type in the word "scholarship" into a search engine and you'll get over 100,000 results. Only a tiny fraction of these results will actually be useful to you. To solve this problem of too much information there are specialized websites that let you search databases of scholarships. For the best of these, you fill out some information about yourself and with the click of a mouse are matched to scholarships that you can apply to win.

Sound too easy? In some ways it is. Don't rely on these websites to find every scholarship that is right for you. Many students make the mistake of assuming that once they do a search they have exhausted all sources for scholarships. The reality is that no matter how many scholarships these websites claim to have in their database none of them even comes close to the total number of scholarships that are available. Don't rely on websites as your only means of finding scholarships. If you do you'll miss some of the best awards that can only be found through your own detective work.

Before we share our list of the best websites to search we want to warn you against using any website that charges you money to perform a search. There are enough good free websites that you should never have to pay for a scholarship search.

Now without further adieu, here are some of the better free websites that we recommend you search:

127. SuperCollege
http://www.supercollege.com

128. moolahSPOT
http://www.moolahspot.com

129. Sallie Mae
http://www.salliemae.com/scholarships

130. Scholarship Experts
http://www.scholarshipexperts.com

131. Zinch
http://www.zinch.com/scholarships

132. The College Board
http://www.collegeboard.com

133. Cornell University Mario Einaudi Center for International Studies
http://einaudi.cornell.edu/funding-opportunities/postdoc
This site is for international students, but many of the fellowships and scholarships listed are also open to non-international students.

134. The Princeton Review
http://www.review.com

135. CollegeXpress
http://www.collegexpress.com

136. Adventures In Education
http://www.aie.org

137. FastWeb
http://www.fastweb.com

138. Scholarships.com
http://www.scholarships.com

Does SuperCollege offer a scholarship?

Yes we do! Each year we use part of the proceeds from the sale of our books to award scholarships to outstanding high school and college students. This award is part of our ongoing mission to help you pay for the college of your dreams. So if you are a high school, college or graduate school student, visit our website to submit your application. There is no age limit, but you need to be a U.S. citizen or legal resident. You may study any major and attend or plan to attend any accredited college or university in the U.S. Visit our website to apply at http://www.supercollege.com.

---

139. Petersons
http://www.petersons.com

140. FastAid
http://www.fastaid.com

141. CollegeNet
http://www.collegenet.com

142.

Hitting up big business

When you think about how many cars Toyota and Chevrolet sell or about how many Cokes the world consumes, you can see why large companies like these take some of their profits and return them to students like you through scholarships. These scholarship programs are often general in nature seeking students who are strong academically and in extracurricular activities, but some have a more specific aim. Tylenol, for example, offers scholarships for students entering health-related professions, which makes sense for a pharmaceutical company.

You have probably heard of many of the companies that offer scholarship programs simply because you buy their products. But one quick way to increase your knowledge of what businesses are out there is to read the business section of your newspaper. You can also find a list of big companies by looking at the Forbes Magazine website at http://www.forbes.com. Once you find some good prospects either email or call their human resources department and ask if they have a foundation or scholarship program. The following is just a sample of the more prominent "Big Business" scholarships. You'll notice that some of these awards don't even require that you have an interest in their industry.

143. Amazon Student Scholarship

https://www.amazon.com/b?ie=UTF8&node=9944643011
Amazon offers this scholarship for high school seniors and undergraduate students based on academic success, community service and leadership experience.

144. AXA Achievement Scholarships

http://www.axa-equitable.com/axa-foundation/community-scholarships.html
Each branch of AXA awards up to twelve $2,000 scholarships to local high school seniors. Students must show "ambition and drive" and "determination to set and reach goals" among other traits.

145. Burger King Scholars Program

http://www.bkmclamorefoundation.org
The *Burger King Scholars Program* helps students who plan to enroll in a two- or four-year college or university, participate in community service and demonstrate financial need. Academic achievement and work experience are also considered.

146. Cargill Community Scholarship Program

http://www.cargill.com/about/citizenship/scholarships.htm
Cargill supports three scholarship programs that award more than $500,000 in scholarships annually. These scholarships are for students who live in and around Cargill communities as well as the children of employees.

147. Coca-Cola Scholars Program

http://www.coca-colascholars.org
The world drinks billions of Cokes each year and in return the

company gives away almost $2 million in scholarships. Begun in 1986 to celebrate the Coca-Cola Centennial, the program is designed to contribute to the nation's future and to assist a wide range of students. Applicants must be high school seniors or community college students. Selection is based on character, leadership, academic achievement and motivation to serve and succeed.

148. Coca-Cola Two-Year College Scholarship
http://www.coca-colascholars.org
This program recognizes students enrolled in two-year programs for their academic achievement and community service. Applicants should be first- or second-year postsecondary students who intend to complete their education at a two-year degree school.

149. Commerce Bank Scholarship Sweepstakes
https://credit.commercebank.com/rewards/?type=scholar
Five awards are given each year to pay for college. Applicants must be 18 years or older and be enrolled at least part-time in a post-secondary educational institution.

150. Dell Scholars Program
http://www.msdf.org
Michael Dell is one of the most famous entrepreneurs to have started his computer business in his college dormroom. Now as a result of his company's success, through the Michael and Susan Dell Foundation, he awards scholarships to underprivileged high school seniors.

151. Dupont Challenge
http://thechallenge.dupont.com
This scholarship essay contest is open to students between grades 7 and 12. It is designed to help promote an interest in scientific studies.

152. Glamour's Top Ten College Women Competition
http://www.glamour.com
Who wouldn't want to be on the cover of Glamour? Not only could your face grace the October issue but you could also walk away with a $1,500 prize and a free trip to New York City. This

competition is open to any woman who is a full-time college junior. Winners are selected based on leadership, involvement on campus and the community, academic excellence and future goals.

153. Hitachi Yoshiyama Award
http://www.hitachifoundation.org
The Yoshiyama Award recognizes exemplary service and community involvement. You must be nominated by a community leader, teacher, principal or clergy member.

154. Intel Science Talent Search
http://www.societyforscience.org/sts/
This is the granddaddy of all science fairs. This science competition is designed to recognize excellence in science among the nation's youth and encourage the exploration of science. A recent winner created a glove that can read sign language. First prize is a scholarship worth $100,000.

155. KFC Colonel's Scholars Program
http://www.kfcscholars.org
KFC provides more than chicken. The restaurant company gives scholarships of up to $20,000 to high school seniors who have entrepreneurial drive and financial need and who plan to attend an in-state public college or university.

156. Microsoft General Scholarships
http://www.microsoft.com/college/ss_overview.mspx
If you have ever used a computer, then you are probably familiar with Microsoft. The international software giant offers several scholarships for students, women and minorities. The scholarships are designed to reward students with a passion for software development and technology. Scholarships cover 100 percent of tuition.

157. Papa Johns Scholars
http://www.papajohns.com
Not at all based on your pizza-throwing ability, this program rewards high school seniors based on creativity, community involvement, academic achievement, quality of character, leadership, obstacles overcome, life goals and interests.

158. Prudential Spirit of Community Awards

http://www.prudential.com/community/spirit/

You need to be nominated by your middle or high school counselor or principal. Remember, you can always ask to be nominated. This award is based on community and volunteer activities.

159. Sam Walton Community Scholarship

http://foundation.walmart.com

The foundation of America's largest retailer rewards students who are active in their communities.

160. Siemens Competition in Math, Science and Technology

http://www.siemens-foundation.org

This science fair on steroids attracts high school students from across the country who are willing to challenge themselves through science research.

161. Toshiba Exploravision Awards

http://www.exploravision.org

Known for its own cutting-edge technology, Toshiba sponsors this competition for K-12 students that encourages combining imagination with the tools of science to create and explore a vision of a future technology.

162. Tylenol Scholarship

http://www.tylenol.com/news/scholarship

Paging future doctors and nurses. You can win one of ten $10,000 or one of 150 $1,000 scholarships from Tylenol if you are an undergraduate or graduate school student who has demonstrated leadership in community and school activities and who intends to enter a health-related field.

163. USA Funds Access to Education Scholarships

http://www.usafunds.org

This need-based scholarship program is open to high school seniors or other individuals who plan to enroll or are enrolled in full- or half-time undergraduate or graduate coursework. Winners are chosen based on their academic performance, leadership, activities, work experience and career and educational goals.

164.

Professional associations will pay you to go to school

Whether you want to be a computer scientist or certified fraud examiner there is a professional organization to support your profession. In fact, in the U.S. alone there are more than 135,000 professional associations. One of the missions of these organizations is to support students who want to enter the field by offering scholarships.

In our scholarship book, *The Ultimate Scholarship Book*, we list some of the best professional associations that offer scholarships. We also recommend that you check out the *Encyclopedia of Associations* published by the Gale Group. This multi-volume set is extremely expensive, but fortunately you can find this book at most college and state libraries. Inside you will find a list of nearly every professional association in the U.S. Simply call or visit the websites of the associations that support your future career to see if they offer scholarships.

Another great way to track down professional associations is to talk to the people who are already in these careers. If you're a pre-med student, spend some time talking to doctors to learn which associations they belong to. You can also go to the library and read trade journals for the profession. Associations often advertise in these publications.

The following list is just a few examples of some professional associations that offer scholarships. Remember, there are more than 135,000 professional associations in existence!

165. Association of Certified Fraud Examiners
http://www.acfe.com
If you want to make a career out of detecting forged checks, you can apply for the *Ritchie-Jennings Memorial Scholarship*, which supports students who want to become Certified Fraud Examiners.

166. Academy of Motion Picture Arts and Sciences
http://www.oscars.org
An Oscar may be in your future, so get a head start on the golden guy with these scholarships. Future filmmakers and screenwriters can apply for the *Don and Gee Nicholl Fellowships in Screenwriting* and the *Student Academy Awards*.

167. Academy of Television Arts and Sciences Foundation

http://www.emmys.org

From the academy that presents the Emmys comes the *College Television Awards* for students who produce original films and videos.

168. Actors' Fund of America

http://www.aflcio.org

It may be hard to make ends meet working as a waiter while waiting for your big break. That's why the *Actors' Work Program* provides tuition and grants for job retraining for members of the entertainment industry.

169. Air Traffic Control Association

http://www.atca.org

If your dream is to someday direct the traffic in the sky, you should check out the *Air Traffic Control Association Scholarship Program.*

170. Aircraft Electronics Association

http://www.aea.net

This association offers a variety of awards for students interested in a career in avionics or aircraft repair. They administer the following awards: *Bendix/King Avionics Scholarship, Bud Glover Memorial Scholarship, David Arver Memorial Scholarship, Dutch and Ginger Arver Scholarship, Garmin Scholarship, Goodrich Aerospace Scholarship, Johnny Davis Memorial Scholarship, Lee Tarbox Memorial Scholarship, Lowell Gaylor Memorial Scholarship* and the *Mid-Continent Instrument Scholarship.*

171. American Angus Association

http://www.angus.org

Like Angus beef? Then you might want to apply for the *Angus Foundation Scholarship* for students who are active with the Angus breed.

172. American Association of Airport Executives

http://www.aaae.org

If you love airports and could think of nothing better than spending 40 hours a week working in one then check out the *AAAE Foundation Scholarship.*

173. American Association of Critical-Care Nurses

http://www.aacn.org

Active RN students and members of the AACN can apply for the *Educational Advancement Scholarship.*

174. American Bar Association

http://www.abanet.org/lsd/

Future lawyers can enter the *ABA Essay and Writing Competitions* or apply for the *Legal Opportunity Scholarship Fund.*

175. American Concrete Institute

http://www.aci-int.org

There is no construction industry without cement. If you are a college senior interested in entering the construction industry, you've got to check out the *Peter D. Courtois Concrete Construction Scholarship.*

176. American Criminal Justice Association

http://www.acjalae.org

What if the professional organization that gives the scholarship requires that I be a member to apply?

Most professional organizations do not require that you be a member to apply for a scholarship. However, if you find one that does and you are serious about the career (and you shouldn't really be applying if you're not), then why not join the association? Many offer discounted student memberships. Also, check with your department since some schools purchase group membership for all of their students. You get a lot out of joining an association so even if you have to pay the dues, it is usually well worth it.

Rewarding future crime fighters, the association offers both the *Scholarship Program* for undergraduate or graduate students who are studying criminal justice and a *Student Paper Competition* for student members.

177. American Culinary Federation

http://www.acfchefs.org

Future chefs take note. If you are in a culinary program take a look at these scholarships: the *Chain des Rotisseurs Scholarship*, the *Chair's Scholarship* and the *Ray and Gertrude Marshall Scholarship*.

178. American Dental Association

http://www.ada.org

If you want to pursue a career in dental hygiene, dental assisting, dentistry or dental laboratory technology take a look at the *Allied Dental Health Scholarship*, *Dental Student Scholarship* and the *Minority Dental Student Scholarship*.

179. American Institute of Chemical Engineers (AIChE)

http://www.aiche.org

If you're a member of an AIChE Student Chapter or Chemical Engineering Club you can apply for the *Donald F. and Mildred Topp Othmer Foundation Scholarship* or the *National Student Design Competition*. If you're not a member but are majoring in chemical engineering you can apply for the *John J. McKetta Scholarship*.

180. American Meteorological Society

http://www.ametsoc.org/AMS/

If you've ever dreamed of making it rain (or at least predicting when it will), look at these scholarships for atmospheric or oceanic studies: *AMS Undergraduate Scholarship*, *AMS Graduate Fellowship in the History of Science*, *Industry Minority Scholarship*, *Industry Undergraduate Scholarship*, *Industry/Government Scholarship* and the *Father James B. Macelwane Annual Awards in Meteorology*.

181. American Nuclear Society

http://www.ans.org

If you are a student in a nuclear-related field, check out the *ANS Graduate Scholarship*, the *ANS Undergraduate Scholarship* and the *John Muriel Landis Scholarship*.

182. American Nursery and Landscape Association

http://www.americanhort.org

If you have a green thumb then the *Timothy Bigelow and Palmer W. Bigelow, Jr. Scholarship* and *Usrey Family Scholarship* may be the perfect awards for you.

183. American Society of Agricultural and Biological Engineers

http://www.asabe.org

Biological or agricultural engineering majors are eligible for the *Adams Scholarship Grant*, the *ASAE Foundation Scholarship* and the *ASAE Student Engineer of the Year Scholarship*.

184. American Society of Ichthyologists and Herpetologists

http://www.asih.org

If you are a future ichthyologist or herpetologist check out the *Gaige Fund Award*, the *Raney Fund Award* and the *Stoye and Storer Award*.

185. American Society of Mechanical Engineers (ASME)

http://www.asme.org

ASME student members can apply to a number of scholarships including: the *ASME Foundation Scholarship*, the *F.W. Beichley Scholarship*, the *Frank and Dorothy Miller ASME Auxiliary Scholarship*, the *Garland Duncan Scholarship*, the *John and Elsa Gracik Scholarship*, the *Kenneth Andrew Roe Scholarship*, the *Melvin R. Green Scholarship* and the *Robert F. Sammataro Pressure Vessel Piping Division Scholarship*. (If you understand what this last scholarship is about you probably deserve to win it!)

186. American Society of Travel Agents Foundation

http://www.asta.org

We see travel in your future. If you do too then take a look at the various scholarship programs offered by this society, which include the *American Express Travel Scholarship*, the *Avis Scholarship*, the *Fernando R. Ayuso Award*, the *Healy Scholarship*, the *Holland America Line-Westours, Inc. Research Grant*, the *Joseph R. Stone Scholarship*, the *Princess Cruises and Princess Tours Scholarship*, the *Simmons Scholarship* and the *Southern California Chapter/Pleasant Hawaiian Holidays Scholarship*.

187. American Society of Women Accountants Scholarship

http://www.aswa.org

Attention number crunchers. If you are a female part-time or full-time student of accounting, contact your local ASWA chapter to receive an application for the *ASWA Scholarship*. You do not have to be a member to apply.

188. American Welding Society Foundation

http://www.aws.org

If you are living your dream of working in the spark-filled welding industry then you'll want to apply for the *James A. Turner, Jr. Memorial Scholarship*.

189. Armed Forces Communications and Electronics Association

http://www.afcea.org

First of all you don't have to be affiliated with the military to apply for these scholarships. However, they are geared toward students studying technical or scientific fields. Check out these awards: the *General John A. Wickham Scholarship*, *Ralph W. Shrader Scholarship* and the *Computer Graphic Design Scholarship*.

190. Associated General Contractors of America

http://www.agc.org

Planning on wearing a hard hat to work? If you are an undergraduate or graduate student in construction or civil engineering program you can apply for the *AGC Undergraduate* or *AGC Graduate Scholarship*.

191. Associated Male Choruses of America

http://amcofa.org

This association offers the *AMCA Music Scholarship* to promote chorus and music students in college.

192. Association for Women in Mathematics

http://www.awm-math.org

To support women who are studying mathematics this organization sponsors both the *Alice T. Schafer Prize* and the *AWM Biographies Contest*.

193. Association for Women in Science

http://www.awis.org

It's no secret that there are more men in the sciences than women. That's why the AWS sponsors the *Science Undergraduate Award* and the *Association for Women in Science Graduate Award* to encourage more women to get into the sciences.

194. Association of Food and Drug Officials

http://www.afdo.org

If your dream is to work for the FDA or if you are studying food, drug or consumer product safety you can apply for the *Association of Food and Drug Officials Scholarship Award.*

195. Association of State Dam Safety Officials

http://www.damsafety.org

Somebody has to keep the dam from bursting. If that person is you then don't ignore the *ASDSO Dam Safety Scholarship.*

196. Broadcast Education Association (BEA)

http://www.beaweb.org

This is the award for future Peter Jennings and Katie Courics. If you are a college junior, senior or graduate student at a BEA member university you may be able to apply for the *Broadcast Education Association Scholarship.* The organization has members who are in the television and radio broadcasting industry as well as in telecommunications and electronic media.

197. Educational Foundation for Women in Accounting

http://www.efwa.org

Do you like working with numbers? If so, the *Women in Transition Scholarships* and *Women in Need Scholarships* both provide financial assistance to female students who are pursuing degrees in accounting. Trying to get a Ph.D. in accounting? You may be interested in the *Laurel Fund.*

198. Emergency Nurses Association

http://www.ena.org

To promote research and education in emergency care this association sponsors the *ENA Foundation Undergraduate Scholarship,* the *Karen O'Neil Endowed Advanced Nursing Practice Scholarship* and the *Medtronic Physio-Control Advanced Nursing Practice Scholarship.*

199. Entomological Society of America

http://www.entsoc.org

The *John Henry Comstock Graduate Student Award, Normand R. Dubois Memorial Scholarship* and *Stan Beck Fellowship* all support graduate and undergraduate students who are studying entomology.

200. Executive Women International (EWI)

http://www.ewiconnect.com

High school students can apply for the *Executive Women International Scholarship Program.* Single parents, individuals just entering the workforce or displaced workers can all apply for an *Adult Students in Scholastic Transition* (ASIST) award.

201. Golf Course Superintendents Association of America Foundation

http://www.gcsaa.org

Do you always find yourself defending golf's place in the sporting kingdom? If the golfing industry is your passion you have your pick of scholarships for every aspect of the golf course industry including: the *GCSAA Footsteps on the Green Award,* the *GCSAA Scholars Program,* the *GCSAA Student Essay Contest* and the *Scotts Company Scholars Program.*

202. Herb Society of America

http://www.herbsociety.org

If you are passionate about studying herbs then you don't want to miss applying for an *HAS Research Grant.*

203. Industrial Designers Society of America

http://www.idsa.org

You may have the next winning design for robotic vacuum cleaners or 100 gigabyte mp3 players in you. Student industrial designers can apply for the *David H. Liu Memorial Graduate Scholarships in Product Design,* the *Gianninoto Graduate Scholarship* and the *IDSA Undergraduate Scholarship.*

204. International Association of Fire Fighters

http://www.iaff.org

Members of the IAFF can apply for the *Harvard University Trade*

Union Program Scholarship. Selection is based on participation in your local IAFF affiliate.

205. International Food Service Executives Association
http://www.ifsea.org
You probably know that there is more to food services than food preparation. The industry needs students who are skilled in management. If you are studying a food service-related major then check out the *IFSEA Scholarship.*

206. The International Society for Optical Engineering
http://www.spie.org
This group offers the *Michael Kidger Memorial Scholarship* for students in the optical design field.

207. Iron and Steel Society
http://www.aistfoundation.org
To attract talented and dedicated students to careers within the iron and steel industries, this organization offers the *ISS Scholarship Foundation Scholarship.*

208. Karla Scherer Foundation Scholarship
http://karlascherer.org
Are you gunning to be a CFO of a major company? This award is for female students majoring only in finance or economics who plan to have corporate business careers.

209. National Association of Chiefs of Police
http://www.aphf.org
The *NACOP Scholarship* is for disabled officers who want to retrain through education. It is also open to the college-bound children of disabled officers.

210. National Association of Women in Construction
http://www.nawic.org
Don't think that only the guys get to have the fun with building things. If you are a female student enrolled in a construction-related degree program you can apply for the *Undergraduate Scholarship* and the *Construction Crafts Scholarship.*

How do I actually win a scholarship?

Winning a scholarship takes both time and effort. To help you increase your chances of winning observe these five "rules." If you want to learn more, take a look at our books, *Get Free Cash for College* and *How to Write a Winning Scholarship Essay*.

Be accurate and complete. More applications are disqualified because applicants didn't follow the directions than for any other reason.

Uncover the mission of the scholarship. Understand what the organization is trying to achieve by giving the scholarship and demonstrate how you match their goal in your application and essay.

Don't write your scholarship essay the night before. Give yourself time to write an essay that shows the judges exactly why you are the best candidate for their award by highlighting an experience or achievement that demonstrates how you match the goals of the scholarship.

Ace the interview. Interviews are often where final decisions are made, so be prepared by practicing your answers.

Don't be afraid to brag. This is not the time to be modest. Throughout your scholarship essay and interview explain why you deserve to win.

211. National Community Pharmacists Association

http://www.ncpanet.org

Students who are enrolled in a college of pharmacy may apply for the $2,000 *NCPA Foundation Presidential Scholarship*.

212. National Press Photographers Foundation

http://www.nppa.org

If you are studying photojournalism or you want to enter this industry take at look at the following awards: the *Bob East Scholarship*, the *College Photographer of the Year Award*, the *Joseph Ehrenreich Scholarship*, the *Kit C. King Graduate Scholarship*, the *NPPF Still Photography Scholarship*, the *NPPF Television News Scholarship* and the *Reid Blackburn Scholarship*.

213. National Restaurant Association Educational Foundation
http://www.edfound.org
Students majoring in a food service- or restaurant-related program may apply for either the *Academic Scholarship for High School Seniors* or the *Academic Scholarship for Undergraduate College Students.*

214. National Scholastic Press Association
http://www.studentpress.org
Stop the presses! If you work on your high school newspaper you may apply for the *Wikoff Scholarship for Editorial Leadership.*

215. National Society of Accountants
http://www.nsacct.org
The *NSA Scholarship* is perfect for you if you're an undergraduate majoring in accounting with a minimum 3.0 GPA.

216. National Society of Professional Engineers
http://www.nspe.org
This association offers a variety of scholarships for future engineers including: the *NSPE Auxiliary Scholarship*, the *Paul H. Robbins, P.E., Honorary Scholarship*, the *Professional Engineers in Government Scholarship*, the *Professional Engineers in Industry Scholarship* and the *Virginia D. Henry Memorial Scholarship.*

217. National Speakers Association
http://www.nsaspeaker.org
Surveys show that people fear speaking in public more than death. The *Bill Gove Scholarship*, the *Cavett Robert Scholarship*, the *Nido Qubein Scholarship* and the *Earl Nightengale Scholarship* are for you if you don't feel that way.

218. National Student Nurses' Association
http://www.nsna.org
Students in a school of nursing or pre-nursing program may apply for the *National Student Nurses' Association Scholarship.*

219. Outdoor Writers Association of America
http://www.owaa.org

If writing, filming or creating art based on the great outdoors is what you love, you just might have a chance at the *Bodie McDowell Scholarship*.

220. Physician Assistant Foundation
http://www.aapa.org
AAPA members who attend an ARC-PA–accredited physician assistant program may apply for the *Physician Assistant Foundation Scholarship*.

221. Plumbing-Heating-Cooling Contractors National Association
http://www.phccweb.org
If you are currently in a p-h-c program (and if you are then you know this means plumbing-heating-cooling) you may be able to apply for either the *Delta Faucet Company Scholarship* or the *PHCC Educational Foundation Scholarship*.

222. Public Relations Student Society of America
http://www.prssa.org
Publicity hounds and members of the PRSSA may apply for the following scholarships: the *Gary Yoshimura Scholarship, Professor Sidney Gross Memorial Award*, the *Betsy Plank/PRSSA Scholarship* and the *Lawrence G. Foster Award for Excellence in Public Relations*.

223. Radio and Television News Directors Association
http://www.rtnda.org
If you plan to enter the fast-paced world of television or radio news broadcasting then you should investigate these awards: the *Abe Schechter Graduate Scholarship*, the *Carole Simpson Scholarship*, the *Ed Bradley Scholarship*, the *Ken Kashiwahara Scholarship*, the *Len Allen Award for Radio Newsroom Management*, the *Lou and Carole Prato Sports Reporting Scholarship*, the *Mike Reynolds Scholarship* and the *Undergraduate Scholarship*.

224. Society of American Registered Architects
http://www.airportnet.org
The group sponsors the *Student Design Competition* to help architecture students.

225. Society of Automotive Engineers
http://www.sae.org
Who knew that fixing up cars and trucks would lead you to a scholarship? This organization offers awards for high school, college and graduate students entering this industry including the *Doctoral Scholars Forgivable Loan Program*, the *Long-Term Member Sponsored Scholarship*, the *SAE Engineering Scholarship* and the *Yanmar/SAE Scholarship*.

226. Society of Exploration Geophysicists
http://students.seg.org
To encourage students who want to journey to the center of the earth (or at least pursue a career in exploration geophysics), this association offers the *SEG Scholarship*.

227. Society of Nuclear Medicine
http://www.snmmi.org
Students in nuclear medicine may apply for the *Paul Cole Scholarship Award*.

228. Society of Plastics Engineers
http://www.4spe.org
If you plan to enter the plastics industry then you are in luck. This organization offers a plethora of awards for future plastic people including the *American Plastics Council (APC)/SPE Plastics Environmental Division Scholarship*, the *Composites Division/Harold Giles Scholarship*, the *Polymer Modifiers and Additives Division Scholarship*, the *SPE General Scholarship*, the *Ted Neward Scholarship*, the *Thermoforming Division Memorial Scholarship*, the *Thermoset Division/James I. MacKenzie Memorial Scholarship* and (our favorite) the *Vinyl Plastics Division Scholarship*.

229. Society of Professional Journalists
http://www.spj.org
This group sponsors the *Mark of Excellence Awards* honoring the best in student journalism. There are awards in 45 categories for print, radio, television and online journalism.

230. SWE Society of Women Engineers
http://www.societyofwomenengineers.org

This organization offers *National SWE Scholarships* for students from freshmen in college through graduate and adult students.

231. University Aviation Association
http://www.uaa.aero
This group offers several awards for aviation students including the *Eugene S. Kropf Scholarship*, the *Gary Kiteley Executive Director Scholarship* and the *Joseph Frasca Excellence in Aviation Scholarship*.

232. Wilson Ornithological Society
http://www.wilsonsociety.org
Helping young avian (bird) students everywhere this society offers the *George A. Hall and Harold F. Mayfield Award*, the *Louis Agassiz Fuertes Award* and the *Paul A. Stewart Award*.

233.

Don't ignore scholarship books
Even though they lack the pizzazz of the Internet, scholarship books should not be overlooked. A good book provides a huge number of awards and an index to help you find them. There are a lot of scholarship books—and most are somewhat pricey—so we recommend that you head to your local library or counseling center and browse through their collection.

One that we recommend, and it is not an impartial opinion by any means, is our book, *The Ultimate Scholarship Book.* We wrote this book after getting frustrated with one too many traditional scholarship books that cost too much and gave too little. We wanted a book that listed awards that most students could win. We also wanted to make sure that we didn't just give you the best directory of scholarships but also that we taught you how to win. In *The Ultimate Scholarship Book* you'll find that the first part of the book is a detailed strategy guide on how to create a winning scholarship application. The second part of the book is a comprehensive scholarship directory to over 2,500 awards that you can apply to win.

Complementing our scholarship directory is our other scholarship book, *How to Write a Winning Scholarship Essay.* In this book you can read the essays of 30 scholarship winners and get tips directly from the scholarship judges who decide whether or not you win.

Regardless of whether you read our books, you should not ignore the value of traditional scholarship directories.

234.

Double your scholarship with Dollars for Scholars

There's only one thing better than winning a scholarship, and that is having that scholarship doubled. This might sound too good to be true, but trust us, it's the real deal. Sponsored by Scholarship America, Dollars for Scholars is a network of more than 1,100 community-based scholarship foundations. These organizations award a variety of scholarships. Some of the awards that you win will probably be through your local Dollars for Scholars chapter. If you win a scholarship through the Dollars for Scholars program and attend a college that is a Dollars for Scholars partner school then the school may automatically match your scholarship thereby doubling its value.

Your first step is to find a Dollars for Scholars foundation in your city. Contact it and see what scholarships are available and apply for those that match your background and interests. If you win, then check with your college to see if they will match your scholarship. Get started by visiting the Dollars for Scholars website at http://www.scholarshipamerica.org.

235.

Awards based on your ethnicity

A common misconception is ethnicity-based scholarships are only for minorities. While there are awards for minorities, there are also scholarships for many ethnicities that are not. When looking for one of these scholarships the best place to start is with organizations dedicated to supporting members of your ethnicity. The National Italian American Foundation or National Association for the Advancement of Colored People (NAACP) are good examples.

However, don't limit yourself only to these kinds of groups. If you are a minority, also look at companies and professional associations.

Some have special scholarships to encourage underrepresented groups to enter a specific career or profession.

Keep in mind that there is no universal definition of who is a minority. Each scholarship defines which ethnic groups–and what qualifies you to be a member of an ethnic group–can apply. In general, the movement is toward "underrepresented" groups, which basically means ethnic groups that given their numbers within the general population are underrepresented in education or an industry. This definition means that an ethnic group that was considered a "minority" 10 years ago may no longer be considered one when it comes to a specific scholarship. It's best that you check eligibility requirements of the scholarship before you apply. The following is a small sampling of ethnicity-based awards.

236. Actuarial Scholarships for Minority Students
http://www.beanactuary.org
This award is sponsored by the Casualty Actuarial Society/ Society of Actuaries. It provides awards for both undergraduate and graduate minority students who are interested in pursuing actuarial careers.

237. American Chemical Society Scholars Program
http://www.chemistry.org
Sponsored by the American Chemical Society, this program helps African American, Hispanic and Native American students who intend to major in chemistry or science.

238. American Indian Scholarship
http://www.dar.org
The National Society Daughters of the American Revolution provides this program to assist Native American students. There is no affiliation with DAR required.

Aren't all scholarships based on financial need?

You could be the son or daughter of Bill Gates and still win a scholarship. It's true! The reason is because there are two kinds of scholarships available: need-based and merit-based.

As the name suggests, need-based scholarships are based on your financial need. To verify the level of your need, scholarship organizations may ask for tax returns or a copy of your Free Application for Federal Student Aid (FAFSA). Remember that the definition of need varies. Not all scholarships require extreme need. In fact, some organizations define families with incomes of up to $100,000 as needy. Also, it's important to know that need-based scholarships are not necessarily given to the most needy students. Many need-based scholarships also consider your academic and extracurricular achievement in addition to your financial situation.

On the other hand, merit-based scholarships do not take into account your financial status. Instead, they are based on other qualities such as your grades, involvement in activities, talents or other achievements. For these kinds of awards, it doesn't matter how many digits are in your family's income. You win these scholarships by showing that your background and achievements make you the most deserving of the award.

239. American Society of Criminology Fellowships for Ethnic Minorities

http://www.asc41.com

The American Society of Criminology sponsors this program for African American, Asian American, Latino or Native American students who are majoring in criminology.

240. Armenian Students' Association of America Scholarship

http://www.asainc.org

This program is for students of Armenian descent who are college sophomores or beyond.

241. Asian American Journalists Association Scholarships
http://www.aaja.org
To increase the presence of historically underrepresented Asian Pacific American groups in journalism, this organization awards scholarships to students from backgrounds including Vietnamese, Cambodians, Hmong and other Southeast Asians, South Asians and Pacific Islanders who are interested in journalism. Scholarships include the *Newhouse National Scholarship and Internship Awards,* the *Mary Moy Quan Ing Memorial Scholarship* and the *National AAJA General Scholarship Award.*

242. Asian and Pacific Islander American Scholarships
http://www.apiasf.org
This award supports Asian and Pacific Islander students who plan to be full-time college freshmen.

243. Brown Foundation Scholarships
http://www.brownvboard.org
The foundation assists minority high school seniors and college juniors who plan to enter careers in teaching.

244. Bureau of Indian Affairs High Education Grant
http://www.bia.gov
American Indian and Alaska Native undergraduate students who are members of a tribe or at least one-quarter degree Indian blood descendants may apply for these grants.

245. Cherokee Nation Undergraduate Scholarship Programs
http://www.cherokee.org
Applicants who are high school senior Cherokee Nation tribal members may apply for this award.

246. Council for Exceptional Children Ethnic Diversity Scholarship
http://www.cec.sped.org
Student CEC members from a minority ethnic background who are currently pursuing degrees in special education can apply for this award.

247. Gates Millennium Scholars Program

http://www.gmsp.org

African American, American Indian/Alaska Native, Asian Pacific Islander American or Hispanic American students can apply for this program.

248. Gillette/National Urban League Scholarship and Intern Program for Minority Students

http://www.nul.org

This program helps outstanding African American undergraduates majoring in engineering and business fields.

249. Hellenic Times Scholarship Fund

http://www.htsfund.org

This scholarship supports undergraduate or graduate students of Greek descent between the ages of 17 and 30.

250. Hispanic College Fund Scholarship

http://www.hispanicfund.org

Hispanic students pursuing their bachelor's degree and majoring in a business- or technology-related field may apply for this award.

251. Hispanic Heritage Awards Foundation

http://www.hispanicheritage.org

Hispanic American youth may apply for scholarships in one of these specific disciplines: Academic Excellence, Sports, the Arts, Literature/Journalism, Mathematics, Leadership/Community Service and Science and Technology.

252. Hispanic Outlook Magazine Scholarship Fund

http://www.hispanicoutlook.com

Hispanic high school seniors can apply for this scholarship.

253. Hispanic Scholarship Fund (HSF)

http://www.hsf.net

Students of Hispanic heritage may apply to this program that has awarded more than 45,000 scholarships over the past 25 years.

254. Japanese American Citizens League

http://www.jacl.org

This organization aids student members with various awards including the *Hawigara Student Aid Award*, the *Japanese American Citizens League Creative and Performing Arts Award*, the *Japanese American Citizens League Entering Freshman Award*, the *Japanese American Citizens League Graduate Award*, the *Japanese American Citizens League Law Scholarship* and the *Japanese American Citizens League Undergraduate Award*.

255. Kosciuszko Tuition Scholarship Program

http://www.thekf.org

Students of Polish descent may apply for this scholarship from the Kosciuszko Foundation.

256. League of United Latin American Citizens Scholarship Fund

http://www.lulac.org

Hispanic students who have applied or are enrolled in a college, university or graduate school may apply for an award.

257. League of United Latin American Citizens GM Fund

http://lulac.org/programs/education/scholarships/

If you are a full-time minority college student majoring in courses that will lead to an engineering career you can apply for an award from the *GM Fund*.

258. National Action Council for Minorities in Engineering

http://www.nacme.org

This group offers a variety of scholarships and pre-college programs including the *United Space Alliance Scholarship* and the *3M Corporation Scholarship*.

259. National Association for the Advancement of Colored People (NAACP)

http://www.naacp.org

The NAACP awards over 100 scholarships each year. Some of the awards include the *Earl Graves Scholarship*, the *Agnes Jones Scholarship*, the *Louis Stokes Scholarship*, the *Sutton Scholarship*, the *Roy Wilkins Scholarship* and the *Willems Scholarship*. You can download applications from the website.

260. National Association of Black Accountants Scholarship Program

http://www.nabainc.org

This program is for African Americans and other minorities who intend to enter accounting or finance professions.

261. National Association of Black Journalists Scholarship Program

http://www.nabj.org

This scholarship supports African American students who are planning to pursue careers in journalism.

262. National Association of Hispanic Journalists Scholarships

http://www.nahj.org

Scholarships include the *Cristina Saralegüi Scholarship*, the *NAHJ Scholarship* and the *Newhouse Scholarship*.

263. National Association of Minority Engineering Program Administrators

http://www.namepa.org

To support minority students who want to become engineers, this association offers the *NAMEPA Scholarship Program*.

264. National Black Police Association

http://www.blackpolice.org

The *Alphonso Deal Scholarship Award* is given to high school seniors who are planning to study law enforcement.

265. National Society of Black Engineers

http://www.nsbe.org

Encouraging black students to enter engineering, this organization offers a variety of scholarships and competitions for students of nearly all levels.

266. Native American Journalists Association Scholarship

http://www.naja.com

This award is for Native American students pursuing journalism degrees.

> ## What happens if I find too many scholarships? How do I know which ones to apply for?
>
> Since there are tens of thousands of scholarships available, your problem may not be finding awards but deciding which ones to apply for and which you have the best chance of winning. Although there is no way to predict if you will win a scholarship, there is one method you can use to select those that fit you best and therefore offer you the best chance of winning.
>
> The key is to realize that almost every scholarship organization has a mission or goal for giving away its money. Few groups give away free money for no reason. For example, a nature group might sponsor a scholarship with the goal of promoting conservation and encouraging students to be environmentally conscious. To this end the group will reward students who have demonstrated a concern for the environment and have some plan to contribute to this cause in the future.
>
> Understanding the mission of the scholarship is important because it will clue you in to the kind of student the organization is looking for. If you have the background, interests and accomplishments that match this mission and are able to convey that in your application, you have a good chance of winning the award.

267. Order Sons of Italy in America
http://www.osia.org
Applicants must be enrolled in an undergraduate or graduate program and be of Italian descent.

268. Organization of Chinese Americans
http://www.ocanational.org
This organization offers various scholarships for African American, Asian American, Hispanic American and Native American high school students including the *Lead Summer Program*, the *OCA Avon College Scholarship*, the *OCA National Essay Contest* and the *OCA/UPS Gold Mountain Scholarship*.

269. Public Relations Student Society of America-Multicultural Affairs Scholarship Program

http://www.prssa.org

Students who are of African American, Hispanic, Asian, Native American, Alaskan Native or Pacific Islander ancestry and studying communications may apply for this award.

270. Ron Brown Scholar Program

http://www.ronbrown.org

This program awards scholarships to academically talented and highly motivated African American high school seniors.

271. Scholarships for Disadvantaged Students in Health Professions

http://www.hrsa.gov/loanscholarships/

The Bureau of Health Professions offers scholarships for students from disadvantaged background who also have financial need and are enrolled in health or nursing programs. Individual schools select the scholarship recipients. Contact your financial aid office for details.

272. Society of Hispanic Professional Engineers

http://www.shpe.org

Hispanic students studying math, science and engineering disciplines may apply for a scholarship.

273. The National Italian American Foundation

http://www.niaf.org

Italian American students who demonstrate outstanding potential and high academic achievement or students of any ethnic background who are majoring or minoring in the Italian language or Italian American studies can apply for this group's scholarship.

274. Thurgood Marshall Scholarship Fund

http://www.thurgoodmarshallfund.org

Students enrolled or planning to enroll as full-time students at one of the 45 historically black public colleges and universities, who have demonstrated a commitment to academic excellence and community service and who show financial need can apply for this award.

275. U.S. Pan Asian American Chamber of Commerce
http://www.uspaacc.com

Asian American students may apply for a variety of awards including: the *Asian American Scholarship Fund Award*, the *Yue-Sai Kan Scholarship*, the *Bernadette Wong-Yu Scholarship*, the *Bruce Lee Scholarship* (no martial arts skills required), the *Cary C. and Debra Y.C. Wu Scholarship*, the *Drs. Poh Shien and Judy Young Scholarship*, the *Jackie Chan Scholarship*, the *Ruth Mu-Lan Chu and James S.C. Chao Scholarship* and the *Telamon Scholarship*.

276. United Negro College Fund Scholarships
http://www.uncf.org

Applicants must be African American, have a minimum 2.5 GPA and must have unmet financial need. The UNCF offers a variety of scholarships and grants.

277.

Scholarships for a disability

Many organizations that work on behalf of specific physical or mental disabilities offer scholarship programs. Contact them directly or visit their websites to see what scholarships are available. The Easter Seal Society, for example, offers scholarships through local chapters for students with disabilities. Contact your local Easter Seal Rehabilitation Center to see what scholarships are available in your area. The same is true of most of the other organizations. Here are a few to get you started.

For the hearing impaired:

278. Alexander Graham Bell Association
Alexander Graham Bell Association Scholarship
http://www.agbell.org

279. Children of Deaf Adults, International
Millie Brother Scholarship
http://www.coda-international.org

280. EAR Foundation
Minnie Pearl Scholarship
http://www.earfoundation.org

281. National Association of the Deaf
William C. Stokoe Scholarship
http://www.nad.org

282. National Fraternal Society of the Deaf
Deaf Scholarship
http://www.nfsd.com

283. Travelers Protective Association
TPA Scholarship Trust for the Deaf and Near Deaf
http://www.tpahq.org/scholarshiptrust/

For the visually impaired:

284. American Foundation for the Blind
Ferdinand Torres and Karen D. Carsel Memorial Scholarship
http://www.afb.org

285. Association for Education and Rehabilitation of the Blind and Visually Impaired
William and Dorothy Ferrell Scholarship
http://www.aerbvi.org

286. Christian Record Services
CRS Scholarship for the Legally Blind
http://www.christianrecord.org

287. National Federation of Music Clubs
The NFMC Hinda Honigman Award for the Blind
http://www.nfmc-music.org

288. National Federation of the Blind
National Federation of the Blind Scholarship
http://www.nfb.org

For physical disabilities:

289. Andre Sobel River of Life Foundation
Andre Sobel Award
http://www.andreriveroflife.org

290. Bank of America
Bank of America ADA Abilities Scholarship Program
http://www.scholarshipprograms.org

291. Chair Scholars
Chair Scholars Scholarship for the Physically Challenged
http://www.chairscholars.org

292. Microsoft Scholarships for Students with Disabilities
Microsoft's award is aimed at current college students who are interested in entering the software industry.
Website: https://www.microsoft.com/en-us/diversity/programs/microsoftdisabilityscholarship.aspx

293. Pfizer
Pfizer Epilepsy Scholarship
http://www.epilepsy-scholarship.com

What's the best way to get an application?

Save your stamps (and time) by downloading the scholarship application directly from the Internet whenever possible. By downloading it from the Internet, you have instant access to the application. When using the mail, students have reported receiving applications late, if at all. This is because many scholarship organizations are composed of volunteers, meaning that they don't have the staff to respond as quickly as they'd like to application requests. So if you have a choice, our recommendation is to take matters into your own hands and download them.

294. Spina Bifida Association of America
SBAA Scholarship Fund
http://www.spinabifidaassociation.org

For learning disabilities:

295. International Dyslexia Association
The IDA offers various scholarships through their local associations.
http://www.interdys.org

296. National Center for Learning Disabilities
Anne Ford Scholarship Program
http://www.ncld.org

297. The P. Buckley Moss Society
Ann and Matt Harbison Scholarship
http://www.mosssociety.org

298. Shire ADHD College Scholarship Program
This program assists students who have been diagnosed with ADHD.
http://www.shireadhdscholarship.com

299. VSA Arts
Young Soloists Awards are for student musicians with mental or physical disabilities.
http://vsarts.org

300.

Awards based on personal challenges and hardships

If you've overcome personal challenges or hardships, you can certainly describe this in your scholarship applications no matter what the award. Almost every scholarship judge will be impressed if you have overcome obstacles and reached your goals despite personal challenges. However, there are a few organizations that are dedicated specifically to recognizing students who have overcome significant challenges.

Two of the better known are the *American Cancer Society College Scholarship Program* and the *Horatio Alger Association Scholarship Program*. The *American Cancer Society College Scholarship Program* offers scholarships for students (usually under the age of 25) who are cancer survivors. Each program is run by a local ACS organization. You can find your local ACS at http://www.cancer.org.

The *Horatio Alger Association Scholarship Program* is for students who have overcome major obstacles in their life, are committed to using their college degrees in service to others and demonstrate financial need. Visit http://www.horatioalger.com to receive more information.

When you write about hardships that you've faced in your application, remember that you need to do more than just describe the challenge. You also need to explain how you have survived or overcome the challenge and what you have learned from the experience. Scholarship winners are not those who have faced the most difficult challenges, but those who have encountered obstacles and grown stronger from the experience.

301.

Turn your hobbies and talents into scholarship gold

Whether it's playing basketball or backgammon, we all have interests and hobbies that we pursue outside of the classroom. While we think of these as enjoyable diversions, sometimes they can also be the basis for winning a scholarship. The way to find out if your interest has a related scholarship is to inquire with organized enthusiast groups.

For example, if your hobby is short-wave radio, check out the website of the Amateur Radio Relay League at http://www.arrlf.org. You'll find that this group offers more than a dozen scholarships.

If you are a member of your school band, you might subscribe to *School Band and Orchestra Magazine*. This publication (http://www.sbomagazine.com) sponsors an essay competition for students in grades 4 through 12 for a scholarship.

If you do some digging around your interests and hobbies, chances are you'll find groups and organizations that want to reward students like you.

302.

Scholarship organizations love leaders

You might be a leader and not even know it. While there are many scholarships for leaders, it's amazing how many students don't think they are a leader simply because they don't have the appropriate title such as "president" or "secretary." Being a leader is not just about being elected. You can be a leader simply for organizing your peers. If you have ever organized an event or special project, that is certainly an example of leadership.

One of the most well-known leadership scholarships is the *Principals Leadership Award Scholarship* sponsored by the National Association of Secondary School Principals (http://www.nassp.org) and Herff Jones (http://www.herff-jones.com). Principals nominate high school senior student leaders based on their leadership skills, participation in service organizations, achievements in the arts and sciences, work experience

---

How do I describe my accomplishments to impress the scholarship judges?

Winning a scholarship is about impressing the judges and showing them why you are the best candidate. Your accomplishments, activities, talents and awards all help to prove that you are the best fit. Since you will probably list your activities on the application form, you can use your essay to expand on one or two of the most important. However, don't just parrot back what is on your application. Use the opportunity to focus on a specific accomplishment, provide detail and to put it into the proper context. Listing on your application that you were a stage manager for a play does not explain that you also had to design and build all of the sets in a week. The essay allows you to expand on an achievement to demonstrate its significance.

and academic record. There are 150 students from all 50 states who win $1,000 scholarships.

Most scholarships whether they say so or not value leadership. In all of your applications and interviews you should cite examples of your leadership skills when possible. Remember, you do not have to be in an elected office to be a leader. Any time you have taken the initiative to organize an activity, you have shown leadership.

303.

Turn your community service into scholarship dollars

Whether you collect canned goods for the homeless or sing for lonely senior citizens, volunteer work makes you feel good. This is a noble use of your time which can lead to scholarships that recognize your commitment to your community.

Many students mistake community service as being measured by hours spent per week or doing traditional service club activities. But serving the community can take many forms including being a coach of a little league team or helping to tutor at a community center. What's more important than the number of hours you serve is the contribution that you make. Don't assume that you cannot complete for a service-based scholarship just because you haven't committed thousands of hours.

For example, Amazon offers the *Amazon Student Scholarship*, giving away 50 scholarships of $5,000 each to high school seniors and college undergraduates based on academic achievement, community service and leadership. More details are at https://www.amazon.com/b?ie=UTF8&node=9944643011.

AmeriCorps sponsors the *Presidential Freedom Scholarships* to promote and recognize leadership in service and citizenship. Applicants must be high school juniors or seniors who have contributed at least 100 hours of service within the past year, demonstrate outstanding citizenship through their service and participation in other community activities and plan to attend an eligible institute of higher learning. Learn more by visiting the Americorps website at: http://www.americorps.gov.

304.

You don't have to be a superstar athlete to win a scholarship

You might think you need to be the next Stephen Curry or Hope Solo to win an athletic scholarship. While superior athletic skills certainly wouldn't hurt, the truth is that you don't have to be an athletic superstar to win a scholarship. Naturally you need to be gifted to get an athletic scholarship to play football for the University of Southern California or Ohio State since they are top ranked teams, but you do not necessarily have to be the best for many other college teams.

Even at schools with strong athletic programs, the sport that you play may not be as competitive. This means that the caliber of athlete they are looking for will be much different than for the nationally ranked programs. Many students have won partial or even full athletic scholarships even though they were not even the best athletes at their high school.

The key to getting an athletic scholarship is to be proactive about contacting the coaches at the colleges you are interested in before you apply. Send an email or letter to coaches and tell them that you are a prospective applicant and are also interested in playing on their team. Be ready to send a portfolio of your athletic accomplishments and also make sure to get a letter from your current coach that will attest not only to your abilities but also to your character as an athlete. To find which schools offer athletic programs in your area, visit the NCAA website at http://www.ncaa.org.

Besides athletic scholarships from the colleges, you can also apply for private athletic scholarships from various sporting associations. Here are a few of the more popular ones, but don't forget about the local associations in your area either:

305. Harness Horse Youth Foundation
Harness Racing Scholarship
http://www.hhyf.org

306. Ice Skating Institute of America (ISIA)
ISIA Education Foundation Scholarship
http://www.skateisi.com

307. National Amateur Baseball Federation
Ronald and Irene McMinn Scholarship
http://www.nabf.com

308. National Archery Association
NAA College Scholarship
http://www.usarchery.org

309. National Athletic Trainers' Association
NATA Scholarship
http://www.nata.org

310. National Rifle Association
NRA Junior Member Scholarship
http://www.nrahq.org

311. Nike
Casey Martin Award
http://www.nikebiz.com

312. Our World-Underwater Scholarship Society
North American Rolex Scholarship
http://www.owuscholarship.org

313. Pop Warner
All-American Scholar Program
http://www.popwarner.com

314. Stonehouse Publishing Company
Stonehouse Golf Youth Scholarship
http://www.stonehousegolf.com

315. Wendy's Restaurants
Wendy's High School Heisman Award
http://www.wendyshighschoolheisman.com

316. Women's Sports Foundation
Linda Riddle/SGMA Scholarship
http://www.womenssportsfoundation.org

317.

Ace your college applications to get more scholarships

You may not realize that your college applications are also scholarship applications. If the colleges really want you, then they will not only offer you admission but will also give you an automatic scholarship. Even if you know that you are a definite admission for the college you are applying to, spend the time and effort to create an outstanding application. That might be the difference between simply getting admitted and getting admitted with a $10,000 scholarship.

If you want to learn more about how to ace your college admission applications, we recommend our books, *Get into Any College* and *Accepted! 50 Successful College Admission Essays*.

318.

Help the colleges help you by providing everything they may need to give you a scholarship

When you apply for a scholarship from a college they may ask you to only complete a simple application form. However, you should always include an essay and resume. The reason is that when the scholarship committee reviews your application they may find that you are also qualified for another scholarship from the college. However, this scholarship may require an essay. If you include an essay it will make it very easy for the college to award you the scholarship. You may be surprised to learn that colleges are always looking for students who match their various scholarship programs. Help them help you by giving them everything they would need to award you a scholarship.

319.

Don't let the colleges take away your scholarship money

When you win a scholarship, you have to report it to your college. Unfortunately, sometimes a college will decrease your financial aid by the amount of scholarship money that you win. Not fair, you say? You're absolutely right! If this happens to you, immediately contact the organization that gave you the scholarship and explain the situation. Some scholarship organizations have policies against giving an award to a student if the college will adjust their financial aid package. With the scholarship organization on your side, approach the college financial aid office. In most cases the financial aid office will back down rather than see you forfeit the scholarship.

If the college insists on adjusting your financial aid package, ask that they lower your "self-help" (e.g. student loan) amounts rather than grants. It's much better for you to have to borrow less in loans anyway. Be firm in making your case and be sure to point out to the college that their policy gives you little incentive to apply for any scholarships in the future.

If none of these strategies work, you should still take the scholarship since the scholarship is guaranteed while any financial aid grants are subject to availability of the funds. Even if you get a grant in one year you might not receive the same amount the next year. But a scholarship, if it's renewable, will pay you the same amount every year.

320.

Strange and offbeat scholarships

You've heard the rumors. Somewhere there is a scholarship just for left-handed students. Maybe you heard from a friend of a friend that you can get a scholarship for being tall. While careful investigation reveals that even though there is a scholarship for lefties (given to students at Juniata College in Huntingdon, Pennsylvania) just because you are left-handed does not mean you automatically win. You still have to beat out all of the other talented lefties. We're sure that once you start your scholarship search you'll find plenty of your own strange scholarships.

Here are a few offbeat scholarships to give you an idea of what's out there. Our point in sharing these awards is to inspire you. No matter what your background, talent or achievements, you can find a scholarship that fits. These scholarships prove it.

321. Collegiate Inventors Competition
http://www.collegiateinventors.org
Have an idea for a new invention? This scholarship supports exploration in invention, science and technology.

322. David Letterman Scholarship
http://www.bsu.edu
He may be most famous for his Top 10 Lists, but David Letterman also has a scholarship for telecommunications students at his alma mater, Ball State University.

323. Duck Calling Con-
http://www.stuttgartar-kansas.org
Quack! Do you have a talent for duck calling? The Chick and Sophie Major Memorial Contest awards the country's best duck calls.

324. Duct Tape Stuck at Prom Scholarship
http://www.stuckat-prom.com
The makers of "Duck" brand duct tape sponsor this award. The prize is a $6,000 award for the

couple that goes to their high school prom in the most original attire made from duct tape, which comes in 17 colors!

325. Little People of America Scholarship
http://www.lpaonline.org
You may have heard of the scholarships for tall people. There are also scholarships for those who are short in stature. You must be no taller than 4'10" and have a medically diagnosed form of dwarfism.

326. Magic Scholarship
http://www.wizards.com
Who knew that playing a card game could win you a scholarships? If you enjoy the *Magic The Gathering* card game then you could enter their annual Junior Super Series competition held in cities around the country. Winners earn thousands of dollars in college scholarships.

327. Marbles Scholarship
http://www.nationalmarblestournament.org
You can win money for almost any interest. During a four-day tournament, "mibsters," or marble shooters, compete in more than 1,200 marble games to win scholarship awards.

328. Million-Dollar Name
http://www.luc.edu
Loyola University in Chicago offers a full-tuition, four-year scholarship to any student who is Catholic and whose last name is Zolp. The last name must appear on both the birth and confirmation certificate.

329. National Candy Technologists Scholarship Program
http://www.aactcandy.org/aactscholarship.asp
Do you love candy? If you have a demonstrated interest in confectionary technology, this may be the scholarship for you.

330. National Potato Council Scholarship
http://www.nationalpotatocouncil.org
Are you thinking of majoring in french fries? Okay, not really.

But if you are a graduate student in agribusiness in a field that supports the potato industry, you could win $5,000.

331. Pokemon Scholarships

http://www.pokemon.com/us/play-pokemon/pokemon-events/pokemon-tournaments/scholarships/

Your Pokemon collection in that old shoe box can finally help you pay for college! Scholarships are given to winners in the national and world championships.

332. Tall Student Scholarship

http://www.tall.org

Awarded each year by Tall Club International, applicants for this $1,000 scholarship must be over 6'2" if you're male or 5'10" if you're female. Tall Club International has more than 200 local clubs across the U.S., many of which offer their own scholarships. The award can be used at any college to study any major.

THREE

Contests For Students

Do You Feel Lucky?

Does the word "contest" conjure up images of Ed McMahon knocking on your door, oversized check in hand? While there are contests based on luck, there are also contests that focus on your abilities within a specific skill—such as art, writing or music.

Unlike scholarship competitions, these contests for students are based on just one criterion—such as your ability to write a short story or paint a picture. Things like grades, test scores and extracurricular activities have no meaning in these contests. You are judged purely on your submission or performance.

What's nice about these contests is that they are open only to students, which greatly reduces the competition and increases your chance of winning. Unlike Publisher's Clearinghouse millions of people are not entering.

The following are some of the larger contests that students can enter. Be sure that you also check locally since we found many contests that are limited to students in specific cities and states that we didn't have the s p a c e to include. Just like scholarships, any backyard contests that you find will give you the best odds of winning.

And just for fun we also included a few contests that are based purely on chance for those of you who are feeling lucky.

Contests For Writers And Poets

Unlike scholarships that require an essay as part of the overall competition, in these contests the essay is the competition. Winners are selected based only on their essays. You'll find that many of these competitions are open to students younger than high school seniors and are a great way to get started earning some money.

333. American Fire Sprinkler Association Essay Contest

http://www.firesprinkler.org

You don't have to be an expert on fire sprinklers to enter this contest, but you do have to write an essay on the importance of fire sprinklers. Here's a sample of a recent essay question: "How do fire sprinklers function and where are they required in your community?" Winners receive $1,000 to $3,000.

334. Ayn Rand Essay Contest–*Anthem*

http://www.aynrand.org/contests/

During the course of high school most of you will read something by Ayn Rand. If you do there is an amazing essay contest based on a number of her books. This essay contest is based on Ayn Rand's *Anthem* and is for students in the eighth, ninth or 10th grade. The first prize is $2,000. There are also additional runner-up prizes.

335. Ayn Rand Essay Contest–*Atlas Shrugged*

http://www.aynrand.org/contests/

If you are in the 12th grade or college and have read *Atlas Shrugged* you can enter this essay contest. The first prize is $5,000, and there are also three second prizes worth $1,000.

336. Ayn Rand Essay Contest–*The Fountainhead*

http://www.aynrand.org/contests/

If you're a junior or senior in high school you can enter this essay contest that is based on Ayn Rand's *The Fountainhead.* The first prize is $10,000.

337. Ayn Rand Essay Contest–*We the Living*

http://www.aynrand.org/contests/

High school sophomores, juniors and seniors are eligible to enter this essay contest that is based on Ayn Rand's *We the Living.* The first prize is $3,000.

338. Guidepost Young Writers Contest

http://www.guideposts.com

To enter you must write a first-person story about a memorable or moving experience. This contest is for high school juniors or seniors. Prizes range from $250 to $10,000.

339. Holocaust Remembrance Project
http://holocaust.hklaw.com/
This is a national essay contest for high school students designed to encourage the study of the Holocaust. The project also serves as a living memorial to the victims of the Holocaust. First-place winners receive a scholarship of up to $5,000.

340. Inverness Corporation "Is All Ears" Essay Contest
http://www.invernesscorp.com
What do Arnold Schwarzenegger and Oprah Winfrey have in common? Not much except that either could be your answer to this contest question. Open to all high school students ages 14 to 19, this contest asks the question: "If you had the ear of any special person, famous or not, what would you tell them and why?" Answers must be a terse 150 words or less. Prizes range from $1,000 to $5,000.

341. John F. Kennedy Profile in Courage Essay Contest
http://www.jfklibrary.org/Education/Profile-in-Courage-Essay-Contest.aspx
This essay contest is open to all students in grades 9 to 12. Each year $6,500 in prizes are awarded. You must write an essay of no more than 1,000 words on one of the provided essay questions. Visit the contest website for official rules and to get this year's questions.

342. L. Ron Hubbard Writers of the Future
http://www.writersofthefuture.com
This is a science fiction short story contest for amateur writers. Prizes range from $500 to $4,000.

343. Mensa Education & Research Foundation Scholarship Program
http://www.mensafoundation.org/scholarships
The brainiacs at Mensa have created an award program that is based only on your written essays. You don't have to be a member of Mensa, and grades and financial need are not a consideration. The scholarship program is managed by each local Mensa group, and you must apply through your local Mensa organization.

344. National Council of Teachers of English Student Writing Awards

http://www.ncte.org

The NCTE sponsors several writing awards including the *Achievement Awards in Writing* that recognizes the writing abilities of high school students. You must be nominated by your school for this award competition. The group also sponsors the *Promising Young Writers Program* that is open to students in the eighth grade. Visit the NCTE website for more information and current deadlines.

345. National Peace Essay Contest

http://www.usip.org/category/course-type/national-peace-essay-contest

Students in grades 9 to 12 may enter an essay into this contest, which as the name suggests is about world peace. You must be sponsored by a school, school club, youth group, community group or religious organization with an adult advisor.

346. National Schools Project Young Poets Contest

http://www.youngpoets.org/Contest.htm

Calling all aspiring poets. This contest recognizes young poetry writers (grades K-12.) To enter you must submit an original poem of 21 lines or less. Winners divide more than $70,000 in prizes.

347. Optimist International Essay Contest

http://www.optimist.org

This essay contest awards $44,000 annually in scholarships. Applicants must be under 19 years of age and submit short essays on the topic of freedom. Begin the process by submitting your essay to your local Optimist Club. You can find your local club through the Optimist Club's website.

348. Playwright Discovery Award

http://education.kennedy-center.org//education/vsa/

Students in grades 6 to 12 can win a scholarship for creating an original one-act play script.

349. Power Poetry Scholarships

http://www.powerpoetry.org

Power Poetry offers scholarship contests year-round for high school and college students who submit poems on provided topics. Recent topics include writing about what has shaped you this past year.

350. Scholastic Art and Writing Awards
http://www.artandwriting.org
Students in grades 7 to 12 can enter this competition. You can read past winners' essays online as well as download an application and current contest rules.

351. Signet Classic Student Scholarship Essay Contest
http://us.penguingroup.com/static/pages/services-academic/essayhome.html
The prospect of winning a scholarship is one way to get you to read literary classics. High school juniors and seniors can enter this contest by writing essays on topics related to literature classics. A recent competition was based on Mary Shelley's book *Frankenstein.* Five winners win $1,000 scholarships that can be used toward college.

352. The Laws of Life Essay Contest
http://www.lawsoflife.org
Unlike most essay contests, this one does not provide a topic. You are encouraged to write from your heart. However, you should understand what this group is about and the principles that it advocates. The contest is open to all elementary, high school and college students. You can learn more about the Laws of Life organization and get more information on how to enter online.

353. UNA-USA National High School Essay Contest on the United Nations
http://www.unausa.org (Click on "Education" and then click on "Programs.")
It's time for your best Miss America impression. What is an issue of global concern to you? This

annual essay contest gives high school students in grades 9 to 12 the opportunity to address an issue of significant global concern. Essays must be 1,500 words or less. You must submit your essay to your local United Nations Association Chapter, which you can find on the organization's website. The first prize is $1,000, and naturally, your essay needs to be a little more thought provoking than a 30-second Miss America answer.

Contests For Performing Arts

If you dream of seeing your names in lights and are fearless of the stage then these contests are for you. The following contests are for musicians, thespians and students involved in speech competitions. Most require submitting an original work such as a speech or composition, and most of the music competitions are performance based.

354. American Society of Composers, Authors and Publishers
http://www.ascapfoundation.org/awards.html
The ASCAP foundation offers several music composition competitions including the *Young Jazz Composer Awards*, the *Heineken Music Initiative* for R&B songwriters, the *Morton Gould Young Composer Awards* and the *Rudolf Nissim Prize*. In addition, you can find a list of music scholarships administered by individual high schools, colleges and conservatories on the website.

355. Arts Recognition and Talent Search (ARTS)
http://www.youngarts.org
If you are a talented high school senior, you can apply to the

---

Where can I find more contests for writers?

If after applying to the writing contests in this chapter you still have more words in you, here is a writer's contests directory with more competitions. Note that these are not specifically for students, but most are open to writers of any age. To see the list just surf on over to http://www.dmoz.org/Arts/Writers_Resources/Contests/.

National YoungArts Foundation program. The YoungArts program identifies young artists in dance, film and video, jazz music, photography, theater visual arts, voice and writing. Each year YoungArts awards more than $3 million in college scholarships. YoungArts program participants can also be named an YoungArts Finalist to compete for the honor of being named Presidential Scholars in the Arts. Also, the jazz, music and voice discipline winners can attend the YoungArts Week in Miami and win additional prizes worth up to $25,000.

356. BMI Foundation Awards
http://www.bmifoundation.org
The BMI Foundation offers a variety of scholarship programs including the *John Lennon Scholarship Program*, which was established by Yoko Ono in 1997. This program recognizes songwriters in any genre who are between the ages of 15 and 25. The *Pete Carpenter Fellowship* gives aspiring TV and film composers

---

How can I make a recording of my performance to send to one of these contests?

Many music and vocal contests require a CD. It's very important that you don't skimp on this since no matter how talented you are if you record in a noisy room with a dog barking in the background, it will affect the quality of your performance. But you don't have to shell out hundreds of dollars to rent a studio either.

Consider these no-cost options. Visit your community college and speak to a professor in the applied music department. Tell the professor what you want to do and ask if he or she will let you borrow the recording studio for an hour. Even easier, if you have friends who are in college they can probably hook you up with another student who has access to the campus music studio. Another option is to visit your local public access cable station. They should be listed in the phone book. You can get a CD made of your performance using their professional sound equipment. You might even be able to get your school's A/V club to help out. As you can see there are a lot of free options for recording your performance.

the opportunity to work with composer Mike Post at his studio in Los Angeles and includes a $2,000 stipend for travel and expenses. The fellowship is open to any composer under the age of 35. The BMI Foundation also sponsors its own *Student Composer Awards*, which are for young composers of classical music. You must be a high school or college student or studying under a music teacher and under the age of 26.

357. Chopin Foundation
http://www.chopin.org
This program is available to any pianists age 14 to 17 who are enrolled in secondary or undergraduate institutions as full-time students.

358. Dizzy Feet Foundation
http://dizzyfeetfoundation.org/scholarships/information/
This program is open to students at least 15 years old who are attending an accredited dance school or institution. Awards of up to $10,000 are given.

359. Donna Reed Performing Arts Scholarships
http://www.donnareed.org
The Donna Reed Festival and Workshops for the Performing Arts includes categories for acting, vocal and musical theater. Three $4,000 scholarships are awarded to high school seniors, which may be used at any college.

360. Educational Theatre Association Thespian Scholarships
http://www.edta.org
Each year this association gives away more than $25,000 in scholarships. To apply for an award you must be a high school senior, be active in the International Thespian Society and plan to continue your thespian education in college. A number of competitions are held at the International Thespian Festival. You must audition for the competition. Another program awards money through your state thespian conference. Contact your state thespian director for details. You can learn more about the scholarships and find a directory of state directors at the EDTA website.

361. Glenn Miller Scholarship Competition

http://www.glennmiller.org

You'll be relieved to know that you don't have to look or sound like Glenn Miller to win this competition. The Glenn Miller Birthplace Society offers four scholarships each year for instrumentalists and vocalists to recognize promising young musicians in any field of applied music. To enter you must be a high school senior or college freshman who intends to make music a part of your career. You must also submit a tape of your musical performance.

362. Joseph S. Rumbaugh Oration Contest

http://www.sar.org/youth/rumbaugh.html

Attention history buffs! The National Society of the Sons of the American Revolution sponsors an oratorical scholarship for high school sophomores through seniors. The topic must address an event or person in the Revolutionary War showing the relationship to America today. You compete through your local or state chapters. Find a list of local chapters on the website. Prizes range from $200 to $3,000.

363. Optimist Oratorical Contest

http://www.optimist.org/e/member/scholarships4.cfm

If you're the type of person who likes public speaking, this scholarship is for you. Students who are younger than 16 years old may enter this oratory competition through their local Optimist Club. Each year more than $159,000 is awarded in scholarships. Prizes range from $500 to $1,500.

364. Young Artist Competition

http://www.minnesotaorchestra.org

Founded in 1956, this program is sponsored by WAMSO (Minnesota Orchestra Volunteer Association) and is designed to encourage musical education. Musicians do not need to be residents of Minnesota but must be under the age of 26 and meet all other eligibility requirements. You must also submit a tape or CD of your performance to be judged in the preliminary rounds. The final round is a live performance competition at Macalester College in St. Paul.

365. Young Concert Artists International

http://www.yca.org

Each year this group holds a competition in which four winners are selected to receive a $5,000 award and perform in the Young Concert Artists Series in New York, Boston and Washington, D.C.

Contests For Artists

Let's shed the starving artist stereotype here. If you are an aspiring artist, there are ways to earn some recognition and bank some future cash for college. There are a number of competitions that require you to submit your artwork (or a photograph of your artwork.) Be sure to look at the judging requirements of each contest since they can give you valuable hints about what the judges are looking for in a winning entry.

366. Christophers

http://www.christophers.org

With its motto, "It's better to light one candle than to curse the darkness," the Christophers sponsors an annual poster contest with prizes of up to $1,000. The contest is open to high school students.

367. College Photographer of the Year

http://www.nppa.org

Sponsored by the National Press Photographers Association, this award supports student work in photojournalism.

368. Federal Duck Jr. Stamp Competition

http://duckstamps.fws.gov

All entrants must be over the age of 18 and must design an original stamp featuring an eligible duck. The national winners receive scholarships up to $4,000, and the first place national winner's design is made into a stamp. Pretty cool.

369. Images of Freedom Student Photography Contest

http://www.abanet.org

Students between the ages of 12 and 18 may submit original photos that depict the Law Day theme. Prizes include national recognition, inclusion in a photo exhibit, a U.S. savings bond and educational materials.

370. National Sculpture Society Scholarship

http://www.nationalsculpture.org

College students of figurative or representational sculpture can apply for these $2,000 scholarships for emerging artists. Scholarships are paid directly to the college through which the student applies.

371. Scholastic Art and Writing Awards

http://www.artandwriting.org

Young writers and artists in grades 7 to 12 can enter this competition sponsored by Scholastic. You can view the winning entries from previous years online.

372. Worldstudio Foundation

http://www.worldstudio.org

This foundation supports undergraduate and graduate students majoring in fine or commercial arts, design or architecture who are minorities or who have financial need.

Contests Of Chance

Some people are born lucky. We have an aunt who always seems to be a magnet for slot machine jackpots in Vegas. On the other hand, one of the luckiest days that I (Kelly) had was when I was a kid and won a call-in radio contest. The prize? I got to ride on top of an elephant at the circus. Unfortunately, unlike the prizes of the following contests, that elephant ride didn't help me pay for college. If you consider yourself lucky or just feel lucky you might want to enter a few contests that are only open to students. On the positive side these contests are very easy to enter. On the negative side your fate is totally beyond your control.

373. eCampusTours $1,000 Scholarship Drawing

http://www.ecampustours.com
You can win one of ten $1,000 scholarships by registering on this website.

374. Next Step Magazine

http://www.nextstepmagazine.com
Winners are randomly selected for this magazine's $5,000 scholarship. You must be 14 years or older to enter.

375. Off to College Scholarship Sweepstakes

http://www.suntrusteducation.com/sweeps
Every two weeks a high school senior wins a $1,000 scholarship and $250 SunTrust gift card in this drawing.

376. Sallie Mae $1,000 Scholarship Drawing

http://www.salliemae.com/scholarships
Each month Sallie Mae selects a registered user to receive a $1,000 scholarship. Registration is free and you also get access to some cool resources such as a free scholarship search.

377. SuperCollege Scholarship

http://www.supercollege.com
Sign up to win this $1,500 scholarship awarded through a random drawing. It doesn't get easier than that!

378. U.S. Bank Internet Scholarship Program

http://www.usbank.com/studentbanking
If you're a high school senior who plans on attending a two- or four-year college you can enter to win a $1,000 scholarship. You can enter online.

379.

Win free meals

Most restaurants offer some type of free meal giveaway. Look for a fishbowl near the cash register. Drop in your business card to enter. You can print your own business cards and carry them with you wherever

---

How do I enter scholarship drawings?

Ready to win? Each contest has its own procedures for entering. Most allow you to enter by signing up on their website. SuperCollege, for example, has a simple application form that takes about a minute to complete. You can enter to win at http://www.supercollege.com.

---

you dine. While you usually win a free meal, one student we know actually won a free pizza each week for a year. Not too shabby.

FOUR

Guaranteed Scholarships

Guaranteed Scholarships Do Exist

We have often warned students and parents that there is no such thing as a guaranteed scholarship. Scholarships are competitions, which you win based on the quality of your application. However, there is one class of scholarships that are virtually guaranteed. These awards are usually based on some object criteria such as your grades or test scores. If you achieve certain standards, you will receive the scholarship—guaranteed.

The majority of guaranteed awards are sponsored by colleges and state governments. It is important that you carefully research your current college or colleges that you are applying to as well as your state to see if they offer any type of guaranteed award.

The following are some examples of guaranteed scholarships. Believe it or not, an amazingly high number of students don't take advantage of guaranteed scholarships simply because they didn't know they existed. After reading this chapter we're sure that you won't make this costly mistake!

380.

National Merit Scholarships

The PSAT can be one of the most lucrative tests you'll ever take. The National Merit program (http://www.nationalmerit.org), administered by the National Merit Scholarship Corporation, a non-profit organization, receives the scores for all high school juniors who take the PSAT. Using these scores they select the highest-scoring students to be named National Merit Semifinalists. About 16,000 students out of the more than 1.2 million students who take the PSAT become Semifinalists.

This alone is an honor because it means that out of all of the juniors who took the PSAT exam you are among the top scoring. Unfortunately you don't automatically win a scholarship yet. However, if you are a National Merit Semifinalist you are invited to compete for a *National Merit Scholarship*. From the 16,000 Semifinalists about 8,000 win a National Merit Scholarship that might be one of the following:

- $2,500 from the *National Merit Scholarships*
- Corporate-sponsored *Merit Scholarship* awards
- College-sponsored *Merit Scholarship* awards

The key to being honored as a National Merit Semifinalist and thus being able to compete for some money is to take the PSAT exam during your junior year. You can learn more about the PSAT including the testing dates at http://www.collegeboard.com.

381.

Automatic scholarships based on your GPA and test scores

As your parents have probably told you since birth, there's a reason to get good grades. One of those reasons is to get a scholarship from a college that automatically gives money to students with certain scores. Such guaranteed awards are based on SAT or ACT scores or GPA.

For example, Saint Joseph's College in Rensselaer, Indiana (http://www.saintjoe.edu), offers an *Honors Scholarship* worth up to $17,000 to all accepted students with certain GPAs and test scores. There is a calculator on the website to see if you qualify. For example, you could have an SAT score of 1300 and GPA of 3.25 to win the scholarship.

Other schools have created a tiered system for awarding guaranteed scholarships. Wilmington College of Ohio (http://www.wilmington.edu) offers guaranteed scholarships to all incoming students who meet the following criteria:

- Up to $10,500 for students with a 2.5-4.0 GPA and an ACT score of 17-36 or minimum SAT score of 900
- Up to $12,500 for students with a 3.0-4.0 GPA and an ACT score of 18-36 or SAT score of 940 or higher

Freshmen who apply to the State University of New York at Potsdam (http://www.potsdam.edu) can receive money through the *Freshman Scholars Program* with a minimum GPA of 88 or SAT score of 1100 or ACT score of 24. The awards start at $1,000. Plus, if you maintain a 3.25 GPA while at SUNY you get this amount each year.

Take a look at your school or the schools you are interested in and see if they offer similar guaranteed scholarships. You'll probably find that many colleges offer such incentives to attract students.

382.

Scholarships for transfer students

If you find that your college is not the right fit for you, transferring may be the answer. Unfortunately, your financial aid package does not automatically transfer from one college to another. In fact, this is something you will need to factor in when considering transferring. Some colleges make the transition easier by giving you a guaranteed transfer scholarship.

For example, Ursuline College in Pepper Pike, Ohio (http://www.ursuline.edu), offers the *Ursuline Full-Time Transfer Scholarships* and *Part-Time Transfer Scholarships* for students who have at least a 3.0 college GPA. The scholarships are up to $10,000 and renewable.

If you are thinking about transferring, speak with the admission office at the colleges you are considering. Ask them what kind of financial aid package you may expect and inquire about transfer scholarships that you may be eligible to receive.

383.

You might be entitled to a state entitlement award

All states have financial aid programs for their residents. Some of these programs effectively reward students who perform at a specific academic level in high school. California, for example, has the CalGrant program that automatically gives money to the top students at each high school to attend a college in the state. Ironically, one of the biggest problems with the program is that many students aren't aware that they are eligible for a CalGrant and don't claim their money.

Many states offer similar entitlement awards. Some are based on academic merit while others on financial need. Awards may be designated for high school seniors, adult students or students in certain fields like nursing, medicine or education. Be aware that some require you to use the money only at colleges within your state.

Take a look at Chapter 11 for a list of the state agencies that manage scholarships. Contact your agency to make sure you are not leaving any money on the table.

384.

Get in-state tuition even if you're an out-of-state student

Getting in-state tuition at a public university can save you thousands of dollars. Take a look at the difference in tuition for the University of California at Berkeley. If you are not a resident of California you will have to pay an additional non-resident fee of $26,682 per year.

If you are an out-of-state student you will need to pay out-of-state tuition until you can establish state residency. This is easier in some states than others. Texas, for example, does not like students who move to their state just to use their fine educational system and then leave. One of the residency requirements is that you live in Texas for 12 months without attending a secondary institution. This makes it impossible for any student who goes directly to college in Texas from high school to gain residency. But then again the state motto is: Don't mess with Texas.

The University of California system, on the other hand, makes it possible but not easy. To become a resident you need to show three things:

I received a letter from a scholarship service that said if I paid a fee I was "guaranteed" to win a scholarship. Is this a scam?

Yes! With the exception of the scholarships described in this chapter, if you encounter a so-called "guaranteed" scholarship it is not a legitimate award. Scholarships are competitions and therefore no one can predict or guarantee that you will win. If you come across an offer for a guaranteed scholarship turn the other way and run!

Physical presence. You must have proof that you remained in the state for more than one year. This means not going home for the summer. You actually have to physically be in the state and be able to prove it.

Intent. You must establish ties to the state of California that show you intend to make California your home. This requires giving up any previous residence and getting proof such as a California driver's license.

Financial independence. If both of your parents are non-residents, you must show that you are financially independent. You qualify if you are at least 24 years old, are a veteran of the U.S. Armed Forces, are a ward of the court or both parents are deceased, have legal dependents besides a spouse, are married or are a single student and have not been claimed as an income tax deduction by your parents for the past year for graduate students or past two years for undergraduate students.

California's rules are fairly common among the states. If you are planning to attend a public college outside of your own state, contact the admission office and make sure you understand what you need to do to get state residency. Once you do you'll save a bundle, and it's just like winning a guaranteed scholarship.

385.

Take advantage of residency discount agreements

Some schools have formed relationships with neighboring states to offer their residents automatic in-state rates from the beginning. The University of Arkansas, for example, offers a *Non-Resident Tuition Award* for entering freshmen from neighboring states that include Texas, Mississippi, Louisiana, Kansas, Missouri, Oklahoma and Tennessee. You must meet the minimum academic criteria of a 3.2 GPA or higher and an ACT score of at least 24 or an SAT score of at least 1160. If you meet these academic qualifications and are from a neighboring state you will be granted in-state tuition, which can save you up to $14,000 a year in fees. If you want to attend a state college in a neighboring state make sure you contact the admission office to find out if any such discount agreements are in effect.

Reward Programs For Students

Save Money By Spending Money

You're probably familiar with airline frequent flyer programs. The idea is simple: You earn frequent flyer miles that you eventually redeem for a free ticket. It's a nice benefit for when you'd fly anyway. It's also good for the airlines since you'll stick with one company as you build up your miles.

Some enterprising companies have brought this concept to college savings. You can earn money for college not by flying but by shopping. These companies rebate a percentage of your purchases from participating retailers into college savings plans. (See Chapter 6 for a description of various savings plans.)

The rebates range from 1 percent to more than 30 percent depending on what you purchase, and most programs allow you to get your family and friends involved. Everybody can then start to contribute to one person's educational savings. These programs offer a nice supplement to your savings, and over time you can rack up a nice chunk of change.

Since all of these student reward programs work in a similar way, look for the one that offers you the best selection of participating retailers and merchants as well as the highest rebate on the purchases you make most. Also keep in mind that these programs are relatively new and are continuously adding merchants so be sure to check their websites for the most current list of participating stores.

Some also offer branded credit cards that allow you to earn rebates on every purchase you make using the card.

386.

Upromise

Upromise is a free service in which companies give you money back for college as a way to earn your loyalty. You can designate your own child, a friend's child, a grandchild, a child you expect to have one day or yourself as the recipient of the reward program. You can change the recipient at any time and enroll relatives and friends to help save for your or your child's education.

After you join Upromise you will need to register your credit or debit cards. As you shop at participating stores a percentage from each purchase is credited to your account, which will be invested in a tax-free 529 Savings Plan. The Upromise system is easy to use since once you register your credit cards you just shop normally and your rewards are automatically credited to your savings plan.

Currently, Upromise has more than 40,000 retail stores and services participating in the program. Visit the Upromise website to get a complete list of participating retail stores and restaurants along with the rebate rates.

Website: http://www.upromise.com

What's the best way to use these reward programs?

As with any savings strategy, time is your ally. The earlier you start the better. If you begin these programs 5, 10 or even 15 years before you need the money then you give them a chance to accumulate. The other important key is to multiply your contributions by recruiting as many friends and family members as possible. The more people who contribute their rebates to your account the better. Hit up all of your relatives and friends who don't have college tuition bills headed their way.

387.

Fidelity Rewards Visa Card

If your parents are planning to use a credit card anyway, you might as well get rewards for it. With this credit card, which has no annual fee, two percent of all of your purchases may be contributed to your 529 plan. Grandparents or other relatives can also get the card and contribute their rewards to your 529 plan. As you might expect, the catch is that it must be a Fidelity 529 plan. So it's important to figure out if Fidelity has the right plan for you. The investment firm offers four plans that are available to all U.S. residents.

Website: http://www.fidelity.com

388.

SAGE Scholars Tuition Rewards

When you invest with one of the program's partners, you earn tuition reward points each year. As the program describes, "Tuition reward points are like frequent flyer miles—but for college tuition." The points may be redeemed at one of more than 300 participating private colleges and universities across the country. Each point is worth $1 in scholarships at the participating institutions, and students may use the points to pay for up to 25 percent of the cost of tuition. There is a list of partner programs that you may invest in on the website, and

---

Can I rely on reward programs to pay for all of my education?

Unless you are the shopper of the century, the short answer is: no. While these programs are a nice enhancement to your overall savings strategy you should not rely on them alone to generate the money you need for college. Think of these programs as one of many tools that you'll use to build your savings future.

it includes the Pennsylvania 529 College Savings Program as well as banks and credit unions.

Website: http://www.tuitionrewards.com

SIX

Save For College

Saving For College

College is an investment in your future. With few exceptions, you are going to have to contribute some of your own money to pay for it. Even though we won a lot of scholarships—more than $100,000 between the two of us—we still had to fork over some of our own money to pay for our tuition. While it is always better to get free cash from scholarships and financial aid, the reality is that the more you save the more options you'll have.

Your personal savings is your best ally when it comes to paying for college. Scholarships will always be competitions with no guarantees that you'll win. Financial aid changes each year depending on the budgets of the government and college. There is no guarantee, even if you deserve it, that you will receive all of the financial aid that you need to pay for school.

Plus, if you were planning to take out a student loan (and most students do borrow some amount to pay for school) your savings will multiply in value. For example, let's say you end up borrowing $50,000 to pay for all four years of college. At 3.76 percent interest over 10 years (the typical term for a student loan) you would end up paying more than $10,065 in interest. But if you were able to save half of that amount and borrowed only $25,000 you would pay only $5,032 in interest. That means your personal savings just helped you to avoid $5,033 in additional interest payments.

There is one last benefit of your savings. Since it is your or your family's hard-earned money, it puts a real value on the price of your education. When we were at Harvard we met students from a variety of backgrounds. For some their parents had so much money that Harvard tuition was a drop in the bucket. For others it seemed like the family had to mortgage everything they owned just to pay for it. Can you guess which students worked harder? The students who felt the enormity of the price of their educations worked much harder and achieved much more than those whose educations were handed to them on a silver platter. This may not seem like much of a consolation now when you are eating Cup-O-Noodles in order to cut expenses, but trust us it does pay off in the long run.

The bottom line is that *your* savings is *your* money. You have total freedom to use it at whichever college you want. Nothing is as flexible as your own money. In this chapter we're going to show you some of the best strategies for building your savings.

Important: Before we begin remember that this information is meant to provide general guidance about your saving options. You should always check with an accountant regarding your individual situation and to make sure that tax laws haven't changed.

The Coverdell Education Savings Account

389.

Grow your money tax-free with the Coverdell Education Savings Account

Saving your money is a good thing, but it's even better when you let your money grow without having to pay the tax collector. This is a benefit of the Coverdell Education Savings Account (ESA). Once you set up the account and name a beneficiary (who must be under the age of 18) you can start contributing up to $2,000 per year to the account under current law to invest in any combination of stocks, bonds, mutual funds, certificates of deposit, money market funds and just plain cash.

As your money grows you are allowed to defer paying federal income taxes. In many states you will not have to pay state taxes either. When you are ready to use the money to pay for the beneficiary's educational expenses, which can include tuition, room and board, books and supplies, computers and transportation, you can withdraw the money tax-free.

The definition of what counts as educational expenses is quite broad for the Coverdell. In fact, your Coverdell savings is not limited to paying for college expenses, but you can also use it to pay for educational expenses for elementary and high school. This can be useful if you think you might need it to pay for private school tuition.

The big disadvantage of the Coverdell is the limits on who can contribute and how much you can contribute each year. You can contribute up to $2,000 a year per child. If you only have a year or two before your child goes to college you're not going to be able to realize a lot of tax-free gains.

Also, to be able to contribute the $2,000 per year maximum you must have a modified adjusted gross income (which is known as MAGI and you'll hear this term a lot) of $95,000 or less if you are a single tax filer or $190,000 or less if you are married and file jointly. If you make more, the amounts of your contributions are gradually reduced. If you earned more than $110,000 as a single filer or $220,000 as a joint filer you cannot contribute to a Coverdell account.

In what could be a positive or a negative depending on your investing skills, the Coverdell requires that you decide how your money is allocated. You'll actually need to pick individual investments. This can be good if you like to trade or bad if you are not comfortable making investment decisions.

Like all special savings plans with tax benefits, if you don't use the money for qualified educational expenses you will have to pay the taxes that you would otherwise owe along with a stiff 10 percent penalty. If for some reason the beneficiary of a Coverdell account does not go to college or use the money for qualified educational expenses by the age of 30, he or she can transfer it to another relative or a member of the family to avoid the penalty.

How do I figure out my modified adjusted gross income (MAGI) to see if I qualify to contribute to a Coverdell ESA?

The Coverdell Education Savings Account as well as all of the various tax breaks for education require that you fall within a certain modified adjusted gross income (MAGI). For most taxpayers, MAGI is simply your adjusted gross income (AGI) from your 1040 tax forms. If you file your taxes using form 1040 then your MAGI is the AGI on line 37 and is modified by adding any foreign earned income exclusion, foreign housing exclusion, exclusion of income for residents of American Samoa and exclusion of income from Puerto Rico. If you file form 1040A then your MAGI is the AGI on line 21.

390.

Opening a Coverdell is as easy as 1-2-3

Banks, brokerage houses, securities firms and mutual fund companies offer Coverdell Education Savings Accounts. While researching where to open your Coverdell, be sure to note any minimums on the account. Some require that you invest a minimum amount each year to avoid paying an account maintenance fee. Also, be sure to understand the fees and commissions of each institution. Once you open an account, you will choose how your money is invested. Here are some places where you can open a Coverdell:

391. American Express
http://www.americanexpress.com

392. Charles Schwab
http://www.schwab.com

393. DWS Investments
http://www.dws-investments.com

394. E-Trade Financial
http://www.etrade.com

395. Franklin Templeton Investments
http://www.franklintempleton.com

396. Janus International Holding
http://www.janus.com

397. JP Morgan Chase
http://www.jpmorgan.com

398. T.D. Ameritrade
http://www.tdameritrade.com

399. T. Rowe Price
http://www.troweprice.com

400. UBS PaineWebber
http://www.ubs.com

401. Wells Fargo
http://www.wellsfargo.com

402.

You can contribute to a Coverdell even if you are over the income limit

If you exceed the income limits of the Coverdell ESA you can still take advantage of the Coverdell by gifting the $2,000 to your child and having him or her open the account. This is also a way for relatives to contribute to your son or daughter's Coverdell. Remember that the total amount that your child can contribute to a Coverdell (regardless of where the money comes from) is $2,000 per year.

403.

Read exciting Coverdell examples by downloading IRS Publication 970

You can download the nitty-gritty details on the Coverdell (as well as 529 Plans and other tax breaks) by getting the latest version of IRS Publication 970. Visit http://www.irs.gov, and search for "Publication 970" on the front page.

While the document is typical of most IRS publications, one nice feature is the examples. Here is one reprinted from the section on the Coverdell, which explains how the contribution limits work when several relatives set up a Coverdell to benefit a single child.

When Maria Luna was born in 2016, three separate Coverdell ESAs were set up for her, one by her parents, one by her grandfather and one by her aunt. In 2017, the total of all contributions to Maria's three Coverdell ESAs cannot be more than $2,000. For example, if her grandfather contributed $2,000 to one of her Coverdell ESAs, no one else could contribute to any of her three accounts. Or, if her parents contributed $1,000 and her aunt $600, her grandfather or someone else could contribute no more than $400. These contributions could be put into any of Maria's Coverdell ESA accounts.

The example goes on and changes the scenario by adding another child to Maria Luna's family. *The facts are the same as in the previous example except that Maria Luna's older brother, Edgar, also has a Coverdell ESA. If their grandfather contributed $2,000 to Maria's Coverdell ESA in 2017, he could also contribute $2,000 to Edgar's Coverdell ESA.*

While IRS publications are far from pleasure reading, the examples they provide help in understanding how the rules apply in the real world.

The 529 Savings Plan

Given the buzz about the 529 Savings Plan, you'd think it was the best thing to come along since the invention of compound interest in helping you pay for college. While there are some real advantages to 529 Savings Plans, they are not magical solutions.

Like any investment, 529 Savings Plans (officially known as qualified tuition programs or QTPs), don't guarantee specific returns and rise and fall with the market. The tax-free benefits, which are really the major benefits of the plan, only apply to the earnings that are generated. This means if you only have a year or two before your child enters college you probably won't notice much of a benefit. But for long-term savings, the right 529 Savings Plan (don't worry we'll show you what to look for when selecting a plan) should help you build your college fund faster. There is also an interesting estate planning benefit to a 529 Savings Plan that your family might be able to take advantage of.

Let's take a look at the much-ballyhooed 529 Savings Plans.

404.

Grow your money tax-free with the 529 Savings Plan

The 529 Savings Plans are the toast of the town among many financial advisors. They are popular not because they have had phenomenal rates of return (many plans lose value during a down stock market) but because they allow families to stock away a lot of money tax-free. Contribution limits are much higher than the Coverdell with some plans capping the contribution at more than $450,000 per student. Plus, there are no income limits to who can contribute to a 529 Plan, which means that every family member can participate including rich Uncle Leo.

529 Savings Plans are offered by every state and the District of Columbia, and many states offer more than one plan. You don't

have to participate in your own state's plan and are free to sign up for any of the 529 Plans that are out there. However, you should check your state's tax regulations since some states allow you to take a state tax deduction on the money you put into a 529 Plan. If you live in one of these states you'll probably find that with these tax savings your state plan will offer you the best deal.

All of the money that you put into your 529 Plan will grow free from federal income tax and depending on your state may also be free from state taxes as long as you use the money for qualified college educational expenses.

Unlike the Coverdell, all of the money that you put into a 529 Plan must be used for college-related expenses or else you not only pay the taxes that you would have owed on any gains but also a stiff 10 percent penalty. Fortunately, 529 Plans are very flexible when it comes to changing the beneficiary since unlike the Coverdell the money stays in your control. Even if you opened a 529 Plan for one child you don't

---

How much will a four-year public college cost when my child graduates from high school?

According to the College Board the average one-year cost for tuition and room and board at a four-year public college is $20,090. Assuming a 7 percent increase in costs each year you can use this table to project what the average total cost will be when your child heads off to school.

Years until student begins college	Total estimated cost of a four-year public education
1	$95,442
2	$102,123
3	$109,272
4	$116,921
5	$125,105
7	$143,233
10	$175,467
12	$200,892
15	$246,101

have to use that money for that child. You can use the money from your 529 Plan for any member of your family including yourself.

So far everything about the 529 Plan sounds good. What about the downside? The disadvantage of the 529 is that your investments are determined by the plan. In other words, you don't manage which specific stocks your money is invested in. Most 529 Plans have different investment tracks such as conservative, moderate and aggressive. In addition, most offer an age-based option that is more aggressive when your child is younger and becomes increasingly conservative as your child gets closer to college age. In this sense a 529 Savings Plan is like a mutual fund where you rely on the fund manager to pick the right mix of investments. But unlike stocks or mutual funds, once you've chosen a track for your 529 Plan, you usually can't modify it for a year. You can also change between different 529 Plans only once a year.

Like any investment, 529 Savings Plans are tied to the market. When the market is good, 529 Savings Plans generally rise in value. When the market is bad, 529 Savings Plans generally fall. Fortunately, with many that offer an age-based program as your child nears high school graduation the funds shift more of your money out of volatile investments and into safer bonds and cash.

It's important to remember that 529 Savings Plans are not a quick fix to your college money needs. To make a 529 Savings Plan work you need to be a consistent saver over a long period of time. You also need good returns on your money since the primary benefit is not having to pay taxes on the gains.

405.

What to consider when choosing a 529 Savings Plan
Since you can participate in any state's 529 Savings Plan regardless of where you live, you have many options. Maybe too many. When you are considering the merits of each plan focus on these areas before you invest:

Low expense ratio and other fees. Know what all of the fees are before you sign up. Pay particular attention to annual account maintenance fees, transfer fees and commissions. The annual account maintenance fee is a percentage and is also known as the expense ratio. We recommend that you try to find a plan that has an expense ratio that is under 1 percent a year.

State benefits. You may be eligible for significant benefits if you invest in your own state's plan. These benefits may include state tax deductions on contributions and/or earnings and can more than make up for other shortcomings of the plan. A few states even offer matching contributions!

Investment track options. More options are usually better. Look for a plan that gives you a good mix of investment tracks. (Remember you can usually switch tracks only once a year.) You want as much flexibility in your plan as possible.

Ease of changing account beneficiary. Make sure you can change the beneficiary in case your child does not need all of the money for college.

Other less important considerations include the minimum amount you need to open the account, conveniences such as online transactions and whether or not the plan accepts contributions at any time in the year.

406.

Beware of the pitfall of 529 Savings Plans

One of the dangers of all 529 Savings Plans is that because the plans are relatively new the rules are still changing. Here is one dangerous trend that you need to be aware of before investing:

A few states have begun to charge a tax on the earnings of 529 Plans sponsored by other states. If you live in one of these states it effectively makes most out-of-state 529 Plans very unattractive. As state budgets shrink you can expect more states to do this to generate additional revenue.

407.

If you live in a state that allows a deduction, take it

If you live in one of the following states your 529 Plans may allow a state tax deduction or credit for contributions to your 529 Plan. This is a huge benefit that you should consider when examining your state's own 529 Plan. Remember that tax laws can change so check with your state tax office or accountant to verify that you can still deduct contributions to your 529 Plans. Also, some states place limits on the maximum amount that can be deducted in one year.

- Alabama
- Arizona
- Arkansas
- Colorado
- Connecticut
- District of Columbia
- Georgia
- Idaho
- Illinois
- Indiana
- Iowa
- Kansas
- Louisiana
- Maine
- Maryland
- Massachusetts
- Michigan
- Mississippi
- Missouri
- Montana
- Nebraska
- New Mexico
- New York
- North Dakota
- Ohio
- Oklahoma
- Oregon
- Pennsylvania
- Rhode Island

- South Carolina
- Utah
- Vermont
- Virginia
- West Virginia
- Wisconsin

Prepaid College Tuition Plans

408.

Pre-pay your education with the Prepaid Tuition Plan

Prepaid College Tuition Plans are the first cousins of 529 Plans. These plans are run by your state's Treasurer's Office and allow you to contribute a fixed amount of money on a monthly or yearly basis to buy

---

How much will a four-year private college cost when my child graduates from high school?

According to the College Board the average one-year cost for tuition and room and board at a four-year private college is $45,370. Assuming a 7 percent increase in costs each year you can use this table to project what the average total cost will be when your child heads off to school.

Years until student begins college	Total estimated cost of a 4-year private education
1	$215,541
2	$230,629
3	$246,773
4	$264,047
5	$282,530
7	$323,469
10	$396,263
12	$453,682
15	$555,780

a fixed number of tuition credits at a public college or university at today's prices. This effectively allows you to pre-pay for your child's tuition.

If prices go up (and you can bet that they will) by the time your child is ready to enter college the prepaid program will cover any increase. Most prepaid plans require that your child be a high school freshman or younger when you start the plan. These plans are good if you think your child will attend your state's college or university. The risk is that your child will want to attend a private college or out-of-state school. In this case you will usually be refunded what you put into the plan along with some interest. Since private or out-of-state public schools often cost more than in-state schools, the amount you get back is usually not enough to pay for the more expensive choice of your child.

It is very important to understand what you are buying with a prepaid plan. Some states' prepaid plans cover tuition but not room and board, which can be a hefty expense. Be sure you also understand what happens if your child decides not to go to that school and if you are able to change beneficiaries.

Your State's 529 And Prepaid Tuition Plans

You don't need to join your state's 529 Savings Plan, and you are free to sign up for any state's plan. Just be sure that you know what state benefits, if any, you may miss by not using your state's plan.

Some states also offer more than one 529 Savings Plan. Most states contract the management of their 529 Plans to investment companies like TIAA-CREF or Fidelity. A good resource to get an overview of all of the state's plans can be found at the College Savings Plans Network at http://www.collegesavings.org. Here is an overview of each state's plan:

409. Alabama

Savings Plan

Fund: CollegeCounts 529 Fund
Administrator: Union Bank & Trust Company

State tax deduction for contributions: Yes
State allows tax-free withdrawals: Yes
Website: http://www.collegecounts529.com
Phone: 866-529-2228

410. Alaska

Savings Plans

Fund: University of Alaska College Savings Plan
Administrator: T. Rowe Price
State tax deduction for contributions: No state income tax
State allows tax-free withdrawals: No state income tax
Website: http://www.uacollegesavings.com
Phone: 866-277-1005

Fund: T. Rowe Price College Savings Plan
Administrator: T. Rowe Price
State tax deduction for contributions: No state income tax
State allows tax-free withdrawals: No state income tax
Website: http://www.price529.com
Phone: 800-369-3641

Fund: John Hancock Freedom 529
Administrator: John Hancock
State tax deduction for contributions: No state income tax
State allows tax-free withdrawals: No state income tax
Website: http://www.jhinvestments.com/College/Overview.aspx
Phone: 866-222-7498

Prepaid Tuition Plan

The University of Alaska College Savings Plan offers as one of its portfolio choices the Advanced College Tuition (ACT) track that allows you to lock in the cost of tuition for the University of Alaska at today's prices.

411. Arizona

Savings Plans

Fund: Arizona Family College Savings Program
Administrator: College Savings Bank
State tax deduction for contributions: Yes
State allows tax-free withdrawals: Yes
Website: http://www.az529.gov
Phone: 800-888-2723

Fund: Fidelity Arizona College Savings Plan
Administrator: Fidelity Investments
State tax deduction for contributions: Yes
State allows tax-free withdrawals: Yes
Website: https://www.fidelity.com/arizona-529/
Phone: 800-544-1262

Fund: Ivy InvestEd 529 Plan
Administrator: Ivy Investment Management Company
State tax deduction for contributions: Yes
State allows tax-free withdrawals: Yes
Website: http://www.ivyinvestments.com/products/ivy-invested-529-plan
Phone: 800-877-6472

412. Arkansas

Savings Plan

Fund: GIFT College Investing Plan
Administrator: Ascensus College Savings
State tax deduction for contributions: Yes
State allows tax-free withdrawals: Yes
Website: http://www.arkansas529.org
Phone: 800-587-7301

Fund: iShares 529 Plan
Administrator: Ascensus Broker Dealer Services Inc.
State tax deduction for contributions: Yes
State allows tax-free withdrawals: Yes

Website: http://www.ishares529.com
Phone: 888-529-9552

413. California

Savings Plan

Fund: ScholarShare College Savings Plan
Administrator: TIAA-CREF Tuition Financing Inc.
State tax deduction for contributions: No
State allows tax-free withdrawals: Yes
Website: http://www.scholarshare.com
Phone: 800-544-5248

414. Colorado

Savings Plans

Fund: Direct Portfolio College Savings Plan
Administrator: Ascensus Broker Dealer Services Inc. and The
Vanguard Group, Inc.
State tax deduction for contributions: Yes
State allows tax-free withdrawals: Yes
Website: http://www.collegeinvest.org
Phone: 800-997-4295

Fund: Scholars Choice College Savings Program
Administrator: Legg Mason Inc.
State tax deduction for contributions: Yes
State allows tax-free withdrawals: Yes
Website: https://www.leggmason.com/en-us/investing/
college-savings/529-audience-filter.html
Phone: 888-572-4652

Fund: Stable Value Plus College Savings Program
Administrator: MetLife
State tax deduction for contributions: Yes
State allows tax-free withdrawals: Yes
Website: http://www.collegeinvest.org
Phone: 800-478-5651

Fund: Smart Choice College Savings Plan
Administrator: FirstBank Holding Company
State tax deduction for contributions: Yes
State allows tax-free withdrawals: Yes
Website: http://www.collegeinvest.org
Phone: 800-964-3444

415. Connecticut

Savings Plan

Fund: Connecticut Higher Education Trust
Administrator: TIAA-CREF Tuition Financing Inc.
State tax deduction for contributions: Yes
State allows tax-free withdrawals: Yes
Website: http://www.aboutchet.com
Phone: 888-799-2438

416. Delaware

Savings Plan

Fund: Delaware College Investment Plan
Administrator: Fidelity Investments
State tax deduction for contributions: No
State allows tax-free withdrawals: Yes
Website: https://www.fidelity.com/delaware-529/
Phone: 800-544-1655

417. District of Columbia

Savings Plan

Fund: DC 529 College Savings Program
Administrator: Calvert Investment Management Inc.
State tax deduction for contributions: Yes
State allows tax-free withdrawals: Yes
Website: http://www.dccollegesavings.com
Phone: 800-987-4859

418. Florida

Savings Plan

Fund: Florida 529 Savings Plan
Administrator: Florida Prepaid College Board
State tax deduction for contributions: No state income tax
State allows tax-free withdrawals: No state income tax
Website: http://www.myfloridaprepaid.com
Phone: 800-552-4723

Prepaid Tuition Plan

Fund: Florida Prepaid College Plan
Administrator: Florida Prepaid College Board
State tax deduction for contributions: No state income tax
State allows tax-free withdrawals: No state income tax
Website: http://www.myfloridaprepaid.com
Phone: 800-552-4723

419. Georgia

Savings Plan

Fund: Path2College 529 Plan
Administrator: TIAA-CREF Tuition Financing Inc.
State tax deduction for contributions: Yes
State allows tax-free withdrawals: Yes
Website: http://www.path2college529.com
Phone: 877-424-4377

420. Hawaii

Savings Plan

Fund: Hawaii's College Savings Program
Administrator: Ascensus College Savings and The Vanguard Group
State tax deduction for contributions: No
State allows tax-free withdrawals: Yes

Website: http://www.hi529.com
Phone: 866-529-3343

421. Idaho

Savings Plan

Fund: Idaho College Savings Program/IDeal
Administrator: Ascensus College Savings
State tax deduction for contributions: Yes
State allows tax-free withdrawals: Yes
Website: http://www.idsaves.org
Phone: 866-433-2533

422. Illinois

Savings Plan

Fund: Bright Start College Savings Program
Administrator: OppenheimerFunds
State tax deduction for contributions: Yes
State allows tax-free withdrawals: Yes
Website: http://www.brightstartsavings.com
Phone: 877-432-7444

Fund: Bright Directions College Savings Program
Administrator: Northern Trust Securities
State tax deduction for contributions: Yes
State allows tax-free withdrawals: Yes
Website: http://www.brightdirections.com
Phone: 866-722-7283

Prepaid Tuition Plan

Fund: College Illinois!
Administrator: Illinois Student Assistance Commission
State tax deduction for contributions: Yes
State allows tax-free withdrawals: Yes
Website: http://www.collegeillinois.org
Phone: 877-877-3724

423. Indiana

Savings Plan

Fund: CollegeChoice 529 Direct Savings Plan
Administrator: Ascensus College Savings
State tax deduction for contributions: Yes
State allows tax-free withdrawals: Yes
Website: https://www.collegechoicedirect.com
Phone: 866-485-9415

Fund: CollegeChoice CD 529 Direct Savings Plan
Administrator: College Savings Bank
State tax deduction for contributions: Yes
State allows tax-free withdrawals: Yes
Website: http://www.collegechoicecd.com
Phone: 888-913-2885

424. Iowa

Savings Plan

Fund: College Savings Iowa
Administrator: State Treasurer of Iowa, Ascensus College
Savings and Vanguard
State tax deduction for contributions: Yes
State allows tax-free withdrawals: Yes
Website: https://www.collegesavingsiowa.com
Phone: 888-672-9116

425. Kansas

Savings Plan

Fund: Schwab 529 College Savings Plan
Administrator: Charles Schwab and American Century
State tax deduction for contributions: Yes
State allows tax-free withdrawals: Yes
Website: http://www.schwab.com/529
Phone: 866-903-3863

Fund: Learning Quest Education Savings Program
Administrator: American Century
State tax deduction for contributions: Yes
State allows tax-free withdrawals: Yes
Website: http://www.learningquest.com
Phone: 800-579-2203

426. Kentucky

Savings Plan

Fund: Kentucky Education Savings Plan Trust
Administrator: TIAA-CREF
State tax deduction for contributions: No
State allows tax-free withdrawals: Yes
Website: http://www.kysaves.com
Phone: 877-598-7878

Prepaid Tuition Plan

Fund: Kentucky's Affordable Prepaid Tuition (KAPT)
Administrator: Kentucky Higher Education Assistance Authority
State tax deduction for contributions: No
State allows tax-free withdrawals: Yes
Website: http://www.getkapt.com
Phone: 888-919-5278
This plan is closed to new investors.

427. Louisiana

Savings Plan

Fund: START Saving Program
Administrator: Louisiana State Treasurer
State tax deduction for contributions: Yes
State allows tax-free withdrawals: Yes
Website: http://www.startsaving.la.gov
Phone: 800-259-5626, ext. 1012

428. Maine

Savings Plan

Fund: NextGen College Investing Plan
Administrator: Merrill Lynch, Pierce, Fenner & Smith Inc.
State tax deduction for contributions: Yes
State allows tax-free withdrawals: Yes
Website: http://www.nextgenforme.com
Phone: 877-463-9843

429. Maryland

Savings Plan

Fund: Maryland College Investment Plan
Administrator: T. Rowe Price
State tax deduction for contributions: Yes
State allows tax-free withdrawals: Yes
Website: http://www.maryland529.com
Phone: 888-463-4723

Prepaid Tuition Plan

Fund: Maryland Prepaid College Trust
Administrator: State
State tax deduction for contributions: Yes
State allows tax-free withdrawals: Yes
Website: http://www.maryland529.com
Phone: 888-463-4723

430. Massachusetts

Savings Plan

Fund: U.Fund College Investing Plan
Administrator: Fidelity Investments
State tax deduction for contributions: Yes (2017-2021)
State allows tax-free withdrawals: Yes
Website: https://www.fidelity.com/massachusetts-529/
Phone: 800-544-2776

Prepaid Tuition Plan

Fund: U.Plan
Administrator: State
You participate in U.Plan by purchasing a special state bond. This bond is free of Massachusetts state income tax. You'll have to check with your accountant, but this state bond may also be free of federal income tax.
Website: http://www.mefa.org/uplan/
Phone: 800-449-6332

431. Michigan

Savings Plan

Fund: Michigan Education Savings Plan
Administrator: TIAA-CREF
State tax deduction for contributions: Yes
State allows tax-free withdrawals: Yes
Website: http://www.misaves.com
Phone: 877-861-6377

Prepaid Tuition Plan

Fund: Michigan Education Trust
Administrator: State
State tax deduction for contributions: Yes
State allows tax-free withdrawals: Yes
Website: http://www.michigan.gov/setwithmet
Phone: 800-MET-4-KID

432. Minnesota

Savings Plan

Fund: Minnesota College Savings Plan
Administrator: TIAA-CREF
State tax deduction for contributions: No
State allows tax-free withdrawals: Yes
Website: http://www.mnsaves.org
Phone: 877-338-4646

433. Mississippi

Savings Plan

Fund: Mississippi Affordable College Savings Program
Administrator: TIAA-CREF
State tax deduction for contributions: Yes
State allows tax-free withdrawals: Yes
Website: http://www.ms529.com
Phone: 800-486-3670

Prepaid Tuition Plan

Fund: Mississippi Prepaid Affordable College Tuition Program
Administrator: State
State tax deduction for contributions: Yes
State allows tax-free withdrawals: Yes
Website: http://www.treasurerlynnfitch.ms.gov/collegesavingsmississippi/
Phone: 800-987-4450

434. Missouri

Savings Plan

Fund: MOST - Missouri's 529 College Savings Plan
Administrator: Ascensus College Savings
State tax deduction for contributions: Yes
State allows tax-free withdrawals: Yes
Website: http://www.missourimost.org
Phone: 888-414-6678

435. Montana

Savings Plans

Fund: Achieve Montana
Administrator: Ascensus College Savings and Vanguard Group

State tax deduction for contributions: Yes
State allows tax-free withdrawals: Yes
Website: https://www.achievemontana.com
Phone: 800-888-2723

436. Nebraska

Savings Plans

Fund: Nebraska Education Savings Trust
Administrator: First National Bank of Omaha
State tax deduction for contributions: Yes
State allows tax-free withdrawals: Yes
Website: https://www.nest529direct.com
Phone: 888-993-3746

Fund: State Farm College Savings Plan
Administrator: OppenheimerFunds
State tax deduction for contributions: Yes
State allows tax-free withdrawals: Yes
Website: http://www.statefarm.com
Phone: 800-321-7520

Fund: TD Ameritrade 529 College Savings Plan
Administrator: TD Ameritrade
State tax deduction for contributions: Yes
State allows tax-free withdrawals: Yes
Website: http://www.tdameritrade.com
Phone: 877-408-4644

437. Nevada

Savings Plans

Fund: Putnam 529 for America
Administrator: Putnam Investments
State tax deductions for contributions: No income tax
State allows tax-free withdrawals: No income tax
Website: http://www.putnam.com
Phone: 877-788-6265

Fund: USAA College Savings Plan
Administrator: USAA Investment Management
State tax deductions for contributions: No income tax
State allows tax-free withdrawals: No income tax
Website: http://www.usaa.com
Phone: 800-531-8722

Fund: SSgA Upromise 529 Plan
Administrator: Ascensus College Savings
State tax deductions for contributions: No income tax
State allows tax-free withdrawals: No income tax
Website: http://www.ssga.upromise529.com
Phone: 800-587-7305

Fund: Vanguard 529 College Savings
Administrator: Vanguard
State tax deductions for contributions: No income tax
State allows tax-free withdrawals: No income tax
Website: http://www.vanguard.com/vanguard529
Phone: 866-734-4530

Prepaid Tuition Plan

Fund: Nevada Prepaid Tuition Program
Administrator: State
State tax deductions for contributions: No income tax
State allows tax-free withdrawals: No income tax
Website: https://www.nvprepaid.gov
Phone: 888-477-2667

438. New Hampshire

Savings Plans

Fund: UNIQUE College Investing
Administrator: Fidelity Investments
State tax deductions for contributions: No income tax
State allows tax-free withdrawals: No income tax
Website: https://www.fidelity.com/new-hampshire-529
Phone: 800-544-1914

Fund: Fidelity Advisor 529 Plan
Administrator: Fidelity Advisor Funds
State tax deductions for contributions: No income tax
State allows tax-free withdrawals: No income tax
Website: http://advisor.fidelity.com
Phone: 877-208-0098

439. New Jersey

Savings Plans

Fund: NJBEST 529 College Savings Plan
Administrator: Franklin Templeton
State tax deductions for contributions: No
State allows tax-free withdrawals: Yes
Website: http://www.njbest.com
Phone: 877-4-NJBEST

Fund: Franklin Templeton 529 College Savings Plan
Administrator: Franklin Templeton
State tax deductions for contributions: No
State allows tax-free withdrawals: Yes
Website: http://www.franklintempleton.com
Phone: 866-362-1597

440. New Mexico

Savings Plans

Fund: The Education Plan's College Savings Program
Administrator: Oppenheimer Funds
State tax deductions for contributions: Yes
State allows tax-free withdrawals: Yes
Website: http://www.theeducationplan.com
Phone: 877-337-5268

Fund: Scholar'sEdge
Administrator: OppenheimerFunds
State tax deductions for contributions: Yes

State allows tax-free withdrawals: Yes
Website: http://www.scholarsedge529.com
Phone: 866-529-7283

441. New York

Savings Plan

Fund: New York's College Savings Program
Administrator: Ascensus College Savings
State tax deductions for contributions: Yes
State allows tax-free withdrawals: Yes
Website: http://www.nysaves.org
Phone: 877-697-2837

442. North Carolina

Savings Plan

Fund: National College Savings Program
Administrator: College Foundation Inc.
State tax deductions for contributions: No
State allows tax-free withdrawals: No
Website: http://www.cfnc.org/savings
Phone: 800-600-3453

443. North Dakota

Savings Plan

Fund: College SAVE
Administrator: Ascensus College Savings
State tax deductions for contributions: Yes
State allows tax-free withdrawals: Yes
Website: http://www.collegesave4u.com
Phone: 866-728-3529

444. Ohio

Savings Plan

Fund: Ohio CollegeAdvantage 529 Savings Plan
Administrator: Ohio Tuition Trust Authority
State tax deductions for contributions: Yes
State allows tax-free withdrawals: Yes
Website: http://www.collegeadvantage.com
Phone: 800-233-6734

Fund: BlackRock CollegeAdvantage
Administrator: BlackRock Advisors LLC
State tax deductions for contributions: Yes
State allows tax-free withdrawals: Yes
Website: http://www.blackrock.com
Phone: 866-529-8582

445. Oklahoma

Savings Plan

Fund: Oklahoma College Savings Plan
Administrator: TIAA-CREF
State tax deductions for contributions: Yes
State allows tax-free withdrawals: Yes
Website: http://www.ok4saving.org
Phone: 877-654-7284

Fund: Oklahoma Dream 529 Plan
Administrator: TIAA-Tuition Financing and Allianz Global
State tax deductions for contributions: Yes
State allows tax-free withdrawals: Yes
Website: http://www.okdream529.com
Phone: 877-529-9299

446. Oregon

Savings Plans

Fund: Oregon College Savings Plan
Administrator: TIAA-CREF
State tax deductions for contributions: Yes
State allows tax-free withdrawals: Yes
Website: http://www.oregoncollegesavings.com
Phone: 866-772-8464

Fund: MFS 529 Savings Plan
Administrator: MFS Fund Distributors Inc.
State tax deductions for contributions: Yes
State allows tax-free withdrawals: Yes
Website: http://www.mfs.com
Phone: 866-637-7526

447. Pennsylvania

Savings Plan

Fund: Pennsylvania 529 Investment Plan
Administrator: Pennsylvania Treasury Department
State tax deductions for contributions: Yes
State allows tax-free withdrawals: Yes
Website: http://www.pa529.com
Phone: 800-440-4000

Prepaid Tuition Plan

Fund: Pennsylvania 529 Guaranteed Savings Plan
Administrator: State
State tax deductions for contributions: Yes
State allows tax-free withdrawals: Yes
Website: http://www.pa529.com
Phone: 800-440-4000

448. Rhode Island

Savings Plans

Fund: CollegeBound Saver
Administrator: Rhode Island General Treasurer
State tax deductions for contributions: Yes
State allows tax-free withdrawals: Yes
Website: https://www.collegeboundsaver.com
Phone: 877-517-4829

449. South Carolina

Savings Plan

Fund: Future Scholar 529 College Savings Plan
Administrator: Columbia Management
State tax deductions for contributions: Yes
State allows tax-free withdrawals: Yes
Website: http://www.futurescholar.com
Phone: 888-244-5674

450. South Dakota

Savings Plans

Fund: College Access 529
Administrator: Allianz Global Investors
State tax deductions for contributions: No income tax
State allows tax-free withdrawals: No income tax
Website: http://www.collegeaccess529.com
Phone: 866-529-7462

451. Tennessee

Savings Plans

Fund: TNStars College Savings 529 Plan
Administrator: State
State tax deductions for contributions: No income tax

State allows tax-free withdrawals: No income tax
Website: http://www.tnstars.com
Phone: 855-386-7827

452. Texas

Savings Plan

Fund: Lonestar 529 Plan
Administrator: NorthStar Financial Services Group LLC
State tax deductions for contributions: No income tax
State allows tax-free withdrawals: No income tax
Website: http://www.lonestar529.com
Phone: 800-445-4723

Fund: Texas College Savings Plan
Administrator: NorthStar Financial Services Group LLC
State tax deductions for contributions: No income tax
State allows tax-free withdrawals: No income tax
Website: http://www.texascollegesavings.com
Phone: 800-445-4723, option 3

Prepaid Tuition Plan

Fund: Texas Tuition Promise Fund
Administrator: State
State tax deductions for contributions: No income tax
State allows tax-free withdrawals: No income tax
Website: http://www.texastuitionpromisefund.com
Phone: 800-445-4723

453. Utah

Savings Plan

Fund: Utah Educational Savings Plan
Administrator: Utah Higher Education Assistance Authority
State tax deductions for contributions: Yes
State allows tax-free withdrawals: Yes
Website: http://www.uesp.org
Phone: 800-418-2551

454. Vermont

Savings Plan

Fund: Vermont Higher Education Investment Plan
Administrator: Vermont Student Assistance Corp and
Intuition College Savings Solutions LLC
State tax deductions for contributions: Yes
State allows tax-free withdrawals: Yes
Website: http://www.vheip.org
Phone: 800-637-5860

455. Virginia

Savings Plans

Fund: CollegeAmerica
Administrator: American Funds
State tax deductions for contributions: Yes
State allows tax-free withdrawals: Yes
Website: http://www.virginia529.com/collegeamerica
Phone: 800-421-4225

Fund: Virginia 529 inVEST
Administrator: Virginia College Savings Plan Board
State tax deductions for contributions: Yes
State allows tax-free withdrawals: Yes
Website: http://www.virginia529.com
Phone: 888-567-0540

Fund: CollegeWealth
Administrator: Virginia College Savings Plan Board
State tax deductions for contributions: Yes
State allows tax-free withdrawals: Yes
Website: http://www.virginia529.com
Phone: 888-567-0540

Prepaid Tuition Plan

Fund: Virginia 529 prePAID
Administrator: State

State tax deductions for contributions: Yes
State allows tax-free withdrawals: Yes
Website: http://www.virginia529.com
Phone: 888-567-0540

456. Washington

Prepaid Tuition Plan

Fund: Guaranteed Education Tuition of Washington (GET)
Administrator: State
State tax deductions for contributions: No income tax
State allows tax-free withdrawals: No income tax
Website: http://www.get.wa.gov
Phone: 800-955-2318

457. West Virginia

Savings Plan

Fund: SMART529 Direct College Savings Plan
Administrator: Hartford Securities
State tax deductions for contributions: Yes
State allows tax-free withdrawals: Yes
Website: http://www.smart529.com
Phone: 866-574-3542

Fund: SMART529 Select
Administrator: Hartford Securities
State tax deductions for contributions: Yes
State allows tax-free withdrawals: Yes
Website: http://www.smart529select.com
Phone: 866-574-3542

Fund: The Hartford SMART529
Administrator: Hartford Securities
State tax deductions for contributions: Yes
State allows tax-free withdrawals: Yes
Website: http://www.hartfordfunds.com
Phone: 866-574-3542

458. Wisconsin

Savings Plans

Fund: EdVest
Administrator: TIAA-CREF Tuition Financing Inc.
State tax deductions for contributions: Yes
State allows tax-free withdrawals: Yes
Website: http://www.edvest.com
Phone: 888-338-3789

Fund: Tomorrow's Scholar
Administrator: Voya Investments Distributor LLC
State tax deductions for contributions: Yes
State allows tax-free withdrawals: Yes
Website: http://529plans.investments.voya.com
Phone: 866-677-6933

459. Wyoming

Savings Plan

Wyoming no longer operates a 529 savings plan.

460.

Consider transferring a custodial account to a 529 Plan

Before 529 Savings Plans were established, the Uniform Transfers to Minors Act (UTMA) or Uniform Gifts to Minors Act (UGMA) were the best way to transfer money from you or a relative to your child and pay the least amount of taxes as possible. However, with the 529 Savings Plan you pay no taxes (and may even be able take a state deduction on your contributions) as long as the money is used to pay for college.

So consider transferring the money currently in a UTMA/UGMA into a 529 Savings Plan. Most 529 Plans accept funds from a custodial account. However, 529 Plans can usually only accept cash, which means any investments in a custodial account must be liquidated and taxes paid on the gains before they can be transferred into a 529 Plan. Be sure you estimate the taxes that you might owe should you cash out a custodial account. Also, remember that the money in a UTMA/UGMA was gifted to your child and therefore will become his or her money at the age of maturity, which is either at age 18 or 21 depending on the laws in your state. Therefore, this money can only be used to pay for your child's education and cannot be switched to another beneficiary.

461.

Jump-start your 529 Savings Plan with a super gift

If you or a relative has a chunk of cash that you want to give your child or grandchild to pay for college, you are limited by the current $14,000 annual gift exclusion. This means that if you give more than $14,000 per year you will be subject to gift tax. However, with a 529 Plan you can actually make five year's worth of gifts in one year. So that means that you could give $70,000 if you are single or $140,000 as a couple to your child or grandchild and count it as a gift made over the next five years. You will not incur any gift taxes, and your beneficiary will have access to this significant sum of money. This may be an excellent way for grandparents to transfer a large part of their estate without incurring additional taxes.

462.

For private colleges consider the Private College 529 Plan

The Private College 529 Plan is a prepaid program sponsored by a consortium of almost 300 private universities and colleges. The program has the same federal tax benefits as state-sponsored 529 Plans. Under the Private College 529 Plan you purchase tuition credits at today's prices. This gives you the ability to freeze tuition at today's rate. As the cost of college increases the plan will cover the difference between what you paid for the credit and what tuition actually costs when your child is ready to attend school. As with all prepaid tuition programs the key risk is that your child may not want to attend one of the participating schools. Also, saving through the Private College 529 Plan does guarantee your child admission into any of the member schools.

We recommend that you check out the program by visiting their website and view the list of participating colleges. This is definitely an innovative twist on the traditional 529 Plan. Website: http://www.privatecollege529plan.com.

463.

Compare Coverdell ESAs, 529 Savings Plans and Prepaid Tuition Plans to pick the right one for you

So far we have discussed the Coverdell Education Savings Account, the 529 Savings Plan and the Prepaid Tuition Plan. Here is a quick summary of the major highlights and lowlights of each to help you decide what is right for you.

Coverdell ESA

■ All distributions are tax-free as long as they are used for qualified educational expenses.

■ You have total control over how your money is invested. You can choose which stocks, bonds or mutual fund to invest your money in or you can hold your money in cash.

■ You can use your money to pay for primary and secondary educational expenses including tuition, room, board, uniforms, tutoring and even computer equipment and software.

■ Coverdell accounts may be owned by the student or the student's parent. Under the Federal methodology which is used by most public universities to determine eligibility for financial aid, Coverdell accounts are considered the asset of the parent which means it will have a small impact on the student's chances of receiving financial aid.

■ The money must be used by the beneficiary or designated to another relative before the beneficiary turns 30.

■ The annual contribution limit is $2,000 per beneficiary, which means you have to start early to make the Coverdell effective.

■ There are income limits on who can contribute to a Coverdell.

529 Savings Plans

■ All distributions are tax-free as long as they are used for qualified college expenses.

■ The funds in the plan are controlled by the contributor. This means that parents can make sure the money is used for college and can also transfer it to another beneficiary if necessary.

■ The contribution limits are very high.

■ There is no income limitation to who can contribute money to a 529 Savings Plan.

■ Some states offer significant state tax savings for using your in-state plan.

■ Investments in a 529 Plan are managed by a fund manager You can't do your own stock picking.

■ The money in a 529 Plan is considered the asset of the contributor, which if it is not the beneficiary will have less negative impact on financial aid.

■ The money can only be used for college or graduate school expenses.

■ 529 Plans are not very flexible. There are restrictions on how often you can switch investment tracks and plans.

■ All 529 Plans are relatively new and have not established a long track record.

Prepaid Tuition Plans

■ These are relatively low-risk plans since you are guaranteed to have your tuition paid as long as you meet the schedule of payments.

■ Prepaid tuition plans are considered an asset of the parent (same as 529 Savings Plans) by the Federal methodology which means it will have a small impact on the student's financial aid.

■ Prepaid plans are not offered by all states. Your state college may not have a prepaid plan.

■ The plan locks you into a specific college system. If you are saving for a young child there is a chance that he or she may not want to go to your state college or that you may move to another state and not be able to transfer the fund.

■ Depending on your plan it may only cover tuition and not room and board, which is often a significant portion of college expenses.

464.

Take advantage of both Coverdell and 529 Savings Plans

There is no reason why you can't do both a Coverdell and 529 Savings Plan. This would give you some diversification of your savings since you have 100 percent control of your Coverdell investments. You can also use the Coverdell for primary and secondary expenses–especially if your child will be attending an expensive private high school.

Having a 529 Savings Plan will allow you to save more than the Coverdell since it has higher limits and you may be able to get more family members to participate by contributing. Depending on your state tax laws you may also enjoy some significant state tax deductions for using your state's own 529 Savings Plan.

Government Savings Bonds

465.

Cash in a bond tax-free

When we were kids, there was no birthday gift that was more disappointing than a savings bond. It was nice to see that the bond would

---

Where can I find some calculators to help me plan my budget and savings?

The best calculators for figuring such things as how much you need to save for college and how much college will cost are found online. There are many good ones available. We like the calculators on SallieMae.com. They not only have the standard calculators but also some useful ones for creating a budget. Visit www.salliemae.com and look for the College Planning Toolbox in the College Planning section.

be worth $100, but to have to wait five to seven years to redeem it seemed like an eternity. As a parent, however, you might want to consider buying bonds for your child's education since you may be able to exclude the interest earned from taxes if you use the proceeds to pay for qualified educational expenses.

Eligible bonds are series EE bonds issued on January 1990 and later, along with all Series I Bonds. To cash in the bonds tax-free you must have been at least 24 years old when you purchased them, and the bonds must be registered in your name or your spouse's name. Your child can be listed as a beneficiary but not as a co-owner. You must also meet specific income limits. For the 2016 tax year your modified gross adjusted income must be less than $77,200 if you are filing single and less than $115,750 if you file jointly. If you make more than this amount your tax benefits will be reduced. If you earn more than $92,200 as a single filer or $145,750 as a joint filer you cannot deduct any interest.

Unfortunately, savings bonds given to your child as a gift aren't eligible for tax-free treatment. Also, any bonds not purchased by you are similarly ineligible. However, if you meet the criteria all you need to do is file form 8815 to figure your education savings bond interest exclusion. For more information, take a look at http://www.savingsbonds.gov.

466.

Convert a savings bond to a 529 Savings Plan

Under the Education Bond Program you can cash in your bonds and use the proceeds to fund a 529 Savings Plan tax-free. The same limitations apply as in the above example of cashing in a bond to pay for educational expenses. You can learn more by visiting the Bureau of the Fiscal Service at https://www.fiscal.treasury.gov.

Individual Development Account Program

467.

Double or triple your savings with an Individual Development Account (IDA)

Individual Development Accounts (IDAs) are designed for low-income workers to quickly save money for school by matching their savings. The idea is that if you are low income and working, the best way for you to improve your status is to build your savings, which can then be used to purchase an asset such as a house, business or education. To help speed this process the Individual Development Account was established and is managed by a network of non-profit organizations. If you qualify for the IDA program you will set up a goal such as saving $2,000 for college and start saving. When you reach that goal the IDA network will match what you saved by a ratio of two, three or even seven times that amount. Matched funds come from financial institutions, foundations, religious congregations and state and local governments.

For example, if you receive a 2:1 match, which is the most common, each time you deposit $10, you will get an additional $20 credited to your goal. When you reach your goal the money is released directly to the college to pay for your tuition. Having your savings matched speeds up the time it takes for you to reach your goal.

IDA programs usually set their own specific participation requirements. In general, you must be within 200 percent of poverty. This works out to less than $23,760 for an individual or $48,600 for a family of four. IDA participants must also be employed and agree to take financial planning classes sponsored by the non-profit organization.

The hardest part of participating in an IDA program is finding them. Since the network of IDA providers is composed of a hodgepodge of agencies, there is no national directory. You will have to do some digging. Start with all of the foundations and non-profits in your area. Also try contacting the manager at your local banks. There is a directory of IDA programs in your state at http://www.idanetwork.org. This is not a complete listing of organizations, but it will give you an idea of what you are looking for.

Once you find one in your area make sure you understand the participation guidelines. If you qualify you can definitely speed your way to your educational goal.

Gifting Money For College

468.

Gifting the old fashion way through UGMA/UTMA and Custodial Accounts

For a long time the Uniform Transfers/Gifts to Minors Acts were the main way parents and grandparents transferred money to a child. With money put into custodial accounts, children under the age of 18 can keep the first $1,000 in unearned income tax free and pay at their tax rate for the next $1,000. This also applies to children up to age 23 if they are full-time dependent students.

With the advent of 529 Savings Plans and the increased contribution limits to the Coverdell ESA, you now have an alternative to transfer money totally tax-free. The only limitation is that the money must be used to pay for educational expenses. If you want to help your child save for a down payment on a house or any non-education related uses, then UGMA/UTMA may still be the best option.

One additional potential advantage of transferring money with a 529 Plan is that the money stays in your control. With a custodial account (and even Coverdell ESAs) the money becomes the property of the child at age 18 or 21, depending on your state's laws. Also, 529 Plans are considered the property of the contributor, which is usually the parent, while custodial accounts are the property of the student, which means that money will have a greater negative impact on the size of any financial aid package.

469.

For big money think Crummey Trust

When you hear the term "trust fund baby" it is usually referring to a Crummey Trust. This is the type of trust that you set up for a minor. Unlike with a custodial account, the person who sets up the trust fund can determine when the beneficiary is allowed to take control of the money. A Crummey Trust is usually established to hold a significant amount of money and is relatively expensive to establish. Plus, the trust is considered the asset of the beneficiary, which means it can hurt your chances of receiving financial aid. However, if you have a trust fund to begin with then there's a good chance you won't qualify for financial aid anyway.

Investing For College

If you choose to use a 529 Plan then most of your investment decisions are done. Once you pick which investment track you want to follow within your plan, the fund manager will take care of all the day-to-day decisions. Like a mutual fund you just keep adding money over time. However, if you plan to open a Coverdell or simply to invest on your own, you'll learn that investing for college is different than for other goals such as retirement. The biggest challenge is that you don't have as much flexibility over when you need the money. You can always defer retirement for five years but not so with a college education. Incorporate the following tips for your own investment strategies.

470.

Set annual goals

You need to know what your goal is before you start investing. Figure out how much college will cost when your child is ready to attend. Be sure to plan for both private and public college educations. Once you have a goal you can set targets for your investment strategy. Plus, as you get closer to your goal you can switch to an increasingly conservative strategy to make sure you don't risk what you worked so hard to build. To get a good estimate for what it will cost for your child to go to college in the future take a look at the College Planning Toolbox on the Sallie Mae website at http://www.salliemae.com. You might want to sit down before you view the final total.

471.

Start early to give your money time to grow

The hardest part of investing is often getting started. You need to fill out paper work to open accounts and select investment options, but the sooner you begin the better your chances are of reaching your goal. Time is on your side. Once you get your investments started you might want to consider making an automatic investment each month. Mutual funds, for example, let you set up automatic investment so that each month a certain amount of additional shares are purchased. But don't be tempted to set these mechanisms up and then forget about them. Pay attention and don't get complacent especially as the time for when you need the money approaches.

472.

Minimize your risk and maximize your return with dollar cost averaging

If you want to be conservative in your investment approach, consider the strategy of dollar cost averaging. This is based on the principle that the market in the long term always rises and trying to time the market is next to impossible. Therefore, it is best to buy a fixed amount of stock or mutual funds each month. Some months you are buying high since the market is up, but some months you are buying at a bargain when the market is down. Over time this will average out and you will have taken advantage of low prices while not investing your entire nest egg when the market was too high. Combined with an automatic investment option this can be a really low maintenance way to invest.

473.

Play it conservatively

You don't want to gamble with your child's future. While there is always risk in any kind of investment, make sure you are not being too aggressive when you are nearing the time you need the money. If you didn't learn your lesson from the dot-com implosion, don't speculate on so-called "sure bets" or "hot tips." Even relatively safe choices start to look too risky if you can't wait out a market downturn.

474.

Diversify to prevent putting all your eggs in one basket

Part of being conservative with your investments is diversifying your portfolio. You don't want to keep all of your money in one stock or even one sector. Spread your money around to make sure a collapse in one part of your portfolio won't sink your entire investment boat.

475.

Take a lesson from age-based 529 Savings Plans

Most 529 Plans offer a conservative age-based approach. When your child is young, the fund invests more aggressively in stocks and mutual funds. As your child gets older more money is shifted into fixed income investments like bonds. When your child is a few years from college most of the money is kept in safe money market funds. You don't want a disaster in the stock market to doom your child's chances of getting an education. As you near the time when you need the money, begin to move out of more risky investments.

476.

Don't neglect your IRAs

Compared to the Coverdell ESA or a good 529 Plan, using an Individual Retirement Account (IRA) is not the best way to save for college since you may have to pay taxes on what you withdraw. However, there are some benefits that make building your IRA a smart idea.

When it comes to determining financial aid, your retirement accounts are exempt from consideration. In other words, colleges can't touch these accounts when they try to determine how much money you can afford to pay for college. Plus, you can withdraw money from an IRA before you turn 59 ½ and avoid the 10 percent early withdrawal penalty as long as the money is used for college expenses. This applies to any IRA you own, whether it is a traditional IRA (including a SEP-IRA), a Roth IRA or a SIMPLE IRA. If you want to learn more about these different IRAs take a look at the IRS's Publication 590. Remember that you might have to pay income tax on part of the money that you withdraw, but at least you avoid the huge 10 percent penalty. Speak with your accountant to determine if this is a good strategy for you.

477.

Purchase zero coupon bonds strategically

These bonds are issued at a discount from their face value. After a specified maturity date the bond can be redeemed for the full face value. You will need to make sure that the maturity date is before the time when you need to use it for college. But these are relatively safe investments, and if you plan correctly you can have bonds mature at each year in which the tuition bills are due.

How much do I have to save each month to be able to reach my goal?

The answer depends on how much your goal is. You want to sock away as much as possible. If you look at this chart you can see how much you will have if you save $50, $100, $250 and $500 per month. This table assumes a 5 percent growth rate on all of your money saved. As you can see, the amount you can save even with a limited budget and in a short amount of time can add up.

Number of years saved	Amount saved per month	Grand total
1	50	616
1	100	1,233
1	250	3,082
1	500	6,165
2	50	1,264
2	100	2,529
2	250	6,322
2	500	12,645
3	50	1,945
3	100	3,891
3	250	9,728
3	500	19,457
4	50	2,661
4	100	5,323
4	250	13,308
4	500	26,617
5	50	3,414
5	100	6,828
5	250	17,072
5	500	34,144
7	50	5,037
7	100	10,074
7	250	25,186
7	500	50,373
10	50	7,796
10	100	15,592
10	250	38,982
10	500	77,964

Saving Money Every Day

Cutting your family expenses means more money that you can save and invest. As the parent of a college-bound student you should be ruthless in your quest to cut family expenses to free up money to save. Here are some ways to do it:

478.

Don't ever think that it's too late to start saving

Given a choice, it is better to start saving for college when your child is 5 instead of 18. But don't throw up your hands in despair even if you have only a year or less to save. Because things like financial aid and scholarships are unpredictable, whatever you can save may be just enough to fill a critical gap. Also, every dollar you save could mean one less dollar you have to borrow. This will save you a lot of money in interest payments. When you think about it, each dollar you save is actually worth a lot more if it helps you borrow less. So no matter how soon you have to pay the first tuition bill, start saving money today.

One last benefit to saving early is that you also begin to train your family to live on less. Parents supporting a child in college can attest to the personal sacrifices they make. If you can learn to live on less now then these sacrifices won't seem as difficult.

479.

Identify and eliminate the non-essential luxuries

For many families the key to saving money is to cut unnecessary expenses. Here is a great exercise. Record for an entire month how much you spend. Write down every dollar you spend from food, to clothes, to going to the movies. At the end of the month add up what's on your list. Where is your money going? What expenses are non-essential or luxuries? Do you really need that $4 cappuccino when you could make it at home instead? Does your family need to eat out that often? It may seem trivial but we bet you can find more than spare change to save when you carefully examine how your family spends its money.

One family we know noticed that they were spending nearly $300 a month on restaurant and fast food. They switched to eating at home and doing barbecues when they wanted something special and were able to add more than $3,000 a year to their college savings.

480.

Put off the big purchases, if you can

Instead of buying a new car, push the old one a few more years. Sure a new kitchen would be nice but so would Johnny graduating without your having to take out a second mortgage. Remember too that big purchases also have long-term consequences. The new car will saddle you with higher insurance payments. Remodeling the bathroom may force you to take out a home equity loan. As long as the purchases are not essential (do spend the money to fix a leaky roof), consider putting them off until after your child graduates from college.

481.

Postpone college for a year to help you save

While we have been focused on ways to save for college, one often overlooked option is to have your child wait and work for a year. You can usually defer for a year before entering college. Doing so can also help you decide if college is the right choice. We know of several students who were not too enthusiastic about college until they took a year off and went to work. What they found in the work world was that without a college degree their future was severely limited. Taking a year off not only allowed them to save some money but it also got them excited about going to school.

If you are planning on taking a year off, we strongly recommend that you still apply to college during your senior year and then after you are accepted defer admission by a year. What this means is that you are already accepted by the college but simply postponing the start date. Your will need to talk to the admission office to make sure this is possible. Knowing that you have a guaranteed spot in college will save you a lot of stress.

SEVEN

Tax Breaks For Students

Get Your Tax Dollars Back

It is said that nothing is certain in life except death and taxes. If you are going to college or are the parent of a college-bound student, then you can add one more certainty to life and that is: tuition bills. Fortunately, Uncle Sam acknowledges this reality and offers several valuable tax credits and deductions. These tax breaks literally put money back in your pocket to help you pay those inevitable tuition bills.

The challenge with tax breaks is two-fold. First, you need to decipher the tax codes to determine if you actually qualify for a tax break. Most have income limits and other requirements that restrict their use. Second, if you qualify to take advantage of multiple tax breaks you need to figure out which combination will give you the most benefit. To complicate matters (and you shouldn't expect anything less from the IRS), some of these tax breaks are mutually exclusive, which means you'll have to choose one over the other.

Before you take advantage of any tax break, do a little long-term planning and create several scenarios to see how each choice affects your bottom line. As you will see there are some situations where electing to take a tax break may impact another area of your personal finances.

The information in this chapter is not meant to be authoritative tax advice or a guide to doing your taxes. Before you take advantage of a tax break, check with your accountant to make sure that you meet all qualifications and that the tax rules have not changed.

Timing Is Everything

The premise for all tax breaks is to refund you money that you have paid out of your pocket for college expenses. To claim a tax credit or deduction you therefore must have spent your own money on your or your child's education. That money can't come from a source that is already tax-free such as Coverdell ESA, scholarships, veteran educational assistance, Pell grants or 529 Savings

Plans. This is because any money that already receives favorable tax treatment cannot be claimed for an additional tax credit. Doing so is known as "double dipping," which is a big "no-no" to the IRS.

Since this is an important concept let's look at an example. Imagine that you have set up a 529 Savings Plan that has a balance of $15,000. During your child's first year of college you spent the entire contribution portion (this is the money you put in) of the 529 Plan so what's left represents the earnings portion. The earning portion is totally tax-free as long as you use it for educational expenses. It just so happens that tuition for this year is $15,000. If you use your entire 529 Savings Plan money to pay for tuition, you cannot claim any tax credits on what you have paid for tuition since you used money that already had a tax benefit. Remember the earnings portion of your 529 Plan is tax deferred. However, if you withdraw only $11,000 from the 529 Plan and pay the remaining $4,000 with money from your own pocket you could claim a tax credit on $4,000. If you use the American Opportunity tax credit (formerly the Hope tax credit) assuming that you meet the income limits, you receive the maximum amount of $2,500. Plus, you still have $4,000 left in your 529 Savings Plan for next year's tuition bill.

The bottom line is you need to plan in advance how you are going to take advantage of your tax breaks before you start paying for college. With a little planning you can dramatically affect the value of these tax breaks, leading to more money in your pocket to pay for college.

Remember too that tax laws as well as their interpretations change each year. Please check the requirements of these tax breaks by downloading the latest version of IRS publication 970 at http://www.irs.gov. With this caution in mind, let's take a look at some of the tax breaks that you may be able to use.

482.

Give yourself up to $2,500 with the American Opportunity tax credit

This tax credit reduces your taxes dollar for dollar and is like putting money directly into your pocket. You may receive up to $2,500 in tax

---

What's the difference between a tax credit and a tax deduction?

Tax credits reduce the amount of tax you owe dollar for dollar. Therefore, a tax credit of $1,000 means you will pay $1,000 less in taxes. A tax deduction reduces the amount of money on which your tax is calculated. A tax deduction of $1,000 may save you $200 in actual taxes depending on your tax bracket.

---

credits per student. The American Opportunity credit may be claimed in all four years of college.

To figure out how much of a American Opportunity tax credit that you can claim per student, look at the total amount of money that you paid out of your own pocket for tuition. The American Opportunity credit can only be used for tuition, not room and board and other expenses. So if you are using 529 or Coverdell money you'll want to use it to pay for room and board and use some of your own to pay for tuition. Once you know how much you've paid out of pocket for tuition, you can claim 100 percent of the first $2,000 and 25 percent of the next $2,000 that you paid. In other words to claim the full $2,500 per student you must have paid at least $4,000 in qualified education expenses for that student.

To claim the American Opportunity tax credit you must also meet the income requirements. For a single taxpayer you can get the full credit if your modified gross adjusted income does not exceed $80,000. If it does but is below $90,000 you can claim a partial credit. For married couples filing jointly you can get the full credit if your income does not exceed $160,000. If you earn more but are still below $180,000 you can claim a partial credit.

To claim a American Opportunity tax credit, file your taxes using Form 1040 or 1040A and attach Form 8863 Education Credits. There are a few other stipulations attached to the American Opportunity credit, which are that the student must be enrolled at least half-time, enrolled in a program that leads to a degree, certificate or other recognized educational credential and must be free of any felony conviction for possessing or distributing a controlled substance.

483.

If you're over the income limit you may get a partial credit

Like all tax credits, the American Opportunity has an income requirement. If you are over the initial limit, which is $80,000 for single filers and $160,000 for joint filers, but still below the maximum limit, which is $90,000 for single filers and $180,000 for joint filers, you can claim a partial credit.

To figure out how much you can claim, take the amount that you are over the limit and divide it by the phase-out range. This tells you by what percentage you are over the initial limit. You can then take the remaining percentage (the percentage by which you are still under the maximum limit) and multiply it again by the American Opportunity credit of $2,500 to figure out how much you can claim.

For example, if you are a single filer and you earn $83,000, you are $3,000 over the initial limit of $80,000. You divide that $3,000 by the phase-out range, which is $10,000. The phase-out range is simply the difference between the maximum limit of $90,000 and the initial limit of $80,000. This gives you 0.3, which means you are 30 percent over the initial limit. You can therefore still claim up to 70 percent of the credit or up to $1,750 ($2,500 maximum credit x 0.7 = $1,750.) The process is the same for joint filers only now the phase-out range is $20,000 since you take the difference between $180,000 and $160,000.

484.

Get up to $2,000 with the Lifetime Learning credit

The Lifetime Learning credit is similar to the American Opportunity credit and reduces the tax you owe dollar for dollar. However, you cannot claim both an American Opportunity and a Lifetime Learning credit on the same student in the same year. It is usually to your advantage to claim the American Opportunity tax credit.

If you are an adult student who has already completed four years of undergraduate work or are taking continuing education courses or if you are a graduate school student, then you have no choice but to take the Lifetime Learning credit.

The maximum amount of the Lifetime Learning credit is $2,000 per tax return, which is figured out by taking 20 percent of what you pay for tuition (not room and board or other expenses) up to $10,000. This means that to claim the full $2,000 credit, you must spend $10,000 or more out of your own pocket on tuition. Remember, money that is already receiving a tax benefit like the earnings portions of Coverdell and 529 Plans or tax-free scholarships don't count in figuring out how much you spent. The IRS doesn't allow double-dipping.

There are income limits for the Lifetime Learning credit. For a single taxpayer you can get the full credit if your modified gross adjusted income does not exceed $55,000. If it does but is below $65,000 you can claim a partial credit. For married couples filing jointly you can get the full credit if your income does not exceed $110,000. If you earn more but are still below $130,000 you can claim a partial credit.

Besides the income limit, you also must pay the tuition and related fees for an eligible student, which can include yourself, your spouse or a dependent for whom you claim an exemption on your tax return. The student does not, however, have to study toward a degree. Eligible courses can be part of a postsecondary degree program or taken by the student to acquire or improve job skills. Eligible educational institutions include any college, university, vocational school or other postsecondary educational institution eligible to participate in a student aid program administered by the Department of Education. This includes virtually all accredited, private or public, non-profit, and proprietary (privately owned, profit-making) postsecondary institutions.

Also, the felony drug conviction rule that might prevent you from getting an American Opportunity credit does not apply for the Lifetime Learning credit.

485.

Choose your tax credit wisely since you can only claim one per student per year

You can claim only one tax credit per student per year, which means you need to decide whether to claim the American Opportunity or

Lifetime Learning credit if you qualify for both. Generally it's better to claim the American Opportunity tax credit if you're eligible:

Lifetime Learning credit

- Up to $2,000 credit per return if you spent $10,000 or more of your own money on qualified tuition expenses. The amount that you can claim is less if you spent less. To figure the credit, take 20 percent of what you spent on qualified expenses up to the maximum of $10,000.

- You can claim a Lifetime Learning credit for all years of postsecondary education (including adult education) and for courses to acquire or improve job skills.

- You do not need to be pursuing a degree or other recognized educational credential.

- The felony drug conviction rule does not apply for the Lifetime Learning credit.

American Opportunity credit

- Up to $2,500 credit per eligible student. To get the maximum amount you must have spent at least $4,000 on qualified tuition expenses.

- If you qualify for both the American Opportunity and Lifetime Learning credits you probably want to take the American Opportunity since you'll receive a larger credit.

- You must be pursuing an undergraduate degree or other recognized educational credential.

- You must be enrolled at least half-time for at least one academic period.

- You cannot have any felony drug convictions.

486.

Be sure to get your tax credits in the right order

Since you can claim only one of the credits for each student per year, make sure you take advantage of them in the right order. If you qualify for both then you probably want to use the American Opportunity credit. The American Opportunity credit lets you qualify for the full amount while using less of your own money. This means you can spend more of your Coverdell or 529 Savings Plan money. In some cases this is a good idea since both affect your chances of receiving financial aid. If you have a large college savings this could adversely affect if or how much aid your child receives. By depleting this account in the first few years of college, you may increase your chances of getting financial aid in your child's last years in college.

487.

Don't carelessly miss getting your credit

If you've been diligently contributing to a 529 Savings Plan or Coverdell Education Savings Account, you may find that you have enough money to pay for all of your child's tuition in the first year. However, if you do this you may not be able to claim an American Opportunity tax credit. Since the earning portions of both 529 and Coverdell money are tax-free you can't claim an American Opportunity tax credit for using them. To get around this, you need to pay for some of the tuition expenses with money that does not come from your 529 or Coverdell accounts or that comes from the contribution part of your 529 or Coverdell since this is money that you've already paid taxes on. If you do this (and pay the rest using your tax-free money) you will be able to claim the tax credit.

488.

Lower your income to claim a tax credit

If you are over the income limits that trigger a phase-out for any tax break, you may be able to change your modified gross adjusted income just enough to qualify for the full credit or a larger partial credit. The key is to boost your "above the line" contributions. If you look at your 1040 tax return you'll notice that your adjusted gross income is on line 37. Anything that appears on lines 23 through 36 are known as "above the line" deductions which will reduce your AGI. For most people the one item they have the most control over is contributions to IRAs including SEP and SIMPLE IRAs. Also, contributions to 401k, 403b or 457 retirement plans reduce your income reported on your W2 and have the same effect of reducing your AGI. By increasing your contributions to these accounts you will lower your adjusted gross income. This might be enough to give you a bigger slice of the tax break pie. Plus, money in your retirement accounts is sheltered from the financial aid calculations, which can increase your chances of getting more financial aid from the college.

489.

Don't forget you can deduct your student loan interest

Tax deductions are not as good as tax credits but they do reduce your taxable income, which means you will still pay less taxes. One of the most common education deductions is for student loan interest. All student loan interest that you pay is tax deductible up to $2,500 per year. The loan must have been used for qualified higher-education expenses, including tuition, fees, room and board, supplies and other related expenses. Also the maximum allowable deduction is gradually reduced for single taxpayers whose modified gross adjusted income exceeds $65,000 but is below $80,000 and for married taxpayers filing jointly whose MAGI exceeds $130,000 but is below $160,000.

You can usually count as interest the loan-origination fees (other than fees for services), capitalized interest, interest on revolving lines of credit and interest on refinanced student loans, which include both consolidated loans and collapsed loans. You can also count any voluntary interest payments that you make. To claim the deduction you should receive Form 1098-E from your lender or loan servicer.

490.

Deduct work-related education

Work-related education may provide you with a tax deduction if it amounts to more than two percent of your adjusted gross income. The education must also meet one of these two tests: it is required by your employer or the law to keep your current job, or it maintains or improves skills necessary in your current work.

You must also be working and itemize your deductions on Schedule A if you are an employee. Self-employed workers must file Schedule C, Schedule C-EZ or Schedule F. The great benefit of this deduction is that you may utilize it even if the education could lead to a degree.

491.

Educational benefits from your employer may be tax-free

If you have a generous employer you might be able to receive up to $5,250 of tax-free employer provided educational assistance benefits each year. This means that you may not have to pay tax on amounts your employer pays for your education including payments for tuition, fees and similar expenses, books, supplies and equipment. This can be used for both undergraduate and graduate-level courses. Plus, the payments do not have to be for work-related courses.

How do I calculate my modified adjusted gross income (MAGI) to see if I can deduct what I paid for tuition and fees?

For most taxpayers, your modified adjusted gross income is simply your adjusted gross income (AGI) on your tax return. If you file Form 1040, your MAGI is the AGI on line 37 without taking into account any amount on lines 34 or 35 (tuition and fees deduction or domestic production activities deduction.) You must add back to your income any foreign earned income exclusion, foreign housing exclusion, foreign housing deduction and the exclusion of income from American Samoa or Puerto Rico.

However, you cannot use any of the tax-free education expenses paid for by your employer as the basis for any other deduction or credit, including the American Opportunity and Lifetime Learning credits.

492.

Cash in your government bonds tax-free

If you cashed in a government savings bond to pay for qualified educational expenses you may be able to exclude the interest earned from your federal incomes taxes. The key is that you must have purchased a series EE bond issued after 1989 or the series I bond. The bond must be issued either in your name or in the name of both you and your spouse. You must have been at least 24 years old at the time when you purchased the bond, and it cannot have been a gift to or be in the name of your child.

If you meet these requirements and your modified adjusted gross income is less than $77,200 if filing a single return or $115,750 if filing a joint return you can deduct the interest used to pay for tuition. If your modified gross income is higher than these amounts but below $92,200 for single filers and $145,750 for joint filers then you will still be able to exclude a portion of the interest. You will need to file Form 8815 to figure out your education savings bond interest exclusion.

493.

Money-saving tax benefits of scholarships and fellowships

If you received an academic scholarship or fellowship that is used for qualified tuition, fees and books then it is generally not taxable. For a scholarship or fellowship to be non-taxable you must meet the following conditions:

- You are a candidate for a degree at an educational institution,
- The amounts you receive as a scholarship or fellowship must be used for tuition and fees required for enrollment or attendance at the educational institution, or for books, supplies and equipment required for courses of instruction and
- The amounts received are not a payment for your services.

You cannot exclude from your taxable income any scholarships or grants that are used to pay for room and board.

494.

Get more tax help

Tax questions are never easy and it is essential that you talk to a professional accountant. In addition, tax laws are constantly changing. To get the latest (and free) information, surf over to the IRS website at http://www.irs.gov or schedule phone or personal appointment. You can call with questions to 800-829-1040, or try the IRS's Everyday Tax Solutions service by calling your local IRS office to set up an in-person appointment. If you have access to TTY/TDD equipment, call 800-829-4059.

How do I calculate my modified adjusted gross income (MAGI) to see if I can deduct my student loan interest payments?

For most taxpayers, your modified adjusted gross income is the adjusted gross income (AGI) from your federal income tax return before subtracting any deduction for student loan interest. If you file Form 1040A, your MAGI is the AGI on line 21 without taking into account any amount on line 18 (student loan interest deduction.) If you file Form 1040, your MAGI is the AGI on line 37 without taking into account any amount on line 33 (student loan interest deduction) or line 35 (Domestic production activities or tuition and fees deduction.) You must add back to your income any foreign earned income exclusion, foreign housing exclusion, foreign housing deduction and the exclusion of income from American Samoa or Puerto Rico.

Glossary

IRS Form 970: This is the form from the IRS that outlines tax benefits for education including scholarships, fellowships, grants and tuition reductions; the American Opportunity tax credit; the Lifetime Learning tax credit; student loan interest deduction; student loan cancellations and repayment assistance; tuition and fees deduction; Coverdell Education Savings Accounts; the Qualified Tuition Program (QTP); the Education Savings Bond Program; employer-provided educational assistance and business deductions for work-related education. The form is available at http://www.irs.gov/publications/p970.

Modified adjusted gross income (MAGI): For most, your MAGI is the adjusted gross income (AGI) from your federal income tax return before subtracting any deduction for student loan interest.

Tax credit: Tax credits reduce the amount of tax you owe dollar for dollar. With a tax credit of $2,500, you will pay $2,500 less in taxes.

Tax deduction: Tax deductions reduce the amount of money on which your tax is calculated. If you are in the 28 percent tax bracket, a tax deduction of $1,000 will save you $280.

Maximize Financial Aid

Get Your Share Of Financial Aid

Federal Financial aid can seem like a big, scary mystery. We've actually met people who had nightmares about it. One involved a despotic financial aid officer sitting on top of an 800-foot high pile of cash. Below, a line of weary parents waited their turn. A lucky few received a small handful of dollars. But most got nothing and walked away with bowed heads. Fortunately, this was just a dream. Reality is far less dark and mysterious. You see financial aid officers are not your arch enemies but your allies in helping you pay for college.

The financial aid system has evolved over many decades and is based on a set of well-established rules. If you understand these rules you will not only feel more in control of the process but you will also insure that you have the best chance to get the most financial aid that you deserve.

The Philosophy of Financial Aid

Before we introduce you to the rules, you need to understand one important philosophical principle about financial aid. It is that a college education is not an entitlement. In other words, unlike a high school education, the government does not guarantee anyone the right to an affordable college education. The government does believe that it is in the best interest of society at large to make college as accessible as possible to the most number of people. So it provides aid but only after you have exhausted nearly all of your own resources. Financial aid is not designed to help you spend less money on college but rather to help you afford to go to a college that you might not have been able to pay for on your own. You also have to keep in mind that since a college education is not an entitlement there is no guarantee that even if you meet every qualification that the government or college will automatically come to your aid.

In practical terms this means that while you should apply for financial aid, you should not view it as a sure thing that will take care of the bills you can't afford. Think of yourself as a mountain climber who has a 90-foot rope. If you want to scale a 110-foot cliff then financial aid might give you that extra 20 feet of rope to do so. But if you want to climb a 150-foot cliff you will find that even with the extra 20 feet of rope from financial aid, you still need to bring more of your own rope. Of course, you can also decide to climb a lower cliff.

Okay, enough with the analogies. Let's see how financial aid works and how to get the most you deserve.

The FAFSA and CSS/PROFILE

The primary job of the college financial aid officer is to look at your family's finances and determine your "financial need." To do so they need to get a sense of your family finances. You will provide this information on a form called the *Free Application for Federal Student Aid* or FAFSA. Using your prior-prior year (PPY) tax returns, you will reveal all of the money that you have in savings, investments and hidden Swiss bank accounts. If you are applying to a private college you may also have to provide additional information through the college's own financial aid form or the College Board's *CSS/Financial Aid PROFILE* form. Like the FAFSA, it asks similar questions about your finances.

You can download a copy of these forms and even complete them online at http://www.fafsa.ed.gov for the FAFSA and http://www.collegeboard.com for the PROFILE.

With a detailed picture of your financial situation, each college financial aid officer will analyze the money you have and based on the cost of the college will figure out your degree of financial need. Once they know how much you need, they put together a financial aid package, which spells out how much and from where you are to get this money.

But first, let's begin by looking at how the colleges figure out that magical number of how much money your family can afford to pay for college.

Step 1: Learn How To Qualify For Financial Aid

The first step to getting financial aid is to understand how the system works. Once you know how the calculations determine if you qualify for financial aid you can look at ways to make sure you are getting the most aid you deserve.

495.

Understand how the Institutional and Federal methodologies determine how much you will pay

Public and private colleges have adopted different formulas and procedures for determining how much money your family can afford to pay for college. Public schools (and some privates, too) use what is known as the Federal methodology. This is the formula provided by the U.S. Department of Education. When you submit the Free Application for Federal Student Aid (FAFSA), the government uses the information you provide to calculate the amount of money that you can put toward college for one year. The Federal methodology looks at things like your income and assets but does not consider assets such as retirement accounts and equity that you have built up in your home.

Some private colleges want to know about your retirement accounts and home equity and will use the Institutional methodology. By completing the College Board's PROFILE form in addition to the FAFSA you will give the colleges some additional financial information. While the Institutional methodology is somewhat stricter than the Federal methodology and will usually result in less financial need, you really don't have a choice in the matter since you need to submit the financial aid applications the colleges require.

The goal of both the Federal and Institutional methodologies is to take the numbers you provide on the FAFSA and PROFILE forms, run a series of calculations and end up with a single number. This number is known as your Expected Family Contribution (EFC). This is the magic number. It represents the amount of money that your family is expected to contribute for one year of your education. This number can range from $0 to infinity.

About two weeks after you submit the FAFSA you will receive the Student Aid Report (SAR), which will tell you your Expected Family Contribution. You might want to be sitting down before you view your SAR. For the PROFILE you will not be told your Expected Family Contribution, but you can guess that it will be somewhat higher than the number on your Student Aid Report.

It's important to understand that the Expected Family Contribution is calculated by simply feeding the numbers you provide into a computer. Every family's situation is run through the same calculation. Two families with identical numbers on their FAFSA will have the same Expected Family Contributions. There are no special circumstances or explanations needed at this stage. It won't do you any good to send a letter along with your FAFSA describing how tough it is for your family to make ends meet. Save that letter for the next step when you deal directly with the financial aid officers at the colleges. At this point you are just providing accurate information on your finances based on your tax returns.

But the game is just beginning. Once your Expected Family Contribution has been determined, it is passed on to the colleges you have applied to or the college you attend and is used to determine if you have financial need. It is also at the college level where the exact composition of your financial aid package is determined. And, it is at this point that the computers are turned off and human beings take over.

496.

How your magic number–a.k.a. your Expected Family Contribution–is determined

At this point you are probably wondering how in the heck the government uses a snapshot of your family's finances to determine how much you can spend on college. Like everything from taxes to Social Security benefits, to calculate your Expected Family Contribution the government uses a formula. Here is the general formula, which can change from year to year, for computing your EFC.

Parents' adjusted income x (up to 47 percent) +
Parents' assets x (up to 5.65 percent) +

Student's income x (up to 50 percent) +
Student's assets x (20 percent) = Expected Family Contribution

There are some factors such as family size and number of children in college at the same time that the government uses to adjust the exact percentage that it will assess against your income and assets. Also, there are income and asset protection figures that prevent the government from touching everything that you have. While we could go into a lot of detail to show you the nitty gritty detail of the calculation, we feel it's better that you have a solid overview since that will help you understand how to get more financial aid.

If you want a really detailed calculation to forecast your Expected Family Contribution then we recommend you use an online EFC calculator. One good calculator is on the College Board website at http://bigfuture.collegeboard.org. You can play with it and try different numbers to simulate various changes in your finances. If you want to do it yourself on paper, you can download an EFC worksheet at http://www.ifap.ed.gov. Click on the heading "Worksheets, Schedules and Tables."

What is the timeline for applying for financial aid?

September-December
Focus on your college applications if you are still in high school.

After October 1
Complete and submit your financial aid applications.

After submitting FAFSA
Review your Student Aid Report, which will be sent to you after you submit your FAFSA.

April
You should receive both your college acceptance letters and financial aid packages. Review and compare your aid packages. Ask for a reassessment, if necessary.

May
This is the typical deadline for accepting all or part of your financial aid package.

But for now let's keep things simple and just consider the above formula. Right away you can see that parents' income, student's income and student's assets are the most heavily assessed. Since most students have low to no income, the heavy factors are really parents' income and student's assets. If you can lower either of these numbers, you may be able to significantly change your Expected Family Contribution.

Before we look at how to lower your Expected Family Contribution, we need to point out just a few more things about what counts as income and assets. When you pay your taxes you don't get taxed on everything that you make. You make deductions and shelter some of your money from the tax collector. The same is true when calculating your Expected Family Contribution. Let's take a quick look at what are legitimate debts that will reduce your income or assets in the eyes of financial aid.

497. Your family expense sheet does not count as debt for financial aid

Debt has always been a touchy subject. Colleges are very strict about what they consider debt that can reduce your income. They will not subsidize a family's expensive habits. If a family makes $8,000 a month in income but has expenses of $7,500 a month for such things as car payments, gardener bills, annual family trips to Europe, dinners at the finest restaurants, payments for the big screen TV, etc. then that's too bad. All of these discretionary expenses are not used to reduce your income. Be careful how you think about your income, and don't assume that your family expenses will be taken out when figuring out your income. The financial aid formula will apply the same income protection number (which is quite conservative) to all families. If most of your paycheck is spent in the same month you receive it, you are going to be surprised at how much the financial aid formula will expect you to pay. If, on the other hand, you are controlling expenses and saving your money, you'll find that the expectations are far more reasonable.

498. Credit card debt is not debt when it comes to the financial aid calculation

If you need one more reason not to carry credit card debt (besides the high interest rate) consider the fact that any credit card balances and interest paid will not lower your income for the purposes of financial aid. In reality these debts certainly take money from your pockets. Many families with high consumer debt are surprised at how much money colleges think they can afford. Remember that these debts are considered discretionary and often reflect a family's living style rather than a necessity.

499. Car payments will not lower your income

Car payments will not lower your income for financial aid. Therefore, the lower your payments the better. If you have a choice, pick a less-expensive car and avoid financing.

500. Mortgage payments will not lower your income

Under both the Federal and Institutional methodologies your home mortgage or home equity loan payments will not reduce your income. The same is true for a passbook loan. However, unlike credit card interest payments you can deduct your mortgage or home equity loan payments from your taxes.

501. Your savings and checking accounts are assets

Under both the Federal and Institutional methodologies anything in your savings or checking accounts are counted as assets that you can use to pay for college. If you look at the calculations you'll notice that compared to income these assets are assessed at a much lower rate. There is no legal way to hide these assets.

502. Your stock and bond portfolios are assets

Under both the Federal and Institutional methodologies any stocks or bonds that you hold, which are not in retirement accounts, are fair game for the colleges to assess as available to pay for college. You should not radically alter your investment strategy or holdings just to get a few extra bucks from financial aid. It is just not worth the trouble, and you'll probably lose more than you'll gain.

503. Your house may or may not be an asset

Under the Federal methodology your home is not considered an asset. However, under the Institutional methodology a portion of your home's value may be considered an asset. This presents an interesting option. If you move money from your savings

Where do I get the FAFSA?

You can get your Free Application for Federal Student Aid by visiting http://www.fafsa.ed.gov or by calling 800-4-FED-AID. Most counseling offices and financial aid offices also have FAFSA forms available.

account, for example, into your home by adding a new roof you are effectively sheltering your assets from at least the Federal methodology and possibly also the Institutional methodology for calculating your Expected Family Contribution. But, and this is a big downside, you are spending money that you might need to pay for college. Remember there is no guarantee that the college will be able to fund your entire financial need. Also, as you will see, financial aid may come in the form of a loan, which would cost you more than if you had just used your savings.

However, consider the case where you have a leaky roof that needs to be replaced. It's your child's junior year in college. If you replace your roof now, as opposed to a year from now, you will reduce your savings account (i.e. your assets) and therefore make yourself more eligible for a higher financial aid package for your child's senior year. If you wait a year then it will be too late since your child will already be in the last year of college. (Remember, financial aid is always based on the previous tax year.) All of this assumes that you are already receiving aid and that you don't need the roof money to pay for living necessities. If you desperately need the money for something else, then it would be better to just live with the bucket in the living room until after your child graduates.

504. Retirement accounts cannot be touched

Under most circumstances money in retirement accounts will not be counted as an asset and therefore cannot be touched by the colleges. Stocks, bond and mutual funds held in normal accounts, even if you intend to use them for retirement, will be counted as an asset. To shelter your retirement money, you need to have it in an IRA or 401k type account.

505.

A quick estimate of your Expected Family Contribution

Income is the biggest determinant of Expected Family Contribution. The following chart shows average Expected Family Contribution levels from Stratagee.

Family income	Average EFC 1 dependent	2 dependents
$50,000	$4,024	$3,106
$75,000	$10,492	$8,766
$100,000	$18,769	$17,215
$125,000	$25,715	$24,212
$150,000	$34,004	$31,980
$175,000	$41,839	$39,866
$200,000	$49,635	$47,662

Obviously, these are just average numbers based on a sample student population. Within each income level is a range of specific Expected Family Contribution amounts. You can get a more accurate estimate of your specific EFC by using an online EFC calculator and plugging in your actual family finances.

506.

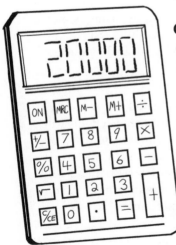

Compute your EFC online–fast and easy

If you want to run a simulation to see what your Expected Family Contribution is, you can do so easily online. One good EFC calculator that we like is at the College Board website. Fill in what you know about your family's finances and it will compute your EFC according to both the Federal and Institutional methods. Find the calculator at https://bigfuture.collegeboard.org/pay-for-college/paying-your-share/expected-family-contribution-calculator.

507.

How to determine your financial need

Once you know your Expected Family Contribution, it's easy to determine your financial need. All you do is take the total cost of attending
a specific college including tuition, room and board, books and travel
expenses and subtract it from your Expected Family Contribution.
The difference is your financial need. It's important to remember that
individual schools, not you, determine the total cost of attendance.

Let's look at an example and assume that your college costs $25,000
per year for tuition and room and board. Add the average expenses
for books, travel and miscellaneous expenses and the total cost of
attendance may be $30,000 per year. You have submitted both the
FAFSA and PROFILE forms. This means that the college has received
your Expected Family Contribution as determined by the Federal
and Institutional methodology. For argument's sake let's assume that
under the Federal methodology your Expected Family Contribution
is $15,000 and under the Institutional methodology it is $16,000.
(Remember the Institutional methodology is usually stricter.) If the
school only uses the Federal methodology it will take the $30,000 for
the total cost of attendance and subtract the $15,000 that your family
is expected to contribute. That leaves your family with a financial need
of $15,000. If the school is a private college that uses the Institutional
methodology, your financial need is $14,000.

It is this amount, your financial need, which the school must now
figure out a way for your family to afford. They can give you money
in the form of grants, student loans and work-study. Or, it is possible
that the school won't be able to find all of the money, leaving you with
"unmet need." The exact composition of your financial aid package
will depend on a variety of factors and will vary by college. This is one
benefit of applying to a number of colleges so that you can compare
different financial aid packages.

Step 2: Lower Your Expected Family Contribution

Now that you understand how the financial aid formula works and
what counts and doesn't count, you can use this information to try
to lower your Expected Family Contribution. It's very important to

remember that the following are generalized strategies that may not be appropriate for your individual situation. These are not solid rules since what might be good for one family may be terrible for another. Before taking any action, you should speak with your accountant to make sure that the strategy will work for your family's individual financial situation.

508.

Keep your child poor

If you look at the calculation for Expected Family Contribution you can see that if you put money into a child's name it will be assessed by 20 percent. But if you keep the money in your name it will only be assessed by up to 5.65 percent. That means for every $100 in the student's name you will be expected to spend $20 to pay for college. However, for every $100 in your name, you will be expected to pay only $5.65 to pay for college. That's a big difference. Any money that is in your child's bank account is considered your child's asset. If a relative would like to give a gift of cash or stock to your child you might want to ask if they are willing to either give it to you or wait until your child graduates from college. Or your generous relative could make the gift directly to your child's 529 Savings Plan.

Here is a chart of common savings accounts and how they are viewed by financial aid formulas:

- 529 Savings Plans (including pre-paid tuition plans) are an asset of the contributor, which is usually the parent.
- Coverdell Education Savings Accounts are an asset of the parents under the Federal and Institutional methodology.
- Custodial accounts are an asset of the student.
- Trust funds are an asset of the student.
- Savings bonds in the name of the student are an asset of the student.

Putting money in your child's name is generally a bad idea when it comes to financial aid. Of course, there may be some good tax reasons for putting money in your child's name especially if you know that

---

Is it worth it to spend my time filling out an application for financial aid?

The short answer is: "ABSOLUTELY!" While it does take some time to fill out a financial aid application, the benefits are well worth the effort. Not only do you try to claim your share of the more than $238 billion in aid that is awarded each year, but you also protect yourself against any future changes to your family's finances. By turning in a financial aid application, you give the college a snapshot of your finances. Should something change in the future this snapshot will be invaluable in helping the college understand how your family is impacted by the change, making it easier for them to respond with additional financial aid.

---

you won't qualify for financial aid. You need to balance the desire to save on taxes with the effect that putting money into a child's name will have on financial aid. It's important to speak with your accountant about your family's individual situation.

509.

Spend UGMA funds three years before your child graduates

Let's say that you have put some money into a custodial account for your child. Why not spend this money while your child is still in high school instead of leaving it to be counted against your financial need? Now if you go crazy and just spend it on things you normally would not have bought, then this won't help. However, let's say that when your child turns 16 and gets his or her license you plan to buy a used car for travel between school and work. Instead of using your own money, let the child use his or her custodial account. As long as you don't spend more than you normally would and buy a BMW instead of a Corolla, then you'll put your child in a better position to receive more financial aid. With the Coverdell, you can't buy a car but you can spend it on any legitimate high school educational expense such as books, uniforms and even a computer.

If you plan to do this, make sure you spend whatever you plan to before January 1 of your student's sophomore year. Remember financial aid is two years behind and you will submit account information based on the prior prior year's tax returns, which for the typical student who enters college in the fall will cover January 1 of the sophomore year through December 31 of the junior year.

510.

Consider deferring bonuses and raises

Imagine this scenario. It's November 2016 and your child is graduating from high school and starting college in the fall of 2018. Your boss tells you that you will get a bonus or significant raise. If you take the bonus now, then that money will be used when determining your child's financial aid package for the 2018-19 school year. Remember

---

In the case of a divorce whose income needs to be reported?

In most divorce situations the financial aid information must come from the parent with whom the student lives the most during the year. Some colleges also require that the non-custodial natural parent complete a separate aid application and these colleges will use their financial information in the aid calculation.

If the parent with whom the student lives remarries, then information must also be included from the stepparent. Regardless of whether or not the stepparent has any intention of supporting the child, his or her financial information will be used when determining financial aid.

The college will consider any special circumstances including if you are not able to locate the non-custodial natural parent. It's important that you communicate any special situations to the financial aid office.

financial aid is always based on the prior prior tax year. If you delay taking your bonus for two months until January 2017, then that money will not be used in your student's financial aid calculations. It will be counted when he or she applies for financial aid for the second year of college. But since you will have spent some (maybe even a significant amount) to pay for the first year you will have fewer assets that will be counted during the second year of college. This also buys you some time to save since you know that the bonus or increase in salary will reduce your financial aid in the following year.

Before you do this, be sure that you are going to get financial aid in the first place. Also consider other factors. Will your boss still be in the mood to give you a bonus next year? Sometimes it's better to just take the money.

This tactic would be much more effective if your child were entering the senior year in college in the fall of 2018. Deferring your raise or bonus in this situation would mean that it would not be counted at all since your son or daughter would be graduating from college.

511.

Consider alternative forms of bonuses

If you have the flexibility, it may make sense to take your bonus or even a pay raise in some other form than cash. Of course, if you need the money then take the cash, but if you are in a situation where there is an equally useful alternative then you might want to take it.

For example, instead of taking a raise you might swap one day a week of working from home which might save you money in other ways such as less childcare costs. Or you might convert your bonus from a cash payment to having your company pay for training or classes that you were planning to pay yourself. A bonus or raise that does not show up as income will not be subjected to financial aid consideration. However, carefully weigh the costs of forgoing a cash bonus or raise. If you can use the money to pay down credit card debt, for example, you are probably much better off doing that.

512.

Time your stock sales

When you sell a stock can have an impact on your financial aid. Let's say you have a stock that has appreciated by $10,000. If you sell the stock after January 1 of your child's sophomore year in high school, the earnings are considered income for your child's first year of college and will be assessed at up to 47 percent. That means that from the $10,000 gain as much as $4,700 can be counted by the financial aid formula as going to pay for college. But let's say that instead you sell the stock before January 1 of your child's sophomore year. The proceeds will not be counted as income but instead show up as an asset. As a parental asset this money can only be assessed at up to 5.65 percent, which means only $565 is considered as available to pay for college.

513.

Build your 401K or IRA accounts

Under both the Federal and Institutional methodologies your retirement accounts are not considered assets that can be used to pay for college. Plus, under current tax laws you can withdraw money from these accounts and use them to pay for college without paying a penalty. So don't neglect your retirement as you save for college.

514.

Declaring your independence

In college, you no longer have a curfew or parents telling you what to do, so why shouldn't you declare yourself independent? Many students mistakenly believe that if they declare their independence from their parents they will get more financial aid. Unfortunately, declaring independence for the purposes of financial aid is based on very strict guidelines. In most cases, you are considered dependent on your parents for support and their income and assets will be considered when determining your financial need. Under certain circumstances, you can be evaluated independently of your parents, and only you and your spouse's (if you have one) income and assets will be taken into account. You're considered independent if one of the following is true:

- You are 24 years or older by December 31 of the current year.
- You're married.
- You're enrolled in a graduate or professional degree program.
- You have legal dependents other than a spouse.
- You're an orphan or ward of the court.
- You're currently serving on active duty in the U.S. Armed Forces.
- You're a veteran of the U.S. Armed Forces.

Your parents may not support you at all, but according to the above guidelines you are still considered a dependent. If this is the case it is vitally important that you include a detailed letter explaining the situation to the college financial aid office.

Step 3: Complete The Financial Aid Application

Since we know you are going to be applying for financial aid, here are a few tips to make sure to fill out the applications correctly and present an accurate picture of your finances to the colleges

515.

Get into the right mindset

When you're sitting in front of the computer, you may have a feeling of dread at the thought of filling out the FAFSA. Tell yourself that it usually takes about 30 to 60 minutes to complete the form. When you think about it, that's a small investment of time for the possible reward!

516.

Colleges run out of money so turn in applications early

The deadlines for turning in your financial aid applications vary by college. You want to turn in your FAFSA as soon as possible after October 1, which if you are applying for aid for the first time is of your senior year in high school. The reason is that colleges have a limited amount of financial aid.

Most colleges use what is known as a "priority" deadline. While the deadline varies by school it is usually sometime in January or February. This date is when the school expects to run out of money. If you get your application turned in by this deadline you should be fine. However, if you application arrives late, or if it was somehow incomplete and you needed to provide more information that pushed you past this deadline, then even if you deserve aid you may not get it simply because the college ran out of money.

517.

Think about financial aid early–before your child is even in high school

Remember that all of the numbers used in financial calculations come from the prior prior tax year. If your child is starting college in September 2018, then your tax return from 2016 will be the basis for that first year. Therefore, if you wait until January 2017 to think about financial aid, it will be too late to do anything that will affect the outcome of your child's first year.

518.

Regardless of your income, don't assume that you won't get any financial aid

The biggest mistake that most families make when it comes to financial aid is they assume they won't qualify and therefore don't make the effort to apply. You'll never know what you truly deserve unless you ap-

---

When should I apply for financial aid?

Apply for financial aid as soon as possible after October 1 of your senior year if you're in high school. Don't wait until after you are accepted by a college to apply. If you do the college may have already allocated all of its money. When it comes to financial aid the early bird does get the worm.

---

ply. You might find that even if you don't get a grant, you are awarded a cushy campus job, special college scholarships or low-interest student loan. You might find that one of these sources of money is just what you need to make paying for college possible.

Here's a chart from a recent U.S. Department of Education study. It is not surprising that as income rises the percentage of students who received financial aid decreases. But even for families that earned over $100,000 per year, more than 71 percent of them still received financial aid.

Family income	Percent of students who received financial aid
Below $20,000	95.6 percent
$20,000-40,000	90.6 percent
$40,000-60,000	90.7 percent
$60,000-80,000	80.3 percent
$80,000-100,000	76.7 percent
Above $100,000	71.6 percent

Another study conducted by an independent education advocacy group found that among today's current college students more than 850,000 qualified to receive federal grants. However, none of these students received a single dime from Uncle Sam. The reason? Because they didn't apply!

The bottom line is that it's dangerous to second-guess the financial aid office. Applying is free and won't take that much time. The rewards can be well worth the effort.

519.

Use your financial aid application as an insurance policy

Nobody can predict the future. Today you may have a great job, but next year you may be out of a job. Or perhaps an elderly grandparent may need to live with your family. Or maybe you will decide to stop working and go back to school. The future is uncertain, which means if something should happen to your family's finances during the year you will want to be able to approach the financial aid office to ask for some help. Your best chance of getting help will depend on whether or not you have applied for financial aid. Without having a FAFSA on record the college has no idea how much of an impact your family has sustained. It makes it much easier for a financial aid officer to give you more money if you have already filled out the FAFSA regardless of whether or not you were given any aid. So think of applying for aid as added insurance against any unexpected changes in your family's future finances.

520.

You must apply for financial aid every year

Financial aid is determined on a year-by-year basis. That means that even if you didn't get financial aid this year you should apply next year since your finances will have changed, especially after paying for one year of tuition. Some families find that after the first or second year of college they have reduced their assets to the point where they qualify for financial aid. There is a Renewal FAFSA that you can use, which saves a lot of time when applying for aid the next year.

521.

Get help completing the FAFSA

If you need help completing the FAFSA, visit the U.S. Department of Education website at http://www.fafsa.ed.gov or call 800-4-FED-AID. The website will take you step by step through the entire process. You might also want to contact your high school counselor or even the financial aid office at your local college. High schools and colleges often hold workshops throughout the spring to help parents and students complete the FAFSA.

Step 4: Work With The Financial Aid Office

All of the information that is used to compute your financial need either through the Federal or Institutional Methodology will eventually be sent to the college financial aid office. There a professional known as the financial aid office will review your information and make the final decision about how much money you will receive. The financial aid officer is an important ally and it's crucial that you know how to work with this professional.

522.

There is a human being behind all financial aid decisions

Up until this point financial aid looks very analytical. It seems like you just plug in the numbers and out pops your Expected Family Contribution. But the story of financial aid does not end with your Expected Family Contribution. After your EFC is computed, the rest of the process becomes a very human process. Your EFC will be sent to every college you are applying to, and this is where the computations end and human beings take over.

At the colleges, financial aid officers use your EFC as a guide when putting together your aid package. The financial aid officer has the ability to raise or lower your EFC for a variety of reasons. Therefore, it is crucial that you are open about your family's true financial situation to the financial aid officer. Remember, too, that all financial aid is based on your prior prior year's taxes. A lot may have happened since then. If you want to share additional information, you can send a letter to the college financial aid office to explain any unusual circumstances that may affect your family's finances. Most colleges actually include a space on their financial aid forms for you to describe any relevant information. When you are thinking about writing this letter consider the following three points.

523. Don't hide the dirty laundry
Many parents when filling out financial forms feel compelled to hide embarrassing circumstances. After all you are revealing your financial strengths and weaknesses to a total stranger. However, if you have extraordinary circumstances such as large medical bills, unemployment, recent or ongoing divorce, siblings attending private elementary or high schools or any additional expenses that may not be reflected in your FAFSA or PROFILE, tell the financial aid officer. Don't be embarrassed. It could cost you big time.

524. Give the college a reason to give you more money
Financial aid officers are numbers people. However, they have wide latitude for interpreting numbers and can apply a variety of standards and make exceptions, which can help or hurt your case. To get the most support from these professionals, make your case with numbers. You can't just say that you don't have enough money. You need to show it. Document with numbers why your tax forms don't accurately reflect your true income or expenses.

525. Be prepared to show the evidence
It's not enough to say that your income has dropped significantly, you need to show it with documentation. Get all your paperwork in order so if the financial aid office requests documentation, you have it.

526. Don't ever try to trick the college
The human being in the financial aid process is also what keeps it safe from trickery. You could, for example, take all of the money in your savings account and plunk it down to buy

---

Should I do the FAFSA online?

Yes, we do recommend that you complete the FAFSA online at http://www.fafsa.ed.gov. The online form will help check calculations and alert you when required information is missing. Plus, you'll receive your results more quickly.

---

an around-the-world vacation. On paper you have no savings. Yet, when the financial aid officer looks at your income, he or she will think it is very odd that someone who earns a decent living and owns a nice house is so cash poor. This is a red flag, and you'll need to provide additional information. Not only would the financial aid officer not give more financial aid but you would also have no money left to pay for college even if you wanted to.

Financial aid officers are experts at reading financial statements. Just by looking at your 1099 interest reports they can get an accurate estimate of the size of your assets. Trying to trick the college will only backfire. Financial aid officers are professionals who have seen every trick in the book. Our best advice on trickery is to not attempt it.

527.

How your financial aid is packaged makes a difference

Let's assume that your Expected Family Contribution is lower than the cost of one year in college and therefore you have financial need. Once that amount is determined it is up to the financial aid office at the college to try to put together a package that will meet that need. The college may not always be able to do it and unless it is the college's policy to meet all financial need of its students, then the college is under no obligation to provide anything. Of course, most colleges will try.

The way in which your aid is packaged will differ not only because your financial need changes with the price of each college but also because colleges have varying amounts of financial aid resources. The following is a detailed description of what you might find in your aid package. Most financial aid packages consist of a combination of these sources.

528. Federal Pell Grants

These grants are for undergraduate study for students who have the most financial need, typically with Expected Family Contributions of $5,234 or less. The amount varies based on your EFC, but the maximum amount for the 2016-17 school year is $5,815. All students who apply for financial aid by completing the FAFSA and are determined to have financial need by their college will be considered for Federal Pell Grants.

529. Federal Supplemental Educational Opportunity Grants

These grants are for undergraduates with the most financial need. The government provides limited funds for individual schools to administer this program. This means there is no guarantee that every eligible student will receive an FSEOG Grant. The amount varies between $100 and $4,000 per year, and the specific amount is determined by the college on a case by case basis.

530. Grants from the college

The college itself has various need-based and merit-based grants. By applying for financial aid you will be considered for these grants.

531. State grants

Your state may offer both need and merit-based grants. While some grants are administered by the state, others are distributed to the colleges to administer.

532. Federal Work-Study

Work-study provides jobs for undergraduate and graduate students with financial need allowing you to earn money while attending school. The focus is on providing work experience in your area of study. Generally, you will work for your school on campus or for a non-profit organization or public agency if you work off campus. You will have a limit on the hours you can work in this program. Your wages are based on the federal minimum wage although it is usually higher.

533. State Work-Study

Besides the federal program, some states also have a work-study program that mirrors the operation of the federal program.

534. Federal Perkins Loans

Federal Perkins Loans are low-interest loans for undergraduate and graduate students with extreme financial need. Your school provides the loan from governmental as well as its own funds. You can borrow up to $5,500 per year as an undergraduate or $8,000 per year as a graduate student. The interest rate is fixed at 5 percent and there are no additional fees.

535. Subsidized and Unsubsidized Federal Direct Loans

There are two types of Direct Loans: Subsidized Direct Loans and Unsubsidized Direct Loans. The U.S. government is the lender. You can borrow up to $5,500 as a freshman (with up to $3,500 of this amount subsidized), $6,500 as a sophomore (with up to $4,500 of this amount subsidized) and $7,500 as a junior or senior dependent undergraduate student (with up to $5,500 of this amount subsidized). If your parents are denied a parent loan or you are an independent student, the school may offer loans of up to $9,500 for freshmen (with up to $3,500 of this amount subsidized), $10,500 for sophomores (up to $4,500 subsidized) and $12,500 for junior and seniors (up to $5,500 subsidized).

Depending on your financial need you may be offered a subsidized or unsubsidized Direct Loan. When the loan is subsidized

---

As a high school student, where can I get my basic questions answered by a financial aid officer?

If you don't want to call a financial aid officer, visit the website of the National Association of Student Financial Aid Administrators. This is a professional organization whose members are college financial aid officers. The website has lots of helpful articles and checklists and information on College Goal Sunday, a free annual program to help students complete the FAFSA. Visit the NASFAA website at http://www.nasfaa.org.

the government pays for the interest that accrues while you are in college and before you start to repay it. For unsubsidized loans you must pay the interest that accrues while you are in college although you don't start making any payments until after you graduate from college. For more detailed information about student loans, see Chapter 12.

Step 5: Compare And Accept Your Financial Aid

A few weeks after you receive your acceptance letters from the colleges you will also get your financial aid award letters. These letters will outline the specific types and dollar amounts that each college is offering. You should compare these award letters and keep the following tips in mind:

536.

You can pick and choose which parts of your financial aid package to accept

When you receive an offer of financial aid you don't have to accept or reject the whole package. You are free to pick and choose the specific pieces of aid you want. If you are offered a grant you'll definitely want to accept it, but you might not want to accept the loan component. When you are analyzing your award package consider each piece separately.

537.

If you need more don't be shy to ask for a re-evaluation

If you feel that the amount of financial aid that you are offered by a college is simply nowhere near enough, you can ask for a re-evaluation. For the re-evaluation to be effective you need to provide the financial aid office with concrete reasons why their initial assessment was wrong. Start with a letter or call to the financial aid office. Be sure that you have all of your documents ready, and remember that the squeaky wheel gets the grease. If you don't say anything about your package the college will assume that you are happy with it. We have a special chapter that is dedicated to asking for a re-evaluation. See Chapter 9 for more details.

538.

Don't lose your financial aid

All financial aid comes with the stipulation that you maintain "satisfactory academic progress." This means that you need to take a minimum number of classes per semester and must have passing grades. If you drop too many classes or take too long to graduate you could jeopardize not only your chances of ever getting a diploma but also your financial aid package.

Asking For More Financial Aid

How To Ask For More Money

L et's get one thing out of the way. College financial aid officers hate the word "negotiate." Perhaps it's because the word conjures up images of haggling with a car salesperson over the cost of floor mats. But regardless of the word you use, it is a well-documented fact that colleges do have wiggle room when it comes to your financial aid package. If you approach them in the right way and provide the right evidence, you may be able to lower the sticker price of your education.

But if you can't use the word "negotiate," what do you call bargaining with the colleges? The word that financial aid officers don't mind is "reassessment." Basically this means you ask the financial aid officers to reconsider the financial aid package that they offered you. But you can't just ask for a reassessment without a reason. You need to provide financial aid officers with concrete reasons for why you deserve a better financial aid package.

If you look at a typical financial aid offer you'll notice that there are two critical areas that determine how much you get.

1. Your Expected Family Contribution. This is the amount that the college has determined that your family can afford to pay. They arrive at this figure by crunching the numbers that you provide on your financial aid application. Once the college determines how much you can pay, all they need to figure out is how to make up for the gap between what you can pay and what it costs to attend their college.

2. The packaging of your award. Your financial aid offer might consist of a combination of grants, work-study and student loans. The composition of your award–called packaging–makes a big difference. Would you rather get $10,000 in grants or $10,000 in student loans?

Your goal when asking for a "reassessment" is to provide reasons for why the Expected Family Contribution is not accurate and makes it extremely difficult or even impossible for you to afford college and/or to increase the amount of grant money in your package. You do this by submitting a letter or scheduling an in-person appointment with the financial aid officer. In your letter or meeting you request a reassessment and provide reasons why the original offer is just not realistic.

The success of your reassessment will depend on the reasons that you give to support your claim that their initial analysis needs fixing. Let's look at some reasons that you can provide to the financial aid office to convince them that they should reassess your financial aid package.

539.

Present any special circumstances not reflected by the numbers in your financial aid application

All the college sees are the numbers that you provide on your financial aid forms. These numbers are based on your income taxes, which are always two years behind. If something has changed recently that affects your family's finances you need to tell the college. Changes to your family's finances may include:

- Unusual medical expenses
- Tuition for a sibling including private secondary or elementary school expenses
- Unemployment of a spouse or parent
- Ongoing divorce or separation
- Care for an aging relative

Whatever the circumstance be sure to explain it in detail in your letter or when you meet with the financial aid officer. Don't just describe the event, but show with numbers how it impacts your family's finances. Financial aid officers like to deal with numbers, which means you need to justify everything with them.

540.

Don't wait for something bad to happen if you know it will

You don't have to wait until something happens to let the financial aid officer know about it. If you know that there will be a change in your parents' employment or if there will be an unavoidable financial expenditure, let the financial aid office know about it now. Like any large organization the college has a limited budget. If you wait until something happens it might be too late for the college to do anything about it. If you let them know in advance they may be able to budget for it and have the money for you when the inevitable occurs.

541.

Play one college off another college

If you have been accepted to several colleges and receive financial aid packages that are vastly different, you may be able to use one to motivate the other to be a little more generous. Let's imagine that your first choice, College A, gives you a smaller aid package or one that is composed of only loans. Not a very attractive offer. However, your second choice, College B, gives you either a bigger package or more of your money in grants. Now you are in a position to ask College A to match the offer of College B.

First, email a letter to College A. Begin by stating that you are extremely excited about being accepted and would very much like to attend the college. Explain that given the financial aid package offered, you may not be able to afford the costs. Justify in real numbers why their offer is not sufficient. This, of course, must be true since the college can see all of your family's finances. Not wanting to spend your money is not a good reason. Not having the money to spend is an excellent reason. There is a big difference between the two.

After you make a case for why you need more financial aid, share the better offer made by College B. Include a copy of the award letter

---

How should I contact the financial aid office to ask for a reassessment?

If you are a high school senior, time is of the essence since you receive admission offers in April and often have to make a decision by May. Even if you are already in college, timing is important because financial aid budgets do get depleted. If you are close to the college, you should try to make an in-person appointment. Otherwise, go with email. Sending snail mail just takes too long. You need to give the college time to respond, so the sooner you can let them know of your request for a reassessment the better.

---

from College B with your letter. Point out to the financial aid officer that given the generous package from College B it makes it hard to turn down. Politely reiterate that you would prefer to attend College A and would like to know if there is anything the financial aid office can do to reassess your aid package.

Throughout the letter you want to be friendly and polite. Remember you are not negotiating for a lower price on a car but asking for a reassessment and providing another college's better offer (as well as your own family's finances) as a basis. You want to avoid sounding confrontational or argumentative. You also need to have concrete reasons why you need more financial aid.

This technique does not guarantee success. In fact, no college is under any obligation to change its original offer. However, if you can present a compelling case, you may find that the college is willing to reassess the initial offer and adjust the aid package. You only want to do this with the college you really want to attend. Don't try to pit a whole bunch of colleges against each other. It will only backfire. Focus on your first choice college, and try to use the better offer of your second choice as leverage. If it doesn't work, you can always attend your second choice college, which offered you the better package.

542.

Be polite and never threaten

Some parents take an aggressive approach to asking for more. This rarely works. Financial aid officers are professionals who believe in the aid package that they have created. They know they are not beyond making mistakes and are happy to take a second look if you present a good reason to do so. However, if you come across as aggressive, abrasive or confrontational, they will have little desire to help.

543.

Have a number in mind

When you present your case to the financial aid officer her or she may surprise you by asking: "So, how much do you need?" This is not the time to be tongue-tied! Have the amount you need in mind!

544.

Always, always be honest

During the entire financial aid process you must be honest. If you try to hide, exaggerate or outright lie about your circumstances you will not only lose any change of getting more aid but you will also be subjected to stiff fines and even jail time. Being dishonest on a financial aid application is the same as cheating on your taxes and carries similar federal penalties. On the other hand, as mentioned earlier don't be modest about your financial problems. Don't hide embarrassing facts such as bad credit that prevents you from taking out a loan. The financial aid officer has seen and heard it all and really does want to help.

545.

Example of a successful financial aid reassessment

You can ask for a reassessment at any time during college when something changes in your family's finances. The following is an actual letter one student wrote to the Harvard financial aid office. Before writing the letter, the student had received only a small loan from Harvard despite the fact that her father had been laid off for over a year. The student composed this letter to explain her family's extenuating circumstances, describing their actual income and expenses. Notice how she substantiates her claims with real dollar examples. Her letter paid off–she got a $6,500 grant per semester for the rest of the year!

Dear Sir or Madam:

I am writing to request that my financial aid package for the fall semester be reconsidered. My family and I were disappointed with the amount we were offered because in addition to my father having been unemployed for over a year, my older sister will be a sophomore in college, and my mother, a part-time teacher, has received no income since June because of summer break.

We understand that nearly every family must undergo an amount of hardship to send its members to college. However, because my parents wish to continue financing my sister's and my education, they are worried about how they will pay for their own expenses. They have been using my mother's income to basically cover their mortgage payments and their savings to pay for everything else. In February, my parents had $33,000 in savings. In the last six months, their savings has decreased by about $15,000. They now have about $18,000 to contribute to my sister's and my college expenses as well as to spend on their and my younger brother's food and basic necessities. They don't know how long their savings will last without a change in the amount of aid I will receive.

At the end of this month, my sister will begin her sophomore year at USC. The cost will be $37,096, and she has received $25,781 in financial aid. One of the things you might be able to address is why my sister's financial aid package was dramatically higher than mine.

Since July of last year my father has been unemployed. His severance pay ended in October, and his unemployment benefits have been depleted since February.

Although he has applied for over a dozen positions, his prospects for finding a job in his specialty are slim.

My parents and I have discussed the possibility of having me take a year off so that I may work to help pay for tuition, but we'd much rather that I finish school now and work after I have received my degree.

Please contact my parents or me with any further questions you may have. Thank you very much for your time and consideration. I hope that this information is helpful in your review of my application.

Sincerely Yours,

There's no guarantee that a letter like this will work, but if the financial situation of your family changes significantly and you can show with numbers how it has affected your ability to pay, you need to get in touch with your financial aid office. There is absolutely no harm in asking.

TEN

Avoid Financial Aid Scams

Keeping Your Money Safe

An important part of saving money for college is keeping your hard-earned cash out of the hands of scam artists. Recently, the Federal Trade Commission reported that there were over 175,000 incidents of financial aid scams, which cost consumers more than $25 million. This represents only the scams that were reported, and we've met hundreds of families that have gotten taken for varying amounts from $20 to more than $1,000 who never reported the incident.

To keep your money safe you need to know what to watch out for in a scam. Most scams begin in the same way. An offer arrives in an official looking envelope from a company with an equally official sounding name. Inside you usually find a letter that appeals to your fear on how you are going to pay for college. Then it makes an almost unbelievable offer. For a small sum of money this company will help you locate unclaimed scholarships, maximize your financial aid package and help you pay for college without any financial pain. It offers the answer you have been looking for and the price is peanuts compared to what you were planning to shell out for tuition.

If you send in a check you have probably just become another statistic for the Federal Trade Commission. We should point out that not all of these offers are illegal, which helps to explain why they exist year after year. But they certainly don't live up to their promises. Often what you get for your money is usually much less than you expected and certainly not worth your hard earned money.

To keep your money safe, you need to understand the difference between what is promised and what you actually will receive. Let's take a look at how some of these scams work and why you should avoid them.

546.

The hook: For a fee we will find "hidden" scholarships that nobody knows about. This virtually guarantees that you will be a winner.

The reality: For all practical purposes there is no such thing as a "hidden" scholarship. There are some obscure scholarships that have criteria that almost nobody can meet so they do go un-awarded. But chances are if 99.99 percent of students can't meet the criteria to enter then neither will you. All legitimate scholarships that have reasonable eligibility requirements go awarded. It is true that some have very few applicants, but these are not the awards that you will get. What you will typically receive is a generic list of scholarships that are anything but hidden or a list of scholarships that have such specific criteria that nobody can qualify.

547.

The hook: To enter our mucho-money scholarship you must pay a tiny application fee. After all, what's $5 or $10 to enter if you can walk away with $1,000 or more in scholarships?

The reality: After paying the fee and sending in the application you'll get a nice card that says, "Sorry but you are not a winner." These companies count on tens of thousands of students sending in the application fee. Then even if they have to randomly award a $1,000 scholarship they still bank a huge sum of money from the fees. The defense against these kinds of fake scholarships is simple: Never pay an application fee. Real scholarships do not require any fee from applicants. Scholarship organizations, after all, are trying to give money away, not take it from those who apply. If a scholarship organization can't afford to process applications without a fee then they have no business giving away a scholarship.

The one exception is for a competition where it is more common to include a fee with your submission, but these are usually limited to musical or artistic compositions and performances. Plus, these competitions are not technically scholarships so our rule is still true: Never pay an entry or application fee for a scholarship.

548.

The hook: You've won our scholarship! All we need is your credit card number to verify your eligibility so we can send you the money.

The reality: You'll get some unexpected and unwanted charges on your credit card. Never give out your credit card information to a scholarship organization.

549.

The hook: We guarantee that you will win at least one scholarship!

The reality: There is no such thing as a guaranteed scholarship. Scholarships are competitive and by definition not every applicant will win. The only way you would have a "guaranteed win" is if you had to pay an entry fee and the prize you won was less than what you paid, but we don't think any of you feel like paying $500 to be a guaranteed winner of a $100 scholarship.

550.

The hook: For a fee we will help you complete the FAFSA application and submit it for you.

The reality: The full name of the FAFSA is the Free Application for Federal Student Aid. Notice how the word free is right there at the beginning. The FAFSA is designed to be completed by students and parents. Now, this is not to say that it is easy. It is similar to doing your taxes and in fact much of the information from your 1040 will be used to complete the FAFSA. However, to pay a company a fee to complete

---

Why do so many scammers succeed?

They feed on your fear of not being able to pay for college. A desperate person is much more likely to pay someone who promises an easy solution. To defend yourself you need to be aware of your emotional desire to find money as well as your logical side, which will alert you to a potential scam. Don't let your fears overcome your better judgment.

---

your form is usually not a good idea since you will be providing them with all of the information you need for the forms anyway. All they do is fill in the numbers after you have done the hard work. A better option might be to use your tax planner or accountant. Since they have all of your pertinent information already, it should be easy for them to fill out the FAFSA.

551.

The hook: Our researchers will put together a customized list of scholarships just for you.

What you get: A standard list of scholarships that you could have easily found on your own. The reality is that you can find thousands of scholarships on your own in books and on the Internet without paying a search fee. Plus, you'll do a much better job.

552.

The hook: Come to our free seminar to learn the secrets of going to college for free.

What you actually get: A sales pitch for any combination of the above. Not all seminars are scams or rip-offs, so you'll have to use your own judgment. However, one giveaway is if the seminar sounds like a sales pitch or contains promises that sound too good to be true. If you feel like the seminar is just a live version of a late-night infomercial, then you are probably looking at a seminar where you will be asked to part with your money for what may be totally worthless information.

General Red Flags

In general the major telltale sign that you are about to be taken by a dubious offer is if you are asked to pay any significant amount of money. Particularly if you are applying for a scholarship, never part with your money. Scholarships are meant to pay you money, not the other way around. Here are a few red flags to watch out for:

553.

Red Flag: Registration, entry or administrative fee

Legitimate scholarship and financial aid programs do not require an upfront fee. Do not pay for anything more than the cost of postage. Remember, real scholarships are about giving you money, not the other way around.

554.

Red Flag: Soliciting your credit card or bank account number

Never give out this kind of financial information to anyone who contacts you. The only reason someone would need this information is so that they can charge you.

555.

Red Flag: Refusal to reveal name, address or phone number

You know that something is wrong when the person on the telephone won't reveal his or her name or contact information. All legitimate organizations have no problem giving you their appropriate contact information.

556.

Double Red Flag: Guarantee

Remember, there is no such thing as a guaranteed scholarship in exchange for a fee. Legitimate scholarships are based on merit or need, not your willingness to pay a registration fee.

If you discover that you have been the victim of one of the scams above, don't be embarrassed. This happens to thousands of parents and students every year. Report your experience to the Better Business Bureau and Federal Trade Commission (http://www.ftc.gov) to help prevent it from happening to others. Also, be sure to write us about it. We maintain lists of dishonest and worthless programs and would like to know if you encounter any new ones. The old adage of consumer protection applies to scholarships: If an offer sounds too good to be true, it probably is.

CHAPTER ELEVEN

Get Your State To Pay

Getting Money From Your State

You may not like it when every time you buy something the state tacks on an extra 4 to 9 percent in sales tax. But you can take some consolation in the fact that you may get back some of these dollars through financial aid programs offered by your state. Every state has an agency or department that helps students pay for college. Many states also administer their own centralized financial aid and scholarship programs. Your state agency is a clearinghouse not only for information but also for actual dollars for college.

Your first step is to find your state agency from the following list and visit their website. On their website you will learn about a variety of assistance programs including scholarships offered by the state. You can also contact the agency directly by phone.

Whether you are surfing their website or speaking to an actual person your goal is to learn about all of the opportunities available to you. While every state operates differently and not all have the same programs, here is a list of things that you should inquire about. These are the most common resources and programs offered by most states.

State Scholarships and Grants
Many states award their own state scholarships and grants. Make sure you understand how the scholarship works, who is eligible and if you need to apply by a certain deadline. Some scholarships are automatically awarded to students who do well academically or do a lot of community service and all you need to do to get your money is claim it.

Private Scholarship List
As a clearinghouse for all things related to paying for college, many state agencies also have a list of private scholarships that are available. On some of the websites we have found such invaluable information as lists of all local civic groups that award scholarships.

State Loan Repayment Programs

Your state might sponsor valuable loan repayment programs depending on what you plan to study. Some states, for example, will help you pay back your loan if you enter specific career areas such as teaching, law enforcement, medicine, nursing or technology. As long as you work within those fields in the state after graduation, the state will help you pay back your student loans.

State Work-Study

Like Federal Work-Study some states have their own work-study programs. These programs subsidize your salary as you work either on campus or for a government or nonprofit agency. Through work-study you can earn thousands of extra dollars while you go to school.

Other Funding Resources and Services

Be sure to ask about all of the other resources and services that your state offers. Some sponsor workshops to help families apply for financial aid while others have their own publications that they will send you for free on how to pay for college.

It's important that you learn all that you can about the various programs offered by your state. Request all of the free information that they offer and take advantage of any resources such as lists of community scholarships that they provide.

Before you head off to find your state agency, here are two federally funded but state-administered programs that are offered in most states.

557.

Tuition Exchange

Some states or state university systems have agreements with other states or specific universities in other states to let each other's residents attend at in-state rates. Paying in-state rates at another state's school can save you thousands of dollars. Often these agreements are made with neighboring states. Check with your state office of higher education listed in this chapter for more information.

558.

Leveraging Educational Assistance Partnership (LEAP)

This partnership between the federal and state governments provides grant money to undergraduate and graduate students who have financial need. Each university elects to participate in the LEAP program and determines who will receive LEAP grants. You should contact your financial aid office at the college you attend for more details. LEAP awards range from $100 to $5,000 per year. Your state agency may be able to provide you with a list of colleges that participate in the LEAP program.

State Aid Programs

559. Alabama
Alabama Commission on Higher Education
P.O. Box 302000
Montgomery, AL 36130-2000
Phone: 334-242-1998
In-state Toll-Free: 800-960-7773
Fax: 334-242-0268
Website: http://www.ache.alabama.gov

560. Alaska
Alaska Commission on Postsecondary Education
P.O. Box 110505
Juneau, AK 99811-0505
Phone: 907-465-2962
Toll-Free: 800-441-2962
Fax: 907-465-5316
TTY: 907-465-3143
Email: customer_service@acpe.state.ak.us
Website: http://alaskadvantage.state.ak.us

561. Arizona
Arizona Commission for Postsecondary Education
Suite 650
2020 North Central Avenue

Phoenix, AZ 85004-4503
Phone: 602-258-2435
Fax: 602-258-2483
Website: https://highered.az.gov

562. Arkansas

Arkansas Department of Higher Education
Five Main Place Building
423 Main Street, Suite 400
Little Rock, AR 72201-3818
Phone: 501-371-2000
Fax: 501-371-2001
Website: http://www.adhe.edu

563. California

California Student Aid Commission
P.O. Box 419027
Rancho Cordova, CA 95741-9027
Phone: 916-526-7590
Toll-Free: 888-224-7268
Fax: 916-526-8004
Email: studentsupport@csac.ca.gov
Website: http://www.csac.ca.gov

564. Colorado

Colorado Department of Higher Education
Suite 1600
1560 Broadway
Denver, CO 80202
Phone: 303-866-2723
Fax: 303-866-4266
Email: executivedirector@dhe.state.co.us
Website: http://highered.colorado.gov

565. Connecticut

Connecticut Department of Higher Education
39 Woodland Street
Hartford, CT 06105-2326
Phone: 860-493-3000
Toll-Free: 800-842-0229
Fax: 860-947-1310

Email: lnegro@ctdhe.org
Website: http://www.ctdhe.org

566. Delaware
Delaware Higher Education Commission
The Townsend Building
401 Federal St, Suite 2
Dover, DE 19901
Phone: 302-735-4120
Toll-Free: 800-292-7935
Fax: 302-739-5894
Email: dhec@doe.k12.de.us
Website: http://www.delawaregoestocollege.org

567. District of Columbia
Office of the State Superintendent of Education (District of Columbia)
9th Floor
801 1st Street NE
Washington, DC 20001
Phone: 202-727-6436
Toll-Free: 877-485-6751
Fax: 202-727-2019
TTY: 202-727-1675
Email: osse@dc.gov
Website: http://osse.dc.gov

568. Florida
Florida Department of Education
Office of Student Financial
Assistance
325 West Gaines Street, Suite 1314
Tallahassee, FL 32399-0040
Toll-Free: 888-827-2004
Email: osfa@fldoe.org
Website: http://www.floridastudentfinancialaid.org

569. Georgia
Nonpublic Postsecondary Education Commission
2082 East Exchange Place
Suite 220

Tucker, GA 30084-5305
Phone: 770-414-3300
Website: https://gnpec.org

570. Hawaii

Hawaii State Postsecondary Authorization Program
Department of Commerce and Consumer Affairs
Room 310
335 Merchant Street
Honolulu, HI 96813
Phone: 808-586-7327
Fax: 808-956-5158
http://cca.hawaii.gov/hpeap

Hawaii Department of Education
The department publishes an annual Scholarship and Financial Aid Bulletin.
http://www.hawaiipublicschools.org

571. Idaho

Idaho State Board of Education
P.O. Box 83720
Boise, ID 83720-0037
Phone: 208-332-6800
Fax: 208-334-2632
Email: board@osbe.idaho.gov
Website: http://sde.idaho.gov

572. Illinois

Illinois Student Assistance Commission
1755 Lake Cook Road
Deerfield, IL 60015-5209
Phone: 847-948-8500
Toll-Free: 800-899-4722
Fax: 847-831-8549
TTY: 800-526-0844
Email: isac.studentservices@isac.illinois.gov
Website: http://www.isac.org

573. Indiana
Indiana Commission for Higher Education
Suite 300
101 West Ohio Street
Indianapolis, IN 46204-1984
Phone: 317-464-4400
Fax: 317-464-4410
Email: tlubbers@che.in.gov
Website: http://www.che.in.gov

574. Iowa
Iowa College Student Aid Commission
Third Floor
430 E. Grand Avenue
Des Moines, IA 50319
Phone: 515-725-3400
Toll-Free: 877-272-4456
Fax: 515-725-3401
Email: info@iowacollegeaid.org
Website: http://www.iowacollegeaid.gov

575. Kansas
Kansas Board of Regents
Curtis State Office Building
Suite 520
1000 SW Jackson Street
Topeka, KS 66612-1368
Phone: 785-296-3421
Fax: 785-296-0983
Website: http://www.kansasregents.org

576. Kentucky
Kentucky Higher Education Assistance Authority
100 Airport Road
Frankfort, KY 40602-0798
Phone: 502-696-7200
Toll-Free: 800-928-8926
Fax: 502-696-7496
TTY: 800-855-2880
Email: studentaid@kheaa.com
Website: http://www.kheaa.com

577. Louisiana
Louisiana Office of Student Financial Assistance
602 North Fifth Street
Baton Rouge, LA 70802
Phone: 225-219-1012
Toll-Free: 800-259-5626 x 1012
Fax: 225-208-1496
Email: custserv@la.gov
Website: http://www.osfa.state.la.us

578. Maine
Maine Education Assistance Division
Finance Authority of Maine (FAME)
P.O. Box 949
Augusta, ME 04332-0949
Phone: 207-623-3263
Toll-Free: 800-228-3734
Fax: 207-213-2661
TTY: 207-626-2717
Email: education@famemaine.com
Website: http://www.famemaine.com

579. Maryland
Maryland Higher Education Commission
6 N. Liberty Street
Baltimore, MD 21201
Phone: 410-767-3301
In-state Toll-Free: 800-974-0203
Fax: 410-260-3200
TTY: 800-735-2258
Website: http://www.mhec.state.md.us

580. Massachusetts
Massachusetts Department of Higher Education
Room 1401
One Ashburton Place
Boston, MA 02108-1696
Phone: 617-994-6950
Fax: 617-727-6397
Email: cmccurdy@osfa.mass.edu
Website: http://www.mass.edu

581. Michigan
Michigan Student Financial Services Bureau
P.O. Box 30047
Lansing, MI 48909-7547
Toll-Free: 800-642-5626 x37054
Fax: 517-241-0155
Email: sfs@michigan.gov
Website: http://www.michigan.gov/mistudentaid

582. Minnesota
Minnesota Office of Higher Education
Suite 350
1450 Energy Park Drive
Saint Paul, MN 55108-5227
Phone: 651-642-0567
Toll-Free: 800-657-3866
Fax: 651-642-0675
TTY: 800-627-3529
Email: larry.pogemiller@state.mn.us
Website: http://www.ohe.state.mn.us

583. Mississippi
Mississippi Institutions of Higher Learning
3825 Ridgewood Road
Jackson, MS 39211-6453
Phone: 601-432-6623
In-state Toll-Free: 800-327-2980
Fax: 601-432-6972
Email: commissioner@ihl.state.ms.us
Website: http://www.ihl.state.ms.us

584. Missouri
Missouri Department of Higher Education
205 Jefferson Street
P.O. Box 1469
Jefferson City, MO 65102
Phone: 573-751-2361
Toll-Free: 800-473-6757
Fax: 573-751-6635
TTY: 800-735-2966
Email: info@dhe.mo.gov
Website: http://www.dhe.mo.gov

585. Montana
Montana University System
2500 Broadway
P.O. Box 203201
Helena, MT 59620-3201
Phone: 406-444-6570
Fax: 406-444-1469
Website: http://www.mus.edu

586. Nebraska
Nebraska Coordinating Commission for Postsecondary Education
Suite 300
140 North Eighth Street
P.O. Box 95005
Lincoln, NE 68509-5005
Phone: 402-471-2847
Fax: 402-471-2886
Website: https://ccpe.nebraska.gov

587. Nevada
Nevada Department of Education
700 East Fifth Street
Carson City, NV 89701
Phone: 775-687-9200
Fax: 775-687-9101
Website: http://www.doe.nv.gov

588. New Hampshire
New Hampshire Postsecondary Education Commission
101 Pleasant Street
Concord, NH 03301-3860
Phone: 603-271-3494
Fax: 603-271-2696
TTY: 800-735-2964
Website: http://www.education.nh.gov/highered/

589. New Jersey
Office of the Secretary of Higher Education
20 West State Street, 4th Floor
P.O. Box 542

Trenton, NJ 08625-0542
Phone: 609-292-4310
Fax: 609-292-7225
Website: http://www.state.nj.us/highereducation/

Higher Education Student Assistance Authority
P.O. Box 545
Four Quakerbridge Plaza
Trenton, NJ 08625-0545
Phone: 609-584-4480
Toll-Free: 800-792-8670
Fax: 609-588-7389
TTY: 609-588-2526
Website: http://www.hesaa.org

590. New Mexico
New Mexico Higher Education Department
300 Don Gaspar Avenue
Santa Fe, NM 87501
Phone: 505-827-5800
Toll-Free: 800-279-9777
Fax: 505-476-8453
TTY: 800-659-8331
Email: highered@state.nm.us
Website: http://ped.state.nm.us

Albuquerque Community Foundation (ACF)
P.O. Box 25266
Albuquerque NM 87125-5266
Phone: 505-883-6240
Email: foundation@albuquerquefoundation.org
Website: http://www.albuquerquefoundation.org

591. New York
New York State Higher Education Services Corporation
99 Washington Avenue
Albany, NY 12255
Phone: 518-473-1574
Toll-Free: 888-697-4372
Fax: 518-474-2839
TTY: 800-445-5234

Email: webmail@hesc.org
Website: https://www.hesc.ny.gov

592. North Carolina
North Carolina State Education Assistance Authority
P.O. Box 13663
Research Triangle Park, NC 27709-3663
Phone: 919-549-8614
In-state Toll-Free: 866-866-2362
Fax: 919-549-8481
Email: information@ncseaa.edu
Website: http://www.cfnc.org

593. North Dakota
North Dakota University System
State Student Financial Assistance Program
Department 215
600 East Boulevard Avenue
Bismarck, ND 58505-0230
Phone: 701-328-2960
Fax: 701-328-2961
Email: robin.putnam@ndus.edu
Website: http://www.ndus.edu

594. Ohio
Ohio Board of Regents
University System of Ohio
25 South Front Street
Columbus, OH 43215
Phone: 614-466-6000
Toll-Free: 888-833-1133
Fax: 614-466-5866
Email: hotline@regents.state.oh.us
Website: http://www.ohiohighered.org/board

Ohio Department of Education
25 South Front Street
Columbus, OH 43215-4183
Toll-Free: 877-644-6338
Website: http://www.ode.state.oh.us

595. Oklahoma
Oklahoma State Regents for Higher Education
Suite 200
655 Research Parkway
Oklahoma City, OK 73104
Phone: 405-225-9100
Toll-Free: 800-858-1840
Fax: 405-225-9230
Email: communicationsdepartment@osrhe.edu
Website: http://www.okhighered.org

596. Oregon
Oregon Office of Student Access and Completion
Suite 100
1500 Valley River Drive
Eugene, OR 97401
Phone: 541-687-7400
Toll-Free: 800-452-8807
Fax: 541-687-7414
Email: public_information@mercury.osac.state.or.us
Website: http://www.oregonstudentaid.gov

597. Pennsylvania
Bureau of Postsecondary and Adult Education
State Department of Education
333 Market Street, 12th Floor
Harrisburg, PA 17126
Phone: 717-787-5532
Fax: 717-783-0583
TTY: 717-783-8445
Website: http://www.education.pa.gov

Pennsylvania Higher Education Assistance Agency
Pennsylvania State Grant Program
P.O. Box 8157
Harrisburg, PA 17105-8157
In-state Toll-Free: 800-692-7392
TDD: Dial 711
Website: http://www.pheaa.org

What can I get from my state higher education agency?

Not only is your state agency a clearinghouse for information on state scholarships and financial aid but also a repository of free tips and advice. Most state agencies have an online or print publication that you can get for free. Inside it will detail all of the various state programs along with instructions for applying. When you contact your state agency be sure to request all of the free information it offers.

---

598. Rhode Island

Rhode Island Higher Education Assistance Authority
560 Jefferson Boulevard, Suite 100
Warwick, RI 02886
Phone: 401-736-1100
Toll-Free: 800-922-9855
TTY: 401-734-9481
Email: info@riheaa.org
Website: http://www.riheaa.org

Rhode Island Office of Higher Education
80 Washington Street, Suite 524
Providence, RI 02903
Phone: 401-456-6000
Fax: 401-462-9345
TTY: 401-456-6028
Website: http://www.ribghe.org

599. South Carolina

South Carolina Commission on Higher Education
Suite 300
1122 Lady Street
Columbia, SC 29201
Phone: 803-737-2260
Toll-Free: 877-349-7183
Email: frontdesk@che.sc.gov
Website: http://www.che.sc.gov

600. South Dakota
South Dakota Board of Regents
Suite 200
306 East Capitol Avenue
Pierre, SD 57501
Phone: 605-773-3134
Fax: 605-773-5320
Email: info@sdbor.edu
Website: http://www.sdbor.edu

601. Tennessee
Tennessee Higher Education Commission
Parkway Towers
Suite 1900
404 James Robertson Parkway
Nashville, TN 37243-0830
Phone: 615-741-3605
Fax: 615-741-6230
Email: lovella.carter@state.tn.gov
Website: http://www.tn.gov/thec

602. Texas
Texas Higher Education Coordinating Board
1200 E. Anderson Lane
Austin, TX 78711
Phone: 512-427-6101
Toll-Free: 800-242-3062
Fax: 512-427-6127
Email: grantinfo@thecb.state.tx.us
Website: http://www.thecb.state.tx.us

603. Utah
Utah State Board of Regents
Gateway Center
60 South 400 West
Salt Lake City, UT 84101
Phone: 801-321-7101
Fax: 801-321-7156
Email: jcottrell@utahsbr.edu
Website: http://www.higheredutah.org

604. Vermont

Vermont Student Assistance Corporation
10 East Allen Street
P.O. Box 2000
Winooski, VT 05404-2601
Phone: 802-655-9602
Toll-Free: 800-642-3177
Fax: 802-654-3765
TTY: 800-281-3341
Email: info@vsac.org
Website: http://www.vsac.org

605. Virginia

State Council of Higher Education for Virginia
James Monroe Building
Tenth Floor
101 North 14th Street
Richmond, VA 23219
Phone: 804-225-2600
Fax: 804-225-2604
Email: kirstennelson@schev.edu
Website: http://www.schev.edu

606. Washington

Washington State Achievement Council
917 Lakeridge Way SW
Olympia, WA 98502
Phone: 360-753-7800
Email: info@wsac.wa.gov
Website: http://www.wsac.wa.gov

Office of Superintendent of Public Instruction
Old Capitol Building
P.O. Box 47200
Olympia, WA 98504-7200
Phone: 360-725-6075
TTY: 360-664-3631
Website: http://www.k12.wa.us

607. West Virginia

West Virginia Higher Education Policy Commission
1018 Kanawha Boulevard, East, Suite 700
Charleston, WV 25301
Phone: 304-558-2101
Fax: 304-558-1011
Email: canderson@hepc.wvnet.edu
Website: http://www.wvhepc.edu

608. Wisconsin

Wisconsin Higher Educational Aids Board
Suite 902
131 West Wilson Street
Madison, WI 53707
Phone: 608-267-2206
Fax: 608-267-2808
Email: cassie.weisensel@wisconsin.gov
Website: http://www.heab.state.wi.us

Wisconsin Department of Public Instruction
125 South Webster Street
P.O. Box 7841
Madison, WI 53707-7841
Phone: 608-266-3390
Toll-Free: 800-441-4563
Website: http://dpi.wi.gov

609. Wyoming

Wyoming Community College Commission
Fifth Floor, Suite B
2300 Capitol Avenue
Cheyenne, WY 82002
Phone: 307-777-7144
Fax: 307-777-6567
Email: jrose@commission.wcc.edu
Website: http://www.commission.wcc.edu

Wyoming Department of Education
2300 Capitol Avenue
Hathaway Building, 2nd Floor
Cheyenne, WY 82002-2060

Phone: 307-777-7675
Fax: 307-777-6234
Website: http://edu.wyoming.gov

U.S. Territories

610. American Samoa
American Samoa Community College
Board of Higher Education
P.O. Box 2609
Pago Pago, AS 96799-2609
Phone: 684-699-9155
Email: info@amsamoa.edu
Website: http://www.amsamoa.edu

611. Commonwealth of the Northern Mariana Islands
Northern Marianas Department of Education
CNMI Public School System
Saipan, MP 96950-1250
Phone: 670-237-3027
Fax: 670-234-1270
Email: boe.admin@cnmipss.org
Website: http://www.cnmipss.org

612. Puerto Rico
Puerto Rico Council on Higher Education
P.O. Box 19900
Ave. Ponce de Leon 268
Edificio Hato Rey Center Piso 15
Hato Rey, PR 00918
Phone: 787-641-7100
Fax: 787-641-2573
Email: mi_wiscovich@ces.gobierno.pr
Website: http://www.ce.pr.gov

613. Republic of the Marshall Islands

Republic of the Marshall Islands
RMI Scholarship Grant and Loan Board
P.O. Box 1436
Majuro, MH 96960
Phone: 692-625-5770
Email: misglb@ntamar.net
Website: http://www.rmischolarship.net

614. Virgin Islands

Virgin Islands Department of Education
1834 Kongens Gade
St. Thomas, VI 00802
Phone: 340-774-2810
Fax: 340-779-7153
Email: lterry@doe.vi
Website: http://www.doe.vi

Borrow Money For College

How To Borrow Money

Going to college is an investment in yourself, and sometimes you will need to borrow some money to pay for this investment. Fortunately, there are many places that are willing to lend you money, often on very generous terms. We'll begin by looking at traditional student loans and then explore a few less well-known places to borrow money.

For most families a federal student loan will be the best and cheapest way to borrow money—unless of course you have the option of an interest-free loan from rich Aunt Emma. To qualify for a student loan you need to apply for financial aid by filling out the Free Application for Federal Student Aid (FAFSA).

There are two types of federal student loans: subsidized and unsubsidized. For subsidized loans, the government pays the interest on your loan while you are in school so that interest doesn't accrue during that time. For unsubsidized loans, interest accrues while you are in school and you'll end up paying that interest once you start repayment. Whether a loan is subsidized or unsubsidized does not affect when you need to start paying back your loans, it only affects how much interest accrues while you are in school.

The Federal Student Loan Programs

Let's take a look at the various federal student loan programs:

615.

The Federal Perkins Loans
The Perkins Loan is a guaranteed 5 percent loan for both undergraduate and graduate students with "exceptional" financial need. The U.S.

Department of Education provides colleges with a specific amount of funding and the schools determine which students have the greatest need. Schools usually add their own funds to the federal funds they receive. To be eligible for this loan you must complete the FAFSA. You do not need to start paying back a Perkins Loan until nine months after you graduate, leave school or attend less than half-time. Also, during the time you are in college you do not accumulate any interest on the loan.

616.

The Federal Direct Loans

The Direct Loans are some of the most common low-interest loans for undergraduate and graduate students. You need to attend an ac-credited school at least half-time in order to qualify and must use the money only to cover qualified expenses such as tuition and fees, room and board, books and supplies, transportation and living expenses. Currently, loans have a fixed interest rate of 3.76 percent for unsub-sidized loans and 3.76 percent for subsidized loans and a fee of up to 1.069 percent of the loan. What makes the Direct Loans so popular is that they are guaranteed by the government, which means that even if you have low or no credit since the loan is guaranteed by rich Uncle Sam you'll have no problem qualifying. There are both subsidized and unsubsidized Direct Loans.

Where does the money for the Direct Loan come from? The federal government is the lender. The application process is easy–you only have to complete the FAFSA.

For most students a Direct Loan will be the cheapest means to bor-rowing money to pay for college.

617.

The Parent Loan for Undergraduate Students (PLUS)

The PLUS loan enables parents to borrow money for each dependent, undergraduate student enrolled in school at least half-time. Parents may finance up to the full cost of each student's education each academic year, minus any grants and financial aid received. Parents do not have to prove financial need; however, a credit check is required. The current interest rate on a PLUS loan is fixed at 4.276 percent.

618.

PLUS Loan for Graduate and Professional Degree Students

This loan program allows graduate and professional degree students to borrow up to the cost of attendance minus other financial aid received. The terms are the same as the Parent Loan for Undergraduate Students. Recipients must not have an adverse credit history, and repayment begins on the date of the last disbursement.

619.

The Nursing Student Loan

This is a fixed-rate, low interest and need-based federal loan. You must be enrolled at least half-time in a program leading to a diploma, associate, baccalaureate or graduate degree in nursing. The amount that you may borrow varies by institution. The interest rate is 5 percent per year and interest is subsidized while you are in school. The term of the loan is up to 10 years. To apply for this loan, contact the financial aid office at the school where you plan to attend or where you are enrolled. Or, visit the website of the U.S. Department of Health and Human Services at http://www.hrsa.gov/loanscholarships/loans/nursing.html.

620.

Health Professions Student Loan (HPSL)

This loan is for financially needy students in the health professions, which include dentistry, optometry, pharmacy, podiatric medicine and veterinary medicine. Individual colleges select loan recipients based on financial need, which is determined from your application for financial aid. The interest rate is fixed at 5 percent. Repayment of the loan begins one year after graduation and can be for a term of up to 10 years. There is no origination fee and no penalty for early repayment. To apply for this loan, contact the financial aid office at the school where you intend to apply or where you are enrolled.

621.

Loan for Disadvantaged Students (LDS)

This loan program provides a low-interest 5 percent loan for financially needy students from disadvantaged backgrounds who are pursuing degrees in allopathic medicine, osteopathic medicine, dentistry, optometry, podiatric medicine, pharmacy or veterinary medicine. Individual colleges select loan recipients based on financial need, which is determined from your application for financial aid. The term of the loan can be up to 10 years. Repayment of the loan begins one year after you graduate. To apply for this loan, contact the financial aid office at the school where you intend to apply or where you are enrolled.

622.

Primary Care Loan (PCL)

This is a low-interest loan of 5 percent for students with financial need who are in the health professions, which include allopathic or osteopathic medicine. Medical students must agree to complete their residency training in primary care within four years after graduation and to practice in primary care for the entire term of the loan. Repayment of the loan begins one year after you graduate, and the term can be up to 10 years. To apply for this loan, contact the financial aid office at the school where you intend to apply or where you are enrolled.

Where can I get more information on government loans for health professions?

A good resource that we found is the Health Resources and Services Administration. Visit their website at http://www.hrsa.gov/loanscholarships to get the skinny on various loan programs.

623.

Lower your monthly payments with a Consolidation Loan

It is very likely that you will borrow from more than one student loan program or take out an additional loan during the course of college or graduate school. Having multiple loans means that each month you have to make payments for each loan. It sometimes makes sense to consolidate your federal student loans into a single loan. This makes it easier to pay since you only make a single payment. Also, if you find that the total monthly payments are difficult to make, a consolidation loan can extend the amount of time that you repay the loan which will lower your monthly payments. Although you will end up paying more interest over the entire life of the loan, you might find that cutting your monthly payments by a third or more may be worth it.

You can consolidate Federal Perkins Loans, Federal Unsubsidized and Subsidized Stafford Loans, Federal Direct Loans, Health Professions Loans and Federal Nursing Student Loans. The term of your new consolidation loan will be based on your total education debt and the interest rate will be the weighted average of the loans being consolidated, rounded up to the nearest 1/8th of a percent.

You can use the following website to enter your student loans and see how much you can lower your monthly payments and at what cost if you consolidated your student loans: http://www.studentloans.gov.

How to Pick the Best Student Loan

When it comes time to select your student loan you need to be a smart shopper since not all loans are the same. Also, when it comes time to repay your loans there may be options that will help to reduce your total interest payments.

624.

Maximize federal loans first

Student loans from the government should be your first option. This is because they almost always have the lowest interest rate available. After tapping out federal student loans, then consider private loans from banks and other financial institutions.

625.

Choose a loan that offers the best "borrower benefits"

If you need to take out a student loan beyond a federal student loan, the biggest choice you'll have to make is who to borrow the money from. In fact, you'll probably find that you have a bunch of banks lining up to offer you money. While money is the same regardless of which bank you choose, you want to be a smart shopper by taking advantage of what are known as "borrower benefits."

As a loan borrower you can get valuable benefits for choosing one bank over another. Often these benefits are money-saving incentives for things such as making on-time payments, making payments via auto-debit or signing up for other services provided by the bank or loan servicer. These incentives may come in the form of partial interest rate reductions or even reductions to the principal balance of your outstanding loans. Usually, you won't need to change anything about the way you repay your loans when an incentive is applied to your account. The monthly payment amount remains the same, and you save money by repaying your loan balance more quickly.

So when you are trying to decide where to get your loan from, compare borrower benefits and then choose the loan that gives you the best benefits.

Repaying Your Student Loans

Eventually all borrowed money will need to be repaid. Fortunately, student loans offer several ways to repay your loans that will help you make your payments without breaking the bank.

626.

Make repayment of your loans easier by choosing the right repayment plan

One of the flexibilities of federal student loans is how you can structure repayment. The basic plan is the *standard repayment plan* with a fixed monthly amount for a term of up to 10 years depending on the size of the loan. Smaller loans are usually paid off in less than 10 years. Besides the standard repayment plan you can also select three alternatives. Each of them lengthens the term of the loan and therefore the total amount of interest that you will pay but lowers the monthly payment:

The extended repayment plan. This plan basically extends the term of the loan to 25 years. Doing so will reduce your monthly payments but will result in your paying more in interest. The extended repayment plan may be a good option if you end up borrowing a large amount of money that would make your monthly payments under the standard plan too high. You may opt for the fixed plan, which offers a fixed rate for the full term, or the graduated plan, in which payments increase every two years.

The graduated repayment plan. This plan has a ten-year repayment period. Your initial payments are smaller, and payments are gradually increased every two years over the term of the loan. This method might be helpful when you first graduate since it increases your payments as your salary grows.

Is there an easy way to figure out how much my loan really costs and also how much I will have to pay each month once I begin repayment after I graduate?

The best way to figure out how much you need to pay each month is to use an online loan payment calculator. We like the Repayment Estimator at https://studentaid.ed.gov/repay-loans/understand/plans. This calculator not only shows you what your monthly payments will be, but it also shows you how much total interest you'll pay. This interest is really the cost of your loan.

The income-driven repayment plans. These plans set your monthly payments according to your income, family size and total amount due. Payments are adjusted each year as your income goes up or down and may be as low as $0 per month. The term of this loan is up to 25 years, and at the end of 25 years, any remaining balance on the loan is discharged.

You can switch from one repayment plan to another once a year as long as the maximum loan term for the new plan is longer than the amount of time you have left under the current plan.

627.

Save money by paying off your loans as early as possible

If you want to save money on your loans, remember that time is your enemy. The longer you hold a loan, the more in interest payments you'll have to make. Consider the following example. Imagine that you borrow $20,000 at 3.76 percent interest. The term of the loan is 10 years. If you made your regular payments, at the end of 10 years you will have paid a total of $24,026, which means you will have paid $4,026 in interest. Now let's assume that you pay a little extra each month so that you end up paying off your loan in eight years. If you did this you would have paid a total of $23,190, or $3,190 in interest, which is a savings of $836. The opposite is also true. If it takes you longer to pay off a loan or if you extend your loan repayment, you will end up paying more in total interest payments.

All federal student loans allow you to pay off the entire loan balance early without any penalties.

628.

Put all your loan payments on hold using deferment

Under certain situations you can put a hold on all payments of your student loan. If you have a Direct Subsidized Loan, the government will continue to make the interest payments for you during deferment. If you have a Direct Unsubsidized Loan, you will still be responsible for all interest that accrues during deferment. To qualify for deferment you must meet one of the following requirements:

- You decide to go back to school at least half-time.
- You become unemployed.
- You are experiencing severe economic hardship.
- You enter into a graduate fellowship program.
- You are involved in rehabilitation training.

Deferment does not mean that you don't ever have to repay your loan, but it gives you a break from making payments. Once your deferment period has ended, you need to resume making your monthly payments.

629.

During tough times reduce the burden of loan payments through forbearance

Forbearance allows you to temporarily postpone your payments, extend the time you have to make payments or make smaller payments for a certain amount of time. You must apply to your lender for forbearance, and they will make the decision of whether or not to grant you forbearance. If granted you will still be responsible for all interest that accrues during the forbearance period.

Typical circumstances under which a lender may grant forbearance include:

- If you encounter "personal problems" or economic hardship that affects your ability to make your regular payments.
- If you are unemployed and have already used the maximum time allowed for deferment.
- If you have poor health or a disability.

Other situations that will allow you to receive forbearance include:

- Your debt amount exceeds your total monthly income.
- You file for bankruptcy.
- You are serving in a public service organization such as AmeriCorps.
- There is a natural disaster.
- There is a local or national emergency.
- You must serve in the military.

These are not the only reasons you may be granted forbearance. Almost any legitimate reason that makes it difficult for you to pay may qualify for forbearance. Consult with your lender or loan servicer if you encounter any special circumstances that make it difficult for you to make your monthly payments.

630.

There are few legitimate ways to cancel a student loan

You may dream that your loans would be miraculously forgiven, but there are really only a few special circumstances when this can happen. Federal student loan debt is cancelled entirely if a student loan or PLUS borrower becomes totally and permanently disabled or dies. Other conditions in which student loan debt may be discharged either partially or in full include bankruptcy filing, school closure, false loan certification or an unpaid refund from the school. As you can see you really don't want any of these conditions to befall you in order to cancel your student loan.

631.

Defaulting on a loan will haunt you for a very long time

Defaulting on any student loan is not a good idea. If you start to miss your monthly payments your loan may go into default. This will affect your credit rating and make it hard for you to take out a consumer loan, car loan, mortgage or even pass a simple credit check when renting an apartment. You will also not be eligible to receive any form of financial aid. Defaulted loans can be used to garnish your wages, subtracting up to 10 percent of your salary to pay for your loan. If you are unable to make your scheduled payments, call your lender immediately. There are often steps that can be taken to avoid defaulting.

Keep in mind that a student loan is a serious commitment. Someone trusts you enough to lend you money to pay for your education. In return they expect to be repaid according to the terms of your loan. Take this responsibility seriously.

Private Loans

Not all student loans are government-backed student loans. Most banks offer private student loans that operate very similar to the federal program. These private loans may allow you to borrow more than a federal loan. There are also loans that are not specifically designed to pay for college but that still make a lot of sense to use. Let's take a look at some of these private loans.

632.

Take advantage of a private student loan

Many banks and financial institutions offer special loans for students. These typically mirror the federal student loans. However, since they are private loans and not guaranteed by the government, their terms are set by the individual lenders. These loans can be extremely useful if you exhaust your federal sources of aid. Plus, since they are private loans you can apply for them at any time during the school year. Examples of these types of loans include Sallie Mae's *Smart Option Student Loans* and Discover's *Student Loans.*

You apply for these loans directly with your lender. The interest rate will often be based on your credit history. The better your credit the lower your interest rate. Most private loans allow you to defer your interest and principal payments until after you graduate. When selecting a private loan, compare the interest rates, repayment options, loan terms and borrower benefits.

633.

Conduct independent research

Your college may provide a list of preferred private lenders, but the truth is that you don't need to use a lender from the list. When it comes to private loans, you are free to use the institution of your choice. If you need a private student loan, conduct your own research to figure out the option that is the best fit for you. By shopping around, you may find a better deal.

634.

Use your home equity to pay for college

If you own your home you may be able to use your home's equity to pay for college. Basically, a home equity loan allows you to tap the equity in your home. You can borrow a lump sum (known as a second mortgage) and make monthly payments or you can establish a line of credit (known as a HELOC) and borrow money as you need it.

When you establish a line of credit you only pay the interest on the amount of money that you actually borrow. For example, if you have a $50,000 line of credit you can write checks against that amount when you need it instead of borrowing the entire lump sum and paying interest from the day you get the money. Interest rates on HELOCs can either be fixed or variable depending on the loan.

Home equity loans have some advantages over other types of consumer borrowing. For one, you get to deduct interest from your taxes. (Typically interest on home equity loans up to $100,000 can be deducted.) Even more important may be the fact that borrowing what you need when you need it will not impact your assets as much as taking it all in one lump sum. This means that a home equity line of credit should have less of an impact on your ability to get financial aid. The lower impact that a HELOC has on your assets combined with the tax deduction you get for interest paid makes this one of the better loans outside of student loans to pay for college.

635.

Why you should probably avoid a second mortgage

Some parents consider taking out a second mortgage on their home and using the money to pay for college. The problem is that when you receive the loan that entire amount is added to your assets, which will negatively impact your chances for financial aid. A home equity loan with a line of credit (HELOC), on the other hand, minimizes this problem since you only borrow what you need as you need it. The one risk of a HELOC is that the interest rate is usually variable instead of fixed and if interest rises while you hold the loan so too will your payments. If you are trying to choose between a second mortgage and a home equity line of credit, weigh carefully any impact that receiving all that money will have on your financial aid package.

636.

Borrow from your whole-life insurance policy before you're gone

If you have a whole-life insurance policy as opposed to a term-life policy you may have built up some cash value that you can borrow against. Usually your beneficiaries would receive this cash value after you die, but some policies let you withdraw some of this money or borrow against it. Just remember that unless you pay it back, this amount is taken from your death benefits, decreasing the amount that your beneficiaries receive.

637.

Dip into your IRA penalty-free

You can make withdrawals from traditional IRAs, Roth IRAs and SIMPLE IRAs and avoid the 10 percent early withdrawal penalty if you use the funds for qualified educational expenses. Depending on the type of account and whether you withdraw contributions or earnings, you may owe income tax on the amount. Keep in mind as well that you are taking away from your retirement nest egg.

638.

If you can stomach the risk you can borrow money from your 401k plan

If you have a 401k retirement plan you can borrow money from it and repay yourself the principal and interest within a five-year period. The risk is that if you lose your job you will have to repay the loan immediately or else face the double whammy of income tax and a penalty on the amount you borrowed.

639.

Borrow money from rich relatives

We all dream of having a rich aunt or uncle who becomes our benefactor. If you are lucky you just may have a relative that likes you enough to let you have or borrow some money to pay for school. The cleanest way is for them to gift you the money (they can gift up to $14,000 per year as an individual without tax consequences or $70,000 if they contribute to your 529 Plan. See Chapter 6 for the details.) In return you will owe them a lifetime worth of gratitude.

Unfortunately, not all relatives are comfortable just giving away money. You might be able to arrange for a private loan with either no or low interest. Be careful since loans over $10,000 must follow IRS rules on the minimum interest charged and there are tax implications for both the lender and borrower. Even more dangerous is the effect a personal loan can have on family relations. What happens if you miss a payment or can't pay back all the money? How will you feel at the next family gathering when you have to face the relative whose loan you are having trouble paying back? This can lead to strained family relationships.

If you are going to borrow money that you intend to pay back with interest, it is best to put all of the terms in writing. Include when you should begin repayment–usually some time after you graduate and can find a job–as well as the consequences of missing a payment–usually a penalty fee.

If you are borrowing a large amount, you might want to purchase a loan agreement from a company like LoanBack (http://www.

Can I ever get my loan totally forgiven?

There are two ways to get your student loan forgiven: the good way and the bad way. The good way is through a loan repayment program (see Chapter 13.) The other way is through default, which is essentially like declaring bankruptcy. If you default on your loan, your credit record will be affected and you will have major difficulty borrowing money in the future. The bank may also decide to take part of your wages to force you to repay your loan.

---

loanback.com) to make it as official as possible. These kinds of companies act as an intermediary between you and Uncle Joe, which can help to keep your financial relationship separate from your personal relationship.

640.

Have grandma write a check to the college

If you want to avoid the estate tax implications of receiving a large gift of cash from a grandparent you can have grandma or grandpa write the check directly to the college. Doing so allows grandma to avoid any estate tax consequences. Even if they write a check for the entire cost of your tuition they will not face any estate taxes (the $14,000 gift tax exclusion does not apply) as long as the check is made directly to the college. Now the only question is, do you have grandparents who are in a position to be this charitable?

641.

In a pinch get some emergency cash from your college

Most colleges have money for students who are in a cash crunch and just need a few emergency bucks to make ends meet. A college usually requires that the loan be paid back by the end of the semester or year. However, depending on your circumstances you may be able to negotiate different terms. Visit your financial aid office if you think you need some emergency cash.

CHAPTER THIRTEEN

Loan Forgiveness Programs

Loan Forgiveness Programs And Scholarships For Service

Under normal circumstances, you can only avoid repaying your student loans if you become disabled or die. We're sure you would much rather pay off your loans than suffer one of these alternatives. However, there is one other way to have your loan cancelled that does not involve death or bodily injury. This is through programs known as loan forgiveness.

Many of these programs are run by state governments as a way to encourage you to enter a specific profession or to work in an underserved area. If you agree to the terms of the program then for each year you meet these obligations the state will pay off a percentage of your loans. Typically after four or five years your loans are completely paid off.

Some state-supported loan repayment programs are reserved only for residents of the state. However, this is not true for all programs. Some allow anyone to participate as long as they work in the state. That means you can go to college in one state, relocate and work in another state with a forgiveness program and still reap the benefits. Check both your own state's programs as well as any states where you might consider working.

Closely related to loan forgiveness programs are scholarships for service. These awards are contingent on your obligation to perform a specific duty. This might include studying and working in a specific field. Or it could be doing volunteer work and community service. There are both national and state-based scholarships for service.

The major catch for both loan forgiveness programs and scholarships for service is that both require you to study specific subjects, enter certain occupations or perform certain volunteer duties. If you want to do these things (or if they fit into your long-term personal or career goals) then these programs are an excellent way to help cut the cost of your education.

National Programs

Let's start by taking a look at the national programs. Most are scholarships for service and are designed to encourage you to dedicate a year or two to volunteer work. Many students consider this an invaluable experience. As a reward for giving your time, these programs offer educational benefits that can help you defray the cost of college.

642.

AmeriCorps and VISTA

Run by the Corporation for National and Community Service, AmeriCorps volunteers serve through more than 2,100 non-profits, public agencies and faith-based organizations. Volunteers perform a range of services including tutoring, building affordable housing, cleaning parks and streams and helping communities respond to disasters. As an AmeriCorps volunteer you will serve either full- or part-time over a 10- to 12-month period.

As a full-time member you can receive $5,815 to pay for college, graduate school or to pay back student loans. You also receive health insurance, training and student loan deferment, and depending on your service even a living allowance. If you volunteer on a part-time basis you receive a partial education award.

You can earn up to two awards, which means that if you serve for two years you can earn more than $11,000 for college or grad school. This goes a long way in helping you pay for college or to cut your student loan payments.

If you are planning to attend school after your AmeriCorps service you may also be able to take advantage of college credit offered by some colleges for your service. For example, the University of Vermont offers both course credit and scholarships for AmeriCorps volunteers. Websites: http://www.americorps.gov and www.nationalservice.gov

If you volunteer 1,700 hours with private, nonprofit groups that help eradicate hunger, homelessness, poverty and illiteracy, you can receive $5,958 toward repayment of your student loans, a living allowance and deferment of student loans. As part of AmeriCorps, VISTA focuses on empowering people in low income areas. As a volunteer you work as a community organizer by doing work such as recruiting volunteers, fundraising or helping to develop a new program.
Website: http://www.americorps.gov

643.

Teach For America

Each year, Teach For America selects 2,000 recent college graduates for training to become full-time, paid teachers in urban and rural public schools. As a Teach For America teacher you will receive a salary and health benefits and insurance similar to other first-year teachers. You can also qualify to receive forbearance on your student loans and the same AmeriCorps education award of $5,815 for each year of service. You can use the education award to pay back your student loans or toward your future education.
Website: http://www.teachforamerica.org

645.

National Defense Education Act

If you become a full-time teacher in an elementary or secondary school that serves students from low-income families you can have a portion of your Perkins Loans forgiven. Contact your school district's administration to see which schools qualify under this program.

646.

Teacher Loan Cancellation

If you qualify, the *Teacher Loan Forgiveness Program* will forgive up to $5,000 of Direct Loan amounts. If you teach in certain fields such as mathematics, science and special education you may be eligible for an increased loan forgiveness amount of up to $17,500. If you have a Perkins Loan you may qualify for the

Federal Perkins Loan Teacher Cancellation Program which will discharge up to 100 percent of your loan amount if you serve in a public or non-profit elementary or secondary school in a low-income area, or as a special education teacher or as a teacher in the field of mathematics, science, foreign languages, bilingual education or in any other field of expertise determined by a state education agency to have a shortage of qualified teachers in that state. You can learn more about these programs at: http://studentaid.ed.gov/PORTALSWebApp/students/english/teachercancel.jsp?tab=repaying.

647.

NIH Loan Repayment Program

This program provides repayment of up to $35,000 per year of educational loan debt and federal and state tax reimbursements for professionals pursuing careers in clinical, pediatric, contraception and infertility or health disparities research. Among the requirements, you must conduct research in one of the fields in a project sponsored by non-profit or government funds for the next two years and have earned an M.D., Ph.D., Pharm.D., D.O., D.D.S., D.M.D., D.P.M., D.C., N.D. or equivalent doctoral degree and be a U.S. citizen or permanent resident.
Website: https://www.lrp.nih.gov

When do I get the money?

Some loan forgiveness programs give you the money before or while you are in school, but most kick in after you graduate. So you need to apply for student loans like everyone else, but your big advantage is that as long as you abide by the terms of the program you won't have to pay back the loans or will pay a significantly reduced amount.

648.

National Health Service Corps

This program pays for tuition, fees, a stipend and supplies for health professional students who work in underserved areas. Applicants must be enrolled, or accepted for enrollment, in a fully accredited U.S. allopathic or osteopathic medical school, family nurse practitioner program (master's degree in nursing, post-master's or post-baccalaureate certificate), nurse-midwifery program (master's degree in nursing, post-master's or post-baccalaureate certificate), physician assistant program (certificate, associate, baccalaureate or master's program) or dental school. Scholars attending medical school are expected to complete residency programs in one of the following specialties: family medicine, general pediatrics, general internal medicine, obstetrics/gynecology, psychiatry or rotating internship (D.O.s only) with a request to complete one of the above specialties. Dental scholars may do residencies in general practice or pediatric dentistry. Recipients must also serve full-time, commit to working in an underserved area for at least two years and be U.S. citizens.
Website: http://nhsc.hrsa.gov

649.

Extramural Loan Repayment Program for Clinical Researchers (LRP-CR)

Physicians and scientists may have up to $35,000 of their loans repaid annually for conducting patient-oriented research. Applicants must be

U.S. citizens or permanent residents; hold an M.D., Ph.D., Pharm. D., Psy.D., D.O., D.D.S., D.M.D., D.P.M., D.C., N.D., O.D., D.V.M. or equivalent degree and have qualifying educational debt. Website: https://www.lrp.nih.gov

650.

Association of American Medical Colleges

There is a directory of loan repayment programs for health-related professionals on the website of the Association of American Medical Colleges in the "Financing your medical education" section at http://www.aamc.org. In exchange for loan repayment, medical professionals must provide service, oftentimes in areas of need.

651.

Indian Health Service (IHS) Loan Repayment Program (LRP)

Health professionals who commit to two years of working at an Indian health program site may have up to $20,000 per year in loans forgiven. More information about the program is available from Indian Health Service at http://www.ihs.gov/loanrepayment/.

652.

Veterinary Medicine Loan Repayment Program (VMLRP)

Doctors of Veterinary Medicine (DVM) who have qualifying educational debt and who work in veterinary shortage areas for three years may have up to $25,000 per year forgiven. Visit the National Institute of Food and Agriculture at https://nifa.usda.gov/vmlrp-general-information for more information.

653.

Child Care Provider Loan Cancellation

You may qualify for cancellation of a Direct Loan if you have a degree in early childhood education, are a childcare provider and work in a facility that serves low-income children.
Website: http://studentaid.ed.gov

654.

Public Service Loan Forgiveness Program

You may have loans made through the Federal Direct Program forgiven if you work for any federal government, state government, local government or tribal government entity or most non-profit employers.
Website: http://studentaid.ed.gov

655.

Law Loan Repayment Programs

There is a directory of loan repayment programs for lawyers who work in public service or underserved areas at the Equal Justice Works website at http://www.equaljusticeworks.org. The programs listed are sponsored by law schools, states and companies. Check if your law school participates in this program.

656.

Business School Loan Forgiveness Programs

Some business graduate schools forgive loans for students who enter public service or non-profit careers. For example, Stanford University and Harvard University both offer loan forgiveness programs. Check with your business school's financial aid office. In addition, companies may provide this as a benefit, requiring you to commit to working a number of years with them.

657.

Peace Corps

While the Peace Corps does not offer a loan forgiveness program, it offers several important educational benefits. With the Master's International Program, you can incorporate Peace Corps service into master's degree programs at more than 40 colleges and universities. Most schools provide students with opportunities for research or teaching assistantships, scholarships or a tuition waiver for the cost of credits earned while in the Peace Corps. The Fellows/USA Program offers volunteers who have returned home scholarships or reduced tuition in advanced-degree programs at more than 25 participating colleges and universities. Volunteers commit to work for two years in an underserved community as they pursue their graduate degree. Website: http://www.peacecorps.gov

658.

Professional Associations

Many professional associations offer loan forgiveness programs to help students who have recently entered the career. The Society of Automotive Engineers (http://www.sae.org), for example, offers the *Doctoral Scholars Forgivable Loan Program,* which can help repay your graduate school student loans. Take a look at the professional organizations listed in Chapter 2 or go to your library and check out the book *Encyclopedia of Associations.*

659.

Federal Student Loan Repayment Program

This program allows federal agencies to repay student loans as a recruitment or retention incentive for candidates or current employees of the agency. The program will repay up to a maximum of $10,000 per year for a lifetime total of $60,000 per employee. If you receive this benefit you will need to sign a service agreement to remain in the service of the repaying agency for a period of at least three years. As with any incentive, this authority is used at the discretion of the agency. Each agency develops its own plan to administer the program. Learn more at: http://www.opm.gov/oca/pay/studentloan/.

State Loan Forgiveness Programs

Many states offer loan forgiveness or scholarships for service as a way to entice students to work in underserved areas of the state or in fields with shortages. Some programs require that you are a resident of or attend a college or university in the state while others just require that you work in the state. Be sure to look not only at the state where you are a resident and will be attending college but also at all of the states where you might work after college.

660. Alaska

Alaska Commission on Postsecondary Education
The state offers loan forgiveness programs for students who become teachers, work in fisheries-related fields or graduate from the WWAMI Medical Education program. The WWAMI program includes the states of Washington, Wyoming, Alaska, Montana and Idaho. For more information, visit http://acpe.alaska.gov.

661. Arizona

The Arizona Loan Repayment Program
This program is for students who become primary health care providers, such as physicians, dentists, nurse practitioners, certi-

fied nurse mid-wives or physician assistants. For more details, visit the Arizona Department of Health Services Bureau of Health Systems Development website at http://www.azdhs.gov.

Law School Loan Repayment Programs
A number of individual law schools in the state offer loan repayment programs for graduates who agree to work at public interest or government agencies. These include Arizona State University and the University of Arizona.

662. Arkansas

The State Teacher Education Program (STEP)
This program provides up to $4,000 per year in loan forgiveness for up to three years to educators teaching in a subject or geographic shortage area in an Arkansas public school. For more information, visit the Arkansas Department of Higher Education at http://www.adhe.edu.

The Rural Physician Incentive Program
This program provides loan forgiveness for physicians who establish practices in communities of less than 15,000 in medically underserved areas. To learn more, visit the website of the Arkansas Department of Health at http://www.healthy. arkansas.gov.

663. California

The State Loan Repayment Program
This program is for students who become primary care health providers, including medical doctors and doctors of osteopathy in family practice, general internal medicine, general pediatrics and OB/GYN. Also eligible are physician assistants, nurse practitioners, certified nurse-midwives, general practice dentists (DDS or DMD), psychiatrists, clinical or counseling psychologists, social workers, marriage and family counselors, mental health counselors and licensed professional counselors. For more information visit the Office of Statewide Health Planning and Development at http://www.oshpd.ca.gov/hwdd/slrp.html.

Health Professions Loan Repayment Program
Those working in health professions such as certified nurse midwives, clinical nurse specialists, dental hygienists, dentists, nurse practitioners and physician assistants may receive loan repayments up to $50,000. Recipients must commit to working at an eligible California facility for 24 months. More information is available from the Health Professions Education Foundation at https://www.oshpd.ca.gov/HPEF/.

Steven M. Thompson Physician Corps Loan Repayment Program
Allopathic or osteopathic physicians who agree to work at an eligible Health Professional Shortage Area (HPSA) in California for at least three years may receive up to $105,000 in loan repayment. Details are available from the Health Professions Education Foundation at http://www.oshpd.ca.gov/hpef/Programs/STLRP.html.

The Child Development Grant Program
This program provides need-based grants to students who work in childcare and development at licensed children's centers after graduating. Recipients must work for one year for each year of the award at an eligible program in the state. Get more information at the website of the California Student Aid Commission at http://www.csac.ca.gov.

Law School Loan Repayment Programs
A number of individual law schools in the state offer loan repayment programs for graduates who agree to work at public interest or government agencies. These include the California Western School of Law, Golden Gate University School of Law, Loyola Law School Loyola Marymount University, Pacific McGeorge School of Law, Pepperdine University School of Law, Santa Clara University School of Law, Southwestern Law School, Stanford University School of Law, University of California Berkeley School of Law, University of California Davis School of Law, University of California Hastings School of Law, University of San Diego School of Law, University of San Francisco Law School, University of Southern California Gould School of Law and Whittier Law School.

Is it worth my time to volunteer for a year or two?

Most students we've met who have taken a year off to volunteer treasure their experience. They were able to travel, learn new skills and, most importantly, work on a project that made a difference. They gained skills that both employers and graduate schools desire such as leadership, organizing others and showing a commitment to a cause. Such experiences are useful throughout life regardless of what profession you enter afterward.

664. Colorado

Colorado Health Services Corps
This loan repayment program is for students who become primary health care providers in a health professional shortage area. For more information, contact the Colorado Department of Public Health and Environment at http://www.colorado. gov/cdphe/.

Law School Loan Repayment Programs
A number of individual law schools in the state offer loan repayment programs for graduates who agree to work at public interest or government agencies. These include the University of Colorado and University of Denver.

665. Connecticut

The Connecticut Minority Teacher Incentive Grant
This program offers grants for up to two years and loan reimbursement for up to four years of teaching in Connecticut public schools. For more details, visit the Connecticut Department of Higher Education at http://www.ctohe.org/sfa/.

Law School Loan Repayment Programs
A number of individual law schools in the state offer loan repayment programs for graduates who agree to work at public interest or government agencies. These include the Yale Law School and Quinnipiac University School of Law.

666. Florida

Florida Bar Foundation Loan Repayment Assistance Program
Lawyers may receive up to $7,500 per year in loan repayment by working full-time or part-time for 12 months at eligible legal aid programs. More information is available at http://www. flabarfndn.org.

Nursing Student Loan Forgiveness Program
Licensed nurses working at sites including State of Florida operated medical and healthcare facilities, public schools and federally sponsored community health centers are eligible to receive loan repayments of up to $4,000 per year. See the Florida Department of Education Office of Student Financial Assistance at http://www.floridastudentfinancialaid.org for more information.

Law School Loan Repayment Programs
A number of individual law schools in the state offer loan repayment programs for graduates who agree to work at public interest or government agencies. These include the St. Thomas University School of Law.

667. Georgia

The Registered Nurse Service-Cancelable Loan Program
This program cancels loans for students who become RNs and work for an eligible health care facility. To learn more about this program, visit the Georgia Student Finance Commission at http://www.gsfc.org.

The University of North Georgia Military Scholarship
This award provides full scholarships for students who serve for four years in the Georgia Army National Guard after graduating from North Georgia College. For more details, visit the Georgia Student Finance Commission at http://www.gsfc.org.

The Georgia Military College State Service Scholarship
This program provides full scholarships for students who serve for two years in the Georgia National Guard after graduating

from Georgia Military College. For more information, visit the Georgia Student Finance Commission at http://www.gsfc.org.

The Scholarship For Engineering Education (SEE)
This program forgives loans for Georgia residents who are engineering students at private accredited engineering universities in the state and who work as engineers in Georgia. To learn more, visit the Georgia Student Finance Commission at http://www.gsfc.org.

Law School Loan Repayment Programs
A number of individual law schools in the state offer loan repayment programs for graduates who agree to work at public interest or government agencies. These include the Emory University School of Law and the University of Georgia.

668. Idaho

Idaho Medical Association
The Idaho Medical Association offers a list of loan forgiveness programs for Idaho students in health services at https://www.idmed.org/IDAHO/Idaho_Public/Resources/Loan_Repayment.aspx.

669. Illinois

Illinois Department of Public Health
The Medical Student Scholarship Program repays the loans of Illinois residents who attend medical school and practice in underserved areas in Illinois for a minimum of two years. Similarly, the Nursing Education Scholarship Program supports nurses, and the Allied Health Care Professional Scholarship Program supports nurse practitioners, physician assistants and certified nurse midwives. To learn more, visit http://www.idph.state.il.us.

Law School Loan Repayment Programs
A number of individual law schools in the state offer loan repayment programs for graduates who agree to work at public interest or government agencies. These include the Chicago-Kent College of Law at the Illinois Institute of Technology, DePaul

University College of Law, Loyola University Chicago School of Law, Northwestern University School of Law, University of Chicago Law School and University of Illinois.

670. Indiana

The Minority Teacher Scholarship
This program gives scholarships of up to $4,000 to students seeking teaching certification, special education teaching certification or occupational or physical therapy certification who are Indiana residents. Preference is given to black or Hispanic students and students enrolling in college for the first time. Recipients must teach full-time at an accredited Indiana elementary or secondary school or practice in the field of occupational or physical therapy in an accredited school, vocational rehabilitation center, community mental retardation or other developmental disabilities center, for three years out of the first five years of certification. To learn more, visit the State Student Assistance Commission of Indiana at http://www.in.gov/ssaci.

Law School Loan Repayment Programs
A number of individual law schools in the state offer loan repayment programs for graduates who agree to work at public interest or government agencies. These include the Indiana University School of Law at Bloomington, Notre Dame Law School and the Valparaiso University School of Law.

671. Iowa

Primary Care Recruitment and Retention Endeavor (PRIMECARRE)
Primary care physicians who work in underserved Iowa communities for four years can have up to $90,000 of their loans paid. The SCPCI program identifies third-year residents and new physicians who are interested in rural and small-town practices. To learn more, visit https://idph.iowa.gov/ohds/rural-health-primary-care/primecarre.

Teacher Shortage Forgivable Loans Program
Eligible Iowa students who attend Iowa colleges or universities and pursue degrees and certification in teaching may have up

to $9,000 of their loans forgiven for working in a shortage area. Get more information at http://www.iowacollegeaid.gov.

The Nursing Education Forgivable Loan Program
This program forgives up to $3,000 in student loans for nursing students who work in rural Iowa communities for three years or who work in health profession shortage areas for 1.5 years. For more details, visit http://www.iowacollegeaid.gov.

Law School Loan Repayment Programs
A number of individual law schools in the state offer loan repayment programs for graduates who agree to work at public interest or government agencies. These include the University of Iowa.

672. Kansas

The Kansas Teacher Service Scholarship
The program provides scholarships of $5,000 per year for undergraduate or graduate study for students who commit to teaching in Kansas in a specified curriculum or underserved geographic area. To learn more about this program, visit the Kansas Board of Regents at http://www.kansasregents.org.

The Nursing Scholarship
This award provides $2,500 scholarships each year for students who enroll in licensed practical nurse programs and $3,500 scholarships each year for students who enroll in registered nurse programs. Recipients commit to practicing as an LPN or RN in a specific Kansas location for one year for each year that they receive the scholarship. For more information, visit the Kansas Board of Regents at http://www.kansasregents.org.

The Kansas Osteopathic Medical Service Scholarship
This award provides up to $15,000 per year for study at nationally accredited osteopathy schools for primary care physicians who practice in rural areas of Kansas one year for each year that they receive the scholarship. For details, visit the Kansas Board of Regents at http://www.kansasregents.org.

The Kansas Optometry Service Scholarship
The award pays the difference between resident and non-resident tuition at out-of-state institutions for recipients who practice in Kansas for one year for each year that they receive the scholarship. Get more information at the website of the Kansas Board of Regents at http://www.kansasregents.org.

The Kansas Dental Education Opportunities Program
This program pays the difference between resident and non-resident tuition at the University of Missouri-Kansas City for recipients who establish dental practices in Kansas. To learn more about this program, visit the Kansas Board of Regents at http://www.kansasregents.org.

University of Kansas Medical Center
The Kansas Bridging Plan forgives loans of up to $26,000 for resident physicians in family practice, general internal medicine, general pediatrics and medicine/pediatrics residency programs in Kansas. Recipients agree to work for three years after their residency training programs in rural areas, which consist of any community in any county in Kansas except Douglas, Johnson, Sedgwick, Shawnee or Wyandotte. To get more information, visit http://www.kumc.edu/community-engagement/rural-health.html.

Are loan forgiveness programs a new invention?

Actually the concept of loan forgiveness programs has been around for a long time. The military has used it to recruit officers through ROTC programs. These programs pay your tuition as long as you agree to serve in the military after you graduate. The state's adoption of this system brought the same benefits to other professions such as medical care and teaching. While a specific program might be relatively new, the concept of loan repayment is well established.

673. Kentucky

The KHEAA Teacher Scholarship Program
The program provides awards to Kentucky residents who are full-time students pursuing their initial teacher certification at eligible Kentucky institutions. Awards are up to $12,500 total for undergraduate students and up to $7,500 total for graduate students. Recipients must teach one semester in the state for each semester or summer session in which they receive aid, with two semesters or summer terms cancelled for each semester that they teach in a critical shortage area. To learn more, visit the Kentucky Higher Education Assistance Authority at http://www.kheaa.com.

The Early Childhood Development Scholarship
This program supports the professional development of child-care workers and trainers by providing awards to Kentucky students who are pursuing associate degrees in early childhood education or bachelor's degrees in interdisciplinary early childhood education or a related program that is approved by the Early Childhood Development Authority, Kentucky Early Childhood Development Director's Certificates or Child Development Associate Credentials. Recipients must work at least 20 hours per week at an eligible early childhood facility or provide early childhood development training at least 12 times per year. Scholarships are up to $1,400. For details, visit the Kentucky Higher Education Assistance Authority at http://www.kheaa.com.

The Osteopathic Medicine Scholarship
The scholarship aids Kentucky students who attend the Pikeville College School of Osteopathic Medicine and practice one year in Kentucky for each year of the scholarship. The award provides the difference between in-state tuition at state medical schools and the tuition at the Pikeville College School of Osteopathic Medicine. To learn more, visit the Kentucky Higher Education Assistance Authority at http://www.kheaa.com.

674. Maine

Educators for Maine Program
This program is a merit-based forgivable loan program for Maine residents pursuing careers in education. Undergraduates can receive up to $3,000 per year and graduate school students can receive up to $1,500 per year. After graduating, recipients must teach in an approved Maine public or private school. The loan is forgiven once the recipients gain their state certification. For more information, contact the Finance Authority of Maine at http://www.famemaine.com.

Health Professions Loan Program
This forgivable loan program is available only to Maine residents. Through the program Maine postgraduate health professions students can borrow forgivable loans from the Finance Authority of Maine. All loans are awarded on the basis of need. You must apply through the financial aid office at your medical school. Loans do not accrue interest while you are in school, residency, fellowship or obligated service. You will not have to repay these loans if you work in general primary care practices in designated underserved areas. For each year of eligible practice, 25 percent of your loan will be canceled. To learn more, visit the Finance Authority of Maine at http://www.famemaine.com.

Maine Veterinary Medicine Loan Program
Maine residents who enter the Tufts University School of Veterinary Medicine are eligible to receive a $12,000 loan to reduce their tuition. This loan is forgiven if the student practices large animal veterinary medicine in a designated underserved area in Maine. The Commissioner of Agriculture determines underserved areas. For more information, contact the Finance Authority of Maine at http://www.famemaine.com.

Dental Education Loan and Loan Repayment Program
This program seeks to increase access to dental care to underserved populations in Maine by providing loan repayment for a student's dental education. By working in an underserved area you can receive loan forgiveness of up to $20,000 per year for up to four years for outstanding education loan debt. For more details, visit the Finance Authority of Maine at http://www.famemaine.com.

Maine Osteopathic Association
This organization offers two scholarships to students who are Maine residents and who are attending eligible colleges of osteopathic medicine. For some of the scholarships, students must plan to practice primary care in Maine or teach at an osteopathic college in New England. To learn more, visit the association's website at http://www.mainedo.org.

Law School Loan Repayment Programs
A number of individual law schools in the state offer loan repayment programs for graduates who agree to work at public interest or government agencies. These include the University of Maine School of Law.

675. Maryland

The Janet L. Hoffman Loan Assistance Repayment Program
This program assists Maryland residents who have graduated from a Maryland college or law school and who work for Maryland's state or local government or non-profit agencies. Current eligible employment fields are lawyers, nurses, physical and occupational therapists, social workers, speech pathologists and teachers with the following areas of certification: technology education (secondary); chemistry; computer science (secondary); earth/space science (secondary); English for speakers of other languages-ESOL (elementary and secondary); mathematics (secondary); physical science (secondary); physics (secondary) and special education: generic (infant to grade 3, grades 6 to adult, hearing impaired) and severely and profoundly handicapped. The program awards up to $7,500 per year. To learn more about this program, visit the Maryland Higher Education Commission at http://www.mhec.state.md.us.

The Loan Assistance Repayment Program for Physicians
The loan repayment program helps primary care physicians and medical residents in a residency program specializing in primary care who have graduated from a college or medical school in Maryland and who work in an underserved area in the state. Physicians receive up to $30,000 per year, and residents receive up to $25,000 per year. Both must work full-time as primary care physicians for two to four years. For more details,

visit the Maryland Higher Education Commission at http://www.mhec.state.md.us.

The Maryland Dent-Care Loan Assistance Repayment Program
This program assists practicing dentists who are Maryland residents and provide care to Maryland Medical Assistance Program (MMAP) recipients. Dentists receive up to $23,000 per year. For more information, visit the Maryland Higher Education Commission at http://www.mhec.state.md.us.

The Workforce Shortage Student Assistance Program
This program supports high school seniors, undergraduate students and graduate students who plan to major or are majoring in a specific career/occupational program. Eligible fields are child care, human services, teaching, nursing, physical and occupational therapy, social work and public service. Students and their parents must be Maryland residents and attend a Maryland college or university. The award is up to $4,000 per year, and recipients must work in service obligation in the field in which the award was given within one year of graduation. For more details, visit the Maryland Higher Education Commission at http://www.mhec.state.md.us.

The Firefighter, Ambulance and Rescue Squad Member Scholarship
This program supports active career or volunteer firefighters, ambulance or rescue squad members who are studying fire service technology and emergency medical technology at a Maryland institution. The award is up to $4,550 per year, and recipients must serve a Maryland community while taking courses and serve for one year after completing the courses. To learn more about this program, visit the Maryland Higher Education Commission at http://www.mhec.state.md.us.

The Sharon Christa McAuliffe Memorial Teacher Education Award
This award helps college students with at least 60 semester credit hours, college graduates and teachers certified in a non-critical shortage area. Students must be Maryland residents and attend a Maryland college or university. The award is up to approximately $13,000, and recipients must work full-time as a classroom teacher in a Maryland public school in a critical shortage area for one year for each year of the award. To learn

information, visit the Maryland Higher Education Commission at http://www.mhec.state.md.us.

The State Nursing Scholarship and Living Expenses Grant
This program is for high school seniors, undergraduate students and graduate students who are enrolled or plan to enroll in a nursing program that leads to a nursing degree. Students must be Maryland residents and attend a Maryland college or university. The award is up to $3,000 per year, and recipients must work as a full-time nurse at an eligible health organization in Maryland for one year for each year of the award. For more details about this program, visit the website of the Maryland Higher Education Commission at http://www.mhec.state.md.us.

The Physical and Occupational Therapists and Assistants Grant Program
This program supports high school seniors, undergraduate students and graduate students who are enrolled or plan to enroll in professional programs in physical therapy, physical therapist assistant, occupational therapy or occupational therapist assistant. Students must be Maryland residents and attend a Maryland college or university. The award is up to $2,000 per year, and recipients must work full-time as a therapist or therapist assistant in a Maryland facility that provides service to handicapped children for one year for each year of the award. For more details, visit the Maryland Higher Education Commission at http://www.mhec.state.md.us.

Law School Loan Repayment Programs
A number of individual law schools in the state offer loan repayment programs for graduates who agree to work at public interest or government agencies. These include the University of Maryland School of Law.

676. Massachusetts

The State Loan Repayment Program
This program assists physicians, nurse practitioners, physician assistants, psychologists, family and marriage therapists, dentists and hygienists who work full-time in underserved areas in the state. To learn more about this program, visit the Department

of Public Health Bureau of Family and Community Health at http://www.mass.gov/dph/.

Tomorrow's Teachers Scholarship Program

This program helps Massachusetts high school students who plan to pursue teaching careers, attend Massachusetts colleges or universities and who agree to teach for four years in Massachusetts public schools. The award provides full tuition at a public college or university or the equivalent amount at a private college or university each year. Priority is given to students who plan to teach in a needed subject area or in a teacher shortage area. For more details, visit the Massachusetts Office of Student Financial Aid at http://www.osfa.mass.edu.

The Incentive Program for Aspiring Teachers Tuition Waiver

This program supports college undergraduates in their third or fourth year who plan to pursue teaching careers, attend one of the nine Massachusetts State Colleges or four campuses of the University of Massachusetts and agree to teach for two years in a Massachusetts public school. The award is a tuition waiver equal to the resident tuition rate at the state college or participating university campus they attend. To learn more, visit the website of the Massachusetts Office of Student Financial Aid at http://www.osfa.mass.edu.

Law School Loan Repayment Programs

A number of individual law schools in the state offer loan repayment programs for graduates who agree to work at public interest or government agencies. These include the Boston College Law School, Boston University School of Law, Harvard Law School, Northeastern University School of Law and Suffolk University Law School.

677. Michigan

The Michigan State Loan Repayment Program (SLRP)

This program assists physicians, dentists, nurse practitioners, nurse midwives and physician assistants who work in primary care in the state's underserved communities. Learn more by visiting the website of the Michigan Department of Community Health at http://www.michigan.gov/mdch.

The Michigan Nursing Scholarship
This award aids Michigan resident students at eligible licensed practical nurse (LPN) certification, associate degree in nursing (ADN) or bachelor of science in nursing (BSN) programs at Michigan colleges or universities. Awards are up to $4,000. Recipients of full-time scholarships must work as direct care nurses in Michigan for one year for each year of the scholarship. For more information, visit the Office of Scholarships and Grants, Bureau of Student Financial Aid at http://www.michigan.gov/mistudentaid/.

Law School Loan Repayment Programs
A number of individual law schools in the state offer loan repayment programs for graduates who agree to work at public interest or government agencies. These include the University of Michigan Law School.

678. Minnesota

The Minnesota State Loan Repayment Program
This program helps primary care providers who practice full-time in eligible non-profit private or public entities in federally designated Health Professional Shortage Areas (HPSAs) in Minnesota for a minimum of two years. Loans are repaid up to $20,000 per year. Eligible primary care providers include physicians within the specialties of family practice, obstetrics and gynecology, internal medicine or pediatrics; dentists; dental hygienists; psychiatrists; clinical psychologists; marriage and family therapists; clinical social workers; licensed professional mental health counselors; psychiatric nurse specialists; primary care physician assistants; nurse practitioners; certified nurse midwives and certified midwives. To get more information on this program, visit the Minnesota Department of Health at http://www.health.state.mn.us.

The Rural Physician Loan Forgiveness Program
This program is designed to assist first-, second- or third-year primary care medical residents planning to practice full-time in eligible rural areas in Minnesota. Recipients may receive up to $10,000 in loan repayment per year for each year of service for up to four years and must serve a minimum of three years.

For details, visit the Minnesota Department of Health at http://www.health.state.mn.us.

The Urban Physician Loan Forgiveness Program

This program supports first-, second- or third-year primary care medical residents planning to practice full-time in an underserved urban area in Minnesota. Eligible professions include family practice, pediatrics, internal medicine, obstetrics and gynecology and psychiatry. Participants may receive up to $10,000 in loan repayment per year for each year of service for up to four years and must serve a minimum of three years. Visit the Minnesota Department of Health at http://www.health.state.mn.us for more information.

The Dentist Loan Forgiveness Program

This program aids students in licensed dentist programs who plan to serve state public program enrollees or patients receiving sliding fee schedule discounts in Minnesota. Students may receive up to $10,000 in loan repayment per year for each year of service for up to four years and must serve a minimum of three years. To learn more, visit the Minnesota Department of Health at http://www.health.state.mn.us.

The Rural Midlevel Practitioner Loan Forgiveness Program

This loan forgiveness program helps students in programs for midlevel practitioners including nurse practitioners, nurse-midwives, nurse anesthetists, advanced clinical nurse specialists and physician assistants who plan to practice in a designated rural area in Minnesota. Participants may receive up to $3,500 in loan repayment per year for each year of service. Practitioners in one-year programs may receive two years of loan repayment, and those in two-year programs may receive four years of loan repayment. To get more information on this program, visit the Minnesota Department of Health at http://www.health.state.mn.us.

The Nurses Who Practice in a Nursing Home or an ICFMR Loan Forgiveness Program

This program assists students in registered nursing or licensed practical nursing programs who plan to practice in nursing homes or Intermediate Care Facilities for Persons with Mental Retardation or Related Conditions (ICFMR) in Minnesota.

Participants may receive up to $3,000 in loan repayment per year for each year of service. Practitioners in one-year programs may receive one year of loan repayment, and those in two-year programs may receive two years of loan repayment. For details, visit the Minnesota Department of Health at http://www.health. state.mn.us.

Law School Loan Repayment Programs
A number of individual law schools in the state offer loan repayment programs for graduates who agree to work at public interest or government agencies. These include the Hamline University School of Law, University of Minnesota Law School, University of St. Thomas School of Law and William Mitchell College of Law.

679. Mississippi

The William Winter Teacher Scholar Loan (WWTS)
This program aids high school seniors planning to attend and junior or senior students currently attending Mississippi colleges or universities who are Mississippi residents and who agree to work as full-time classroom teachers in public schools in a critical teacher shortage area of the state. A limited number of awards may be available for freshmen and sophomore students. Recipients must serve for one year for each year of the loan received. The award is up to $3,000 per year. For more information, visit the Mississippi Board of Trustees of State Institutions of Higher Learning at http://riseupms.com/state-aid. The program is not offering loans for the current year.

The Nursing Education Loan/Scholarship (NELS)
This program helps junior and senior students pursuing undergraduate degrees in nursing and licensed registered nurses continuing their education to undergraduate degrees, master's or Ph.D.s. Applicants must be Mississippi residents attending an eligible Mississippi institution who agree to work in professional nursing in the state for one year for each year of the award. The NELS-BSN award is for applicants who are seeking a baccalaureate nursing degree (BSN) and is up to $2,000 per year. The NELS-RN to BSN is for applicants who hold a current nursing license (RN) and are seeking a baccalaureate nursing

degree (BSN) and is up to $1,500 per year for up to two years. The NELS-MSN is for applicants who are licensed registered nurses, hold the BSN degree and are seeking a master's of science degree in nursing (MSN) and is up to $3,000 for one year. The NELS-Ph.D. is for applicants who are licensed registered nurses, have completed the MSN degree requirements and who are seeking Ph.D.s in nursing and is up to $10,000 per year for up to two years. Visit the Mississippi Board of Trustees of State Institutions of Higher Learning at http://riseupms.com/state-aid for details. The program is not offering loans for the current year.

The Southern Regional Education Board Loan/Scholarship
This program aids students who are Mississippi residents, who plan to attend an approved out-of-state school for the study of optometry or osteopathic medicine and who agree to work in Mississippi in the area of specialty. Recipients must serve at least one year for each year of the award, and the award is for up to four years. For more details, visit the Mississippi Institutions of Higher Learning at http://riseupms.com/state-aid.

The Health Care Professions Loan/Scholarship
This program assists Mississippi resident students who are juniors, seniors or graduate students at Mississippi colleges or universities, are majoring in speech pathology or psychology or if in graduate school are majoring in physical therapy or occupational therapy. Recipients must serve at least one year for each year of the award. The award is up to $1,500 per year for undergraduate students and up to $3,000 per year for graduate students for up to two years. For details, visit the Mississippi Institutions of Higher Learning at http://riseupms.com/state-aid. The program is not offering loans for the current year.

680. Missouri

The Missouri Teacher Education Scholarship Program and Minority Teaching Scholarship Program
These programs are for students who plan to become teachers and commit to working in Missouri schools. Learn more about these two programs by visiting the website of the Department of Elementary and Secondary Education at http://dhe.mo.gov/ppc/grants/.

> ## What happens if I don't fulfill the obligations of a loan repayment program?
>
> Loan forgiveness programs are designed so that you take out a student loan just like any other student to pay for your education. After you graduate you must begin to pay back these loans. However, if you participate in a loan forgiveness program, as long as you fulfill the requirements the program will pay back your loans. If you stop fulfilling the requirements then the program stops paying back your loans and you'll need to start making payments again. For scholarships for service if you receive money while you are in school and then renege on your agreement after you graduate, you will have to pay back the money as if it were a loan.

The Physicians Student Loan Repayment Program and Missouri Nurse Loan Repayment Program
Both of these programs repay the loans of physicians and nurses who practice in Missouri. Learn more about them by visiting the Department of Health and Senior Services website at http://www.dhss.mo.gov.

John R. Justice Grant
This program provides loan repayment for federal public defenders and state prosecutors who agree to stay employed as public defenders and prosecutors for at least 36 months. More information is available from the Missouri Department of Public Safety at http://dps.mo.gov.

Law School Loan Repayment Programs
A number of individual law schools in the state offer loan repayment programs for graduates who agree to work at public interest or government agencies. These include the Washington University School of Law.

681. Montana

The Rural Physician Incentive Program
This program assists physicians who practice in underserved ar-

eas of the state. Physicians receive up to $45,000 over a five-year period. Learn more about this program by visiting the website of the Montana Office of Commissioner of Higher Education at http://www.mus.edu.

682. Nebraska

The Nebraska Loan Repayment Program
This program helps physicians, physician assistants, nurse practitioners, mental health professionals, occupational and physical therapists, pharmacists and dentists who practice for three years in a state-designated shortage area. Up to $20,000 per year for doctorate practitioners and up to $10,000 per year for mid-level practitioners and allied health participants is repaid. For more information, visit the Nebraska Health and Human Services website at http://dhhs.ne.gov.

The Nebraska Student Loan Program
This program assists medical, dental and physician assistant students who commit to practicing underserved areas of the state. Applicants must attend a Nebraska school. For more information visit the Nebraska Health and Human Services at http://dhhs.ne.gov.

Law School Loan Repayment Programs
A number of individual law schools in the state offer loan repayment programs for graduates who agree to work at public interest or government agencies. These include the Creighton University School of Law.

683. Nevada

The State Loan Repayment Program (SLRP)
This program aids primary care health professionals who work full-time in federally designated Health Professional Shortage Areas in the state. Get more information on this program by visiting the website of the Nevada Office of Rural Health at http://med.unr.edu/rural-health.

684. New Hampshire

The New Hampshire State Loan Repayment Program (SLRP)
This program assists full-time and part-time health care professionals who work in medically underserved areas of the state. Full-time professionals commit to three years of service and receive up to $75,000 in loan forgiveness over that period. Part-time professionals commit to two years of service and receive up to $27,500 over that period. For more information, visit the New Hampshire Department of Health and Human Services at http://www.dhhs.nh.gov/dphs/bchs/rhpc/repayment.htm.

Law School Loan Repayment Programs
A number of individual law schools in the state offer loan repayment programs for graduates who agree to work at public interest or government agencies. These include the University of New Hampshire School of Law.

685. New Mexico

The Allied Health Student Loan-For-Service
This program provides loans of up to $12,000 per year to allied health professionals who commit to practicing in designated shortage areas in the state. Applicants must be New Mexico residents attending New Mexico postsecondary institutions and major in physical therapy, occupational therapy, speech-language pathology, audiology, pharmacy, nutrition, respiratory care, laboratory technology, radiologic technology, mental health services, emergency medical services or an eligible licensed or certified health profession. For more information, contact the New Mexico Commission on Higher Education at http://hed.state.nm.us.

The Medical Student Loan-For-Service
This program provides loans of up to $12,000 per year to physicians and physician assistants who commit to practicing in designated shortage areas in the state. Applicants must be New Mexico residents attending a U.S. public school of medicine. Preference is given for students who attend the UNM School of Medicine. For details, visit the New Mexico Commission on Higher Education at http://hed.state.nm.us.

The Nursing Student Loan-For-Service
This loan repayment program provides loans of up to $12,000 per year to nursing students who commit to practicing in designated shortage areas in the state. Applicants must be New Mexico residents attending New Mexico postsecondary institutions. To learn more, visit the New Mexico Commission on Higher Education at http://hed.state.nm.us.

The Health Professional Loan Repayment Program
This program provides loan repayment of up to $12,500 per year to practicing health professionals who commit to practicing in designated shortage areas in the state. Applicants must be New Mexico residents and must be practicing allied health professionals, physicians and physician assistants, advanced practical nurses, osteopathic physicians and osteopathic physician assistants, dentists, optometrists or podiatrists. For more details, visit the New Mexico Commission on Higher Education at http://hed.state.nm.us.

The Minority Doctoral Assistance Loan-For-Service
This program provides loans of up to $25,000 per year to ethnic minorities and women who teach in academic disciplines in which they are underrepresented in New Mexico public colleges and universities and who commit to teaching at the sponsoring New Mexico institution for at least one year for each year of the loan. Applicants must be New Mexico residents who have a bachelor's or master's degree from a New Mexico four-year public postsecondary institution and must attend a doctoral program full-time at an eligible institution. For more information, contact the New Mexico Commission on Higher Education at http://hed.state.nm.us.

The Teacher Loan Repayment Program
This program is aimed at pre-K-12 teachers in high-risk positions at public schools in New Mexico. The amount depends on the school's need and the amount of the loan. Recipients must serve for at least two years. To learn more, visit the New Mexico Commission on Higher Education at http://hed.state.nm.us.

Law School Loan Repayment Programs
A number of individual law schools in the state offer loan repayment programs for graduates who agree to work at public

interest or government agencies. These include the University of New Mexico School of Law.

686. New York

The NYS Regents Physician Loan Forgiveness Award Program
This program supports medical and dental students with awards of up to $10,000 a year, for up to four years. Applicants must be full-time students in eligible programs at New York State schools and be New York State residents. Recipients must work one year for each year of the award in a designated physician-shortage area of the state, and the minimum amount of service is two years even if the award is only received for one year. Priority is given to students who are economically disadvantaged or members of a historically underrepresented minority group and graduates of the SEEK, College Discovery, EOP or HEOP programs. For more information, visit the New York Higher Education Services Corporation at http://www.highered.nysed. gov/kiap/scholarships/.

NYC Teaching Fellows
This program has placed over 3,000 teachers in New York City's public schools. Recipients teach and receive a regular teacher's salary and benefits, AmeriCorps program benefits of up to $4,725 a year and a subsidized master's of education at an eligible New York City college or university. Priority is given to high-need areas, including math, science, special education and bilingual education. For details, visit http://www. nycteachingfellows.org.

Law School Loan Repayment Programs
A number of individual law schools in the state offer loan repayment programs for graduates who agree to work at public interest or government agencies. These include Albany Law School of Union University, Benjamin N. Cardozo School of Law at Yeshiva University, Brooklyn Law School, City University of New York School of Law at Queens College, Columbia University School of Law, Cornell Law School, Fordham University School of Law, Hofstra University School of Law*, New York Law School, New York University School of Law, Pace University School of Law and Touro College Jacob D. Fuchsberg Law Center.

687. North Carolina

NCMS Foundation Community Practitioner Program
This program assists health professionals who provide care to the state's underserved communities. Through Federal Loan Repayment, up to $50,000 for a two-year commitment and up to $35,000 each for up to two additional years may be repaid. For State Loan Repayment, the amount is up to $100,000 for physicians doing OB for a four-year commitment and up to $70,000 for physicians not doing OB work for a four-year commitment. In addition, the programs add a 39 percent tax stipend to offset increased tax liability. For recipients with low loans or no loans, the *High Needs Service Bonus* provides up to $50,000 for physicians doing OB work for a four-year commitment and up to $35,000 for physicians not doing OB work for a four-year commitment. For details, visit http://www.ncmedsoc.org.

The Master's Nurse Scholars Program (M-NSP) Graduate Program
This program helps North Carolina residents who attend an eligible master's nursing program in North Carolina. Selection is based on academics, leadership potential and desire to practice nursing. The award is up to $6,000 per year for full-time students and up to $3,000 per year for part-time students, and it is renewable. Recipients must agree to work full-time as a master's-prepared nurse or to teach in a nurse education program in North Carolina one year for each year of the award. For more information, visit the North Carolina State Education Assistance Authority at http://www.ncseaa.edu/orc_nsp.htm.

The Nurse Scholars Program (NSP), Undergraduate Program
This program aids North Carolina residents who attend an eligible Registered Nurse (RN) program at a North Carolina college, university or hospital. Selection is based on academics, leadership potential and desire to practice nursing. The award is up to $5,000 per year and is renewable. Recipients agree to work full-time as a Registered Nurse in North Carolina for one year for each year of the award. For details, visit the College Foundation of North Carolina at http://www.cfnc.org.

Law School Loan Repayment Programs
A number of individual law schools in the state offer loan repayment programs for graduates who agree to work at public inter-

est or government agencies. These include the Duke University School of Law, North Carolina Central University School of Law, University of North Carolina School of Law and Wake Forest School of Law.

688. North Dakota

The STEM Occupations Student Loan Program
This program helps students who have graduated in a technology-related field, interned with a North Dakota business and worked in a technology occupation in the state for one year. The awards forgive up to $1,000 per year for each year of eligible employment up to a maximum of five years. For details, visit the North Dakota University System website at http://www.ndus.edu.

The Teacher Shortage Loan Forgiveness Program
This program assists students who teach grade levels or subject areas with teacher shortages in North Dakota. The awards forgive up to $1,000 per year for each year of eligible employment up to a maximum of five years. For more details, visit the North Dakota University System website at http://www.ndus.edu.

The Physician State/Community Matching Loan Repayment Program
Dentist Loan Repayment Program
Long Term Care Nursing Scholarship and Loan Repayment Program
Nurse Practitioners, Physician Assistants and Certified Nurse Midwives State/Community Matching Loan Repayment Program
These programs are all for health professionals who work at eligible facilities in the state. For more information, visit the North Dakota Department of Health, Office of Community Assistance website at http://www.ndhealth.gov.

689. Ohio

The Nurse Education Assistance Loan Program (NEALP)
This program helps Ohio students who plan to attend or are currently attending an eligible Ohio nurse education program. The loans are up to $3,000 per year for up to four years and may be cancelled at 20 percent per year for a maximum of

five years when recipients work in nursing in Ohio. For more information on this program, visit the Ohio Board of Regents website at http://www.odh.ohio.gov.

The Ohio Physician Loan Repayment Program (OPLRP)
This repayment program supports primary care physicians in family practice, internal medicine, pediatrics or OB/GYN who agree to practice full-time in a Health Professional Shortage Area (HPSA) and to treat a percentage of Medicaid and Medicare patients equal to the percentage in their service area in Ohio. The physicians receive up to $20,000 per year in loan repayment for up to four years and must work a minimum of two years. For more details, visit the Ohio Board of Regents website at http://www.odh.ohio.gov.

Law School Loan Repayment Programs
A number of individual law schools in the state offer loan repayment programs for graduates who agree to work at public interest or government agencies. These include the Capital University Law School, Case Western Reserve University School of Law and Ohio State University Michael E. Moritz College of Law.

690. Oklahoma

The Family Practice Resident Rural Scholarship Program
This scholarship assists Oklahoma residents who attend an accredited family practice or family medicine residency program in the state. Participants receive a $1,000 loan per month that is forgiven after they complete their residency training and work for one month for each month of the loan in an approved rural community. Participants must work for at least 12 months to receive credit on their loans. For more information, visit the Physician Manpower Training Commission website at http://www.pmtc.ok.gov/famprac.htm.

The Nursing Student Assistance Program
This program helps Oklahoma nursing students pursuing LPN, ADN, BSN or MSN degrees who agree to practice in Oklahoma communities, with an emphasis on rural communities. Participants receive loans of up to $2,500 per year. One year of the

loan amount is forgiven for each year that the participants work in an approved health institution. For more details, visit the Physician Manpower Training Commission website at http://www.pmtc.ok.gov/nsap.htm.

The Physician/Community Match Loan Program

The program aids primary care physicians who set up practices in eligible Oklahoma communities, typically with populations of less than 10,000. Physicians may receive a $20,000 lump sum for which they must work at least two years in the community or a lump sum of $40,000 for which they must work at least three years. To learn more, visit the Physician Manpower Training Commission website at http://www.pmtc.ok.gov/physcmp.htm.

The Rural Medical Education Scholarship Loan Program

This program supports Oklahoma residents who are enrolled in medical school in primary care specialties and who plan to practice medicine in rural communities of the state with populations of 7,500 or less. The loan is up to $42,000 over four years. One year is forgiven for each year of practice in the eligible community with a minimum of two years of service. For more information, visit the Physician Manpower Training Commission website at http://www.pmtc.state.ok.us.

The Future Teachers Scholarship

This award helps Oklahoma resident students who plan to teach the critical shortage areas of special education, math, foreign language, science and English in Oklahoma public schools for

---

Are loan forgiveness programs only for state residents?

It all depends on the program. Some programs are only for state residents while others are for any student who is studying or working in the state. You need to be sure to look at the programs not only in your home state but also in any of the states that you might consider working in after you graduate from school.

a minimum of three years. Students must be nominated by their college based on high school GPA or ranking, ACT or SAT score, admission into a professional education program or undergraduate record. The amount of the scholarship is from $500 to $1,500 per year. For more details, visit the Oklahoma State Department of Education website at http://www.okhighered.org/admin-fac/FinAidResources/fts.shtml.

The Teacher Shortage Employment Incentive Program (TSEIP)
This program assists students who graduate from an Oklahoma accredited teacher education program with teaching certification in math or science and who agree to teach in Oklahoma public secondary schools for a minimum of five years. The program reimburses student loans or pays cash to recipients. To learn more, visit the Oklahoma State Department of Education website at http://www.okhighered.org/otc/tseip.shtml.

691. Oregon

The Teacher Loan Forgiveness Program
This program forgives up to $5,000 of recipients' eligible loans. Recipients must have been employed a minimum of five consecutive years as full-time teachers in designated elementary or secondary schools. To learn more, visit the Oregon Student Assistance Commission website at http://www.ode.state.or.us.

The Rural Health Services (RHS) Program
This program supports physicians, nurse practitioners and physician assistants who practice in rural areas in the state. Participants receive loan repayments of up to $25,000 per year. Physicians may have up to 20 percent of their loans repaid for up to five years and must work at least three years in an eligible area. Nurse practitioners and physician assistants may have up to 25 percent of their loans repaid for up to four years and must work at least two years in an eligible area. To learn more, visit the Oregon Office of Rural Health website at http://www.ohsu.edu/xd/outreach/oregon-rural-health/.

Law School Loan Repayment Programs
A number of individual law schools in the state offer loan repayment programs for graduates who agree to work at public interest or government agencies. These include the Lewis and Clark Law School and University of Oregon School of Law.

692. Pennsylvania

The Primary Health Care Practitioners Loan Repayment Program
This program assists practitioners who agree to serve in designated Health Professional Shortage Areas (HPSAs), especially at non-profit community-based or hospital-based primary care centers. Physicians may practice in the following primary care specialties: family practice, internal medicine, pediatrics, obstetrics/gynecology, osteopathic general practice, general dentists, certified registered nurse practitioners (CRNPs) practicing in the above primary care specialties, physician assistants (PA-C) practicing in the above primary care specialties and certified nurse midwives (CNM). Practitioners must work for at least three years at an eligible site and a minimum of four years for the maximum amount of loan repayment. The amount repaid per year is $6,000 to $22,400 depending on the number of years of service and experience. To learn more about this program, visit the Pennsylvania Department of Health website at http://www.dsf.health.state.pa.us/health.

Law School Loan Repayment Programs
A number of individual law schools in the state offer loan repayment programs for graduates who agree to work at public interest or government agencies. These include the Duquesne University School of Law, Pennsylvania State University Dickinson School of Law, Temple University James E. Beasley School of Law, University of Pennsylvania Law School and Villanova University School of Law.

693. Rhode Island

Rhode Island Department of Health
The Health Professional Loan Repayment Program (RI HPLRP) assists health professionals who agree to serve full-time for two

years in approved public or non-profit agencies serving health professional shortage areas. Participants may work in the field as physicians, dentists, nurse practitioners, certified nurse midwives, physician assistants and registered dental hygienists. Recent amounts repaid per year are up to $35,000 for physicians and dentists, up to $8,500 for physician assistants, nurse practitioners and certified midwives and up to $7,000 for registered dental hygienists. For more information, visit the department's website at http://www.health.state.ri.us.

694. South Carolina

South Carolina Center for Teacher Recruitment
The Teaching Fellows Program awards fellowships to up to 200 high school seniors with high academic achievement, a history of service to the school and community and a desire to teach in South Carolina. Teaching Fellows participate in advanced enrichment programs including opportunities in professional development during summer, are involved with communities and businesses and receive up to $6,000 in annual scholarships for four years while studying to earn teacher certification. Fellows agree to teach in South Carolina one year for each year that they receive the fellowship. Get more information at http://www.cerra.org.

695. South Dakota

South Dakota Department of Health
The Rural Healthcare Facility Recruitment Assistance Program awards $5,000 to health professionals who agree to serve full-time for two years at eligible employing facilities in South Dakota. Eligible practitioners include dietitians, nutritionists, nurses, occupational, respiratory, laboratory, and physical therapists, laboratory, medical, and radiologic technologists, pharmacists and paramedics. For details, visit http://www.doh.sd.gov.

696. Tennessee

Tennessee Student Assistance Corporation
The Minority Teaching Fellows Program assists high school senior and continuing college students who are minority residents of Tennessee entering the teaching field. Recipients are awarded $5,000 per year while pursuing a teacher certification and must agree to teach at a K-12 level in a Tennessee public school for one year for each award year. Visit http://www.tn.gov/collegepays/ for more information.

Tennessee Teaching Scholars Program
The Tennessee Teaching Scholars Program aids college juniors, seniors and post baccalaureate candidates who are residents of Tennessee and are admitted to state-approved teacher education programs at eligible Tennessee colleges or universities. Recipients must agree to teach for one year in a Tennessee public school for each award year. For details, visit http://www.tn.gov/collegepays/.

Tennessee Department of Health
The State Loan Repayment Program assists health and dental physicians and mid-level practitioners who serve a minimum of three years in local, underserved areas. Grants are given to preventative medicine physicians, internists, obstetricians, pediatricians, psychiatrists, nurse practitioners, nurse midwives and physician assistants. For details, visit http://health.state.tn.us.

697. Texas

The Teach for Texas Loan Repayment Program (TFTLRP)
This program assists current Texas teachers who agree to teach full-time for five years at a Texas public school located in either a critical shortage field or a designated community experiencing a critical shortage of teachers. The amount repaid per year is the greater of $1,200 or the calculated amount required to repay the loan within 10 years. For more information, visit the Texas Higher Education Coordinating Board website at http://www.collegeforalltexans.com.

The Nursing Education Loan Repayment Program (NELRP)
This program assists full-time employed, registered nurses in repaying educational loans in exchange for their commitment to serve full-time for two or three years at an eligible facility located in a shortage area. Applicants must be U.S. citizens. For more details, visit the Texas Higher Education Coordinating Board website at http://www.collegeforalltexans.com.

The Physician Education Loan Repayment Program Part III (Texas Family Practice Residency Training Program)
This program supports second- or third-year, licensed residents in approved Texas Family Practice Residency Training Programs or full-time faculty who've completed an approved Texas Family Practice Residency Training Program after the July 1, 1994. If the applicants are still in training, they must agree to practice full-time for a year per award year in a shortage area or rural county or work as a faculty member in an approved Texas Family Practice Residency Training Program, starting within three months of residency completion. If the applicants are faculty members, they must agree to begin serving full-time for a year per award year in an approved Texas Family Practice Residency Training Program within three months of the application deadline. Physician recipients must agree to serve full-time at a site located in a Texas Primary Care Health Professional Shortage Area, a rural Texas county or an approved Texas Family Practice Residency Training Program. The minimum amount repaid per year is $9,000 for up to two years. For more information and this program, visit the Texas Higher Education Coordinating Board website at http://www.collegeforalltexans.com.

The Physician Education Loan Repayment Program Parts I and II (For Post Residency Practicing Physicians) (PELRP I and II)
This program aids currently licensed physicians who have earned board certification within the past six years in an approved specialty or who have satisfactorily completed an approved postgraduate program. Recipients must agree to work for at least a year in an approved specialty at an approved practice site. The amount repaid per year is up to $9,000. For more details, visit the Texas Higher Education Coordinating Board website at http://www.collegeforalltexans.com.

The Professional Nurses' Student Loan Repayment Program
This program assists Texas, non-resident or qualified foreign resident licensed nurses who demonstrate financial need and have been practicing in Texas for no less than a year immediately preceding repayment of loans. Recipients must have registered for Selective Service or otherwise be exempt from its requirements. The amount repaid to the student will not exceed the outstanding unpaid principal and interest or $2,000. For more information, visit the Texas Higher Education Coordinating Board website at http://www.collegeforalltexans.com.

698. Utah

Utah Higher Education Assistance Authority
The Terrel H. Bell Teaching Incentive Loan (TIL) aids high school seniors and postsecondary students in pursuit of a degree in teacher education. Students must complete the requisite number of credit hours designated by their particular institutions. The TIL will cover up to four years (eight semesters) of the costs of full-time tuition and general fees. Recipients must be Utah residents, attend a participating Utah institution and agree to teach in a Utah public or private school. For more information, visit https://uheaa.org.

The Utah Health Care Workforce Financial Assistance Program
This program offers professional education scholarships and loan repayment assistance to health care professionals in Utah's underserved areas. Fully-licensed professionals who are eligible for this program include dentists, non-physician mental health therapists, nurses, physicians and physician assistants, although primary care specialties will receive priority. Recipients must agree to work at least two years in a state of Utah-designated underserved area. To learn more, visit the Utah Office of Primary Care and Rural Health at http://health.utah.gov/primarycare/.

The Nursing Education Loan Repayment Program (NELRP)
This program aids registered nurses in repaying their educational loans in exchange for their commitment to serve in areas designated as experiencing a shortage of nurses. To learn more, visit the Utah Office of Primary Care and Rural Health at http://health.utah.gov/primarycare/.

How do states decide which careers to offer loan forgiveness programs for?

Loan forgiveness programs are established by states either to encourage more students to enter specific career fields where there is a shortage or to entice students to work in underserved areas—often inner cities or rural communities. If you want to work in one of these professions then these programs are great deals. Especially when you start out in a career it can be a wonderful experience to work in an area where you are needed the most.

---

699. Vermont

The Vermont Educational Loan Repayment Program
This program assists primary care practitioner, nursing and dental students at schools in Vermont who agree to work in the state for at least one year. Selection is based on essays, recommendations and commitment to working in Vermont. To learn more, visit the website of the Office of Primary Care and Area Health Education Centers (AHEC) Program at http://www.uvm.edu/medicine/ahec/.

700. Virginia

The VDOT Engineering Scholarship Program
This program offers internship opportunities and scholarships to undergraduates studying civil engineering in exchange for their employment during summers and upon graduation. The program prepares students to enter the Engineering Development Program after graduating with their B.S. in civil engineering. For more details, visit the website of the State Council of Higher Education for Virginia at http://www.schev.edu.

The Nursing Scholarship Program
This program assists students who agree to serve in the nursing profession in Virginia. The amount repaid is based on the duration of the recipient's service, with every $100 of aid warranting one month of service. To learn more, visit the website of the

State Council of Higher Education for Virginia at http://www. schev.edu for more information.

The Virginia Teaching Scholarship Loan Program (VTSLP)
This program offers scholarship-loans of up to $3,720 to Virginia resident students who wish to teach in an underserved area of Virginia. Males seeking to teach at the elementary or middle school level as well as minorities in all teaching fields are eligible. Loans are totally forgiven when students agree to teach for four semesters in a Virginia public school located in a designated critical shortage field. Applicants must be full- or part-time students beyond their sophomore year and maintain a grade point average of no less than 2.7. To learn more about this program, visit the website of the State Council of Higher Education for Virginia at http://www.schev.edu.

The NHSC Virginia Loan Repayment Program
The loan forgiveness program offers assistance to students who agree to practice in a designated Health Professional Shortage Area. For more details, visit the Virginia Department of Health website at http://www.vdh.virginia.gov.

The Virginia Loan Repayment Program
This program aids students who serve in either a state-designated Health Professional Shortage Area (HPSA) or a Virginia Medically Underserved Area. Visit the Virginia Department of Health website at http://www.vdh.virginia.gov for more information.

The National Health Service Corp-Virginia Loan Repayment Program (NHSC-VRLP) and the Virginia Loan Repayment Program
This program aids primary care clinicians in exchange for their commitment to practice full-time for at least two years at an eligible site located in one of Virginia's underserved area. Applicants must be fully trained allopathic and osteopathic physicians with specialties in family/general practice, general internal medicine, general pediatrics, obstetrics/gynecology or psychiatry, primary care physician assistants, or for NHSC-VRLP only, primary care physician assistants or primary care nurse practitioners. Applicants must be U.S. citizens and work full-time in primary care or psychiatry services. The amount repaid is up to $50,000 for two years of service and up to $85,000 for three years of service. For more information, visit

the Virginia Department of Health website at http://www.vdh.
virginia.gov.

Law School Loan Repayment Programs
A number of individual law schools in the state offer loan re-
payment programs for graduates who agree to work at public
interest or government agencies. These include the Regent
University School of Law, University of Virginia School of Law,
Washington and Lee University School of Law and William &
Mary School of Law.

701. Washington

Health Professional Loan Repayment
Licensed primary health care professionals can receive assistance if they agree to provide primary health care service
in underserved areas as designated by the state. The program
offers up to $25,000 per year for the first three years and up to
$35,000 each for the fourth and fifth year. Applicants must make
a match with an eligible site and need not be residents of the
state of Washington. To learn more, visit the Washington Student Achievement Council website at http://www.wsac.wa.gov.

Washington Student Achievement Council
The council offers a list of loan forgiveness programs for Washington students on its website. Visit http://www.wsac.wa.gov
to learn more.

Law School Loan Repayment Programs
A number of individual law schools in the state offer loan re-
payment programs for graduates who agree to work at public
interest or government agencies. These include the Gonzaga
University School of Law, Seattle University School of Law and
University of Washington School of Law.

702. West Virginia

West Virginia Higher Education Policy Commission
The Medical Student Loan Program offers loans of up to $5,000
to students who have been accepted or are enrolled full-time in

a West Virginia school of medicine or osteopathy. Applicants must not be in default on any previous loan. The award is renewable based on availability and eligibility. Students must repay the loan at 8 percent interest or loans may be forgiven up to $5,000 for each year of full-time practice in an eligible underserved area or critical shortage field in West Virginia. For more information, visit http://www.cfwv.com.

703. Wisconsin

The Minority Teacher Loan Program
This program offers assistance to minority residents of the state of Wisconsin who are undergraduate juniors or seniors at an independent or University of Wisconsin institution in a program leading to teacher licensure. Recipients must agree to teach in a Wisconsin school district in which minority students make up 29 percent or more of the total enrollment or in a district that participates in the inter-district pupil transfer program. One-quarter of the loan is forgiven for each year in an eligible district, or if the recipient does not teach in an eligible district, the loan must be repaid at 5 percent interest. To learn more, visit the State of Wisconsin Higher Educational Aids Board at http://heab.state.wi.us.

The Nursing Student Loan Program
This program provides assistance to residents of Wisconsin who are enrolled at least half-time at an eligible in-state institution in a program leading to nurse licensure. Up to $3,000 a year can be awarded, with a maximum of $15,000 overall. Recipients must agree to work as licensed nurses in the state of Wisconsin, and for each of the first two years recipients meet eligibility requirements, 25 percent of the loan is forgiven. The remaining balance must be repaid at no more than 5 percent interest. For more details, visit the State of Wisconsin Higher Educational Aids Board at http://heab.state.wi.us.

The Teacher Education Loan Program
This program offers loans to residents of the state of Wisconsin who are enrolled in teacher education programs at the Milwaukee Teacher Education Center (MTEC). Recipients must agree to teach in the Wisconsin school district operating

under Chapter 119 of the Wisconsin State Statutes, First Class City School System (currently consisting of only Milwaukee Public Schools). One-half of the loan is forgiven for each year the recipient teaches in the eligible school district, or recipients must repay the loan at an interest rate of 5 percent. For more information, visit the State of Wisconsin Higher Educational Aids Board at http://heab.state.wi.us.

The Teacher of the Visually Impaired Loan Program
This program provides assistance to Wisconsin residents who are enrolled at least half-time at an in-state or eligible out-of-state institution in a program leading to licensure in teaching of the visually impaired or as orientation and mobility instructors. Up to $10,000 can be awarded per year with a maximum award of $40,000 overall. Recipients must agree to be licensed teachers or orientation or mobility instructors in a Wisconsin school district, the Wisconsin Center for the Blind and Visually Impaired or a cooperative educational service agency. One-quarter of the loan is forgiven for each of the first two years recipients teach and meet the eligibility criteria, and 50 percent is forgiven for the third year. Otherwise the loan must be repaid at an interest rate of 5 percent. To learn more, visit the State of Wisconsin Higher Educational Aids Board at http://heab.state.wi.us.

Wisconsin's Health Professions Loan Assistance Program
This program awards up to $50,000 to health care professionals, including general and pediatric dentists, dental hygienists, primary care physicians, obstetricians, psychiatrists, physician assistants, nurse practitioners and certified nurse midwives. There is a three-year service obligation. Primary care professional applicants must practice in Health Professional Shortage Areas designated federally by the state of Wisconsin. Dentists and dental hygienists must practice in Dental Health Professional Shortage Areas. For more information, visit the Wisconsin Office of Rural Health at http://www.worh.org.

Law School Loan Repayment Programs
A number of individual law schools in the state offer loan repayment programs for graduates who agree to work at public interest or government agencies. These include the Marquette University School of Law and University of Wisconsin Law School.

704. Wyoming

University of Wyoming
The University of Wyoming participates in the Washington, Wyoming, Alaska, Montana and Idaho (WWAMI) program that places 10 Wyoming resident medical students at the University of Wyoming for their first year of study and at the University of Washington for their second. Third and fourth years are spent in clinical sites around the WWAMI area. Applicants must reimburse the University of Wyoming for the costs of education plus interest or complete a minimum of three years of practice following the completion of their medical education. Visit http://www.uwyo.edu/wwami/ for more information.

If I take advantage of one of these loan forgiveness programs, how long will it take for me to pay off my loan?

Each program has its own rules, but in general most programs are set up to pay back all of your loans within four or five years. As long as your loan amount does not exceed the maximum that the program will pay, you will be forgiven anywhere from 20 to 25 percent of what you owe each year. Be sure to check the specific details of each program since most have a maximum amount that they will pay out. If your loan exceeds the maximum you may still have to pay that amount yourself.

Military Options

Soldiering Your Way To An Education

The military has long provided many opportunities to get an education. Not only does the military run its own higher education academies, but all service members also are eligible to receive a variety of educational benefits. The military isn't only interested in helping former members transition back into civilian life. It needs highly educated soldiers. To meet this need it offers to pay for your education before you enter the military through the extensive Reserve Officers Training Corps programs (ROTC), which are established at most colleges. There is also an additional benefit when it comes to life after the military, which is that most employers view the experience gained from military service to be a huge personal asset.

The major requirement for taking advantage of these educational opportunities is that you must serve in the military. Not all service has to be in the full-time, active-duty military. Some benefits are directed to those who serve part-time in the Reserves and National Guard. There are also some benefits designed for the spouses and children of military service people. There are even a few scholarships for the grandchildren of service members.

So pay attention soldier, and you just might get your education for free.

705.

The Reserve Officers Training Corps Program

Each branch of the military runs its own ROTC (pronounced ROT-SEE) program that basically pays for most or all of your tuition and related expenses at almost any college. In exchange you must attend training during the school year and, often, for part of your summers. There are usually two ways to enter ROTC. First, while you are still in high school you can compete for a four-year, full-tuition ROTC scholarship. Second, once you are in college you can take ROTC courses as an elective and if you want to continue with the program you can compete for a ROTC scholarship that will cover your remaining years in college.

If you receive a ROTC scholarship, when you graduate from school you must also serve in the military for a specific number of years. Often it is based on the number of years you received the scholarship. If the Army ROTC, for example, paid for four years of your education then you owe the Army four years of service. You can fulfill this obligation either by joining as an active-duty soldier or through serving in the Reserves or the Army National Guard. However, if you elect to serve through non-active duty you will usually have to commit more time.

Besides paying your way through college, the other major advantage of all ROTC programs is that because of your training during college when you graduate you enter the military as an officer. In fact, most of the officers in the military come through the ROTC program. Each branch of the armed forces runs its ROTC program slightly differently. You can learn more by visiting the appropriate service's website or recruiting center.

706. Navy and Marine ROTC

http://www.navy.com/careers/nrotc/

The Navy ROTC provides tuition support and prepares you for service as a commissioned officer in the Naval or Marine Corps. There are both four-year and two- and three-year scholarships available. The scholarships cover your tuition expenses, books, fees and a living allowance stipend. The Navy also runs the Navy Nurse Corps scholarship program which is only for students pursuing bachelor's degrees in nursing (BSN). When you graduate you will be commissioned as an Ensign in the Naval Reserve or Second Lieutenant in the Marine Corps Reserve. You will typically have to serve for eight years with at least three to four years in active duty status. You can apply directly on the Navy ROTC website or pick up an application at a Navy recruiting center. To apply you must be a U.S. citizen between the ages of 17 and 23 and graduate from high school or receive your GED. You must also meet minimum SAT or ACT test scores.

707. Army ROTC

http://www.armyrotc.com

The Army ROTC program creates more than 75 percent of all Army officers. You can apply at one of 600 schools for scholarships worth up to $70,000 for tuition, fees and monthly stipends. The awards are based on merit including academic achievements, extracurricular activities and interviews. The Army also offers the Army ROTC Nurse Officer Program, which has four-, three- and two-year scholarships. When you graduate from the ROTC program you will be commissioned as a Second Lieutenant and must either serve part-time in the Army National Guard or Army Reserve or full-time on active duty. You can apply for the four-year ROTC scholarship directly on the Army ROTC website or by visiting your nearest Army recruiting center.

708. Air Force ROTC

http://www.afrotc.com

The Air Force ROTC offers scholarships for entering college freshmen and students who are already in college. There are three types of scholarships for high school students. Type 1 scholarships pay full college tuition, most fees and $900 per year for books. Type 2 scholarships pay college tuition and most fees up to $18,000 and $900 per year for books. Most of the recipients of Type 1 and Type 2 scholarships are in technical fields such as engineering, chemistry and meteorology. Type 7 scholarships pay college tuition up to the equivalent of the in-state rate and $900 per year for books. All three scholarships also provide a monthly stipend to recipients. You can apply directly on the Air Force ROTC website or by visiting an Air Force recruiting center. You must be a U.S. citizen, graduate from high school or hold an equivalent certificate, be between the ages of 17 and 30, complete a physical exam and meet minimum SAT or ACT scores.

709.

The Montgomery G.I. Bill

The Montgomery G.I. Bill–affectionately called MGIB–was signed into law on June 22, 1944, by President Franklin D. Roosevelt. Originally known as the "G.I. Bill of Rights," it provided a variety of educational benefits for returning veterans from World War II. Since then the bill has been amended several times and benefits expanded to not only help veterans return to civilian life but also as an incentive to encourage enlistment in today's all-volunteer military forces.

710. G.I. Bill–Active Duty

http://www.benefits.va.gov/gibill/
The G.I. Bill provides up to three years of education benefits for veterans for degree and certificate programs, flight training, apprenticeship, on-the-job training and correspondence courses. If you have served in the active-duty military you will need to take advantage of your G.I. Bill within 10 years of being discharged.

711. G.I. Bill–Selected Reserve

http://www.benefits.va.gov/gibill/
Like the G.I. Bill for active duty service members, the MGIB for Selected Reserve covers the Army Reserve, Navy Reserve, Air Force Reserve, Marine Corps Reserve and Coast Guard Reserve, the Army National Guard and the Air National Guard. You must continue to serve in the Reserves during the time that you take advantage of the benefits.

712. G.I. Bill–Survivors' and Dependents' Educational Assistance Program (DEA)

http://www.benefits.va.gov/gibill/
The G.I. Bill provides what is known as the Survivors' and Dependents' Educational Assistance Program (DEA), which gives up to 45 months of education benefits for eligible dependents of veterans who are permanently and totally disabled or who died while on active duty or as a result of a service-related condition.

713.

Veterans Educational Assistance Program (VEAP)

While in the military you can elect to participate in VEAP, which deducts money from your military pay each month. Uncle Sam will match your contributions on a $2 for $1 basis. You can use this money for degree, certificate, correspondence, apprenticeship, on-the-job training programs and vocational flight training programs. You have 10 years to use your VEAP benefits and if you have money left over, your portion of the remaining contribution is refunded. Learn more at http://www.benefits.va.gov/gibill/.

714.

State-sponsored National Guard benefits

As a member of the National Guard, you already qualify for the Montgomery G.I. Bill for Selected Reserve. Some states offer additional benefits to supplement the G.I. Bill. For example, the Wisconsin *Army National Guard Tuition Grant* provides up to eight semesters of full tuition benefits. You can even use your benefits at select schools outside of the Wisconsin.

Get more information about your state's National Guard benefits by visiting these websites. For the Air National Guard visit http://www.ang.af.mil and for the Army National Guard visit https://www.nationalguard.com.

715.

Other state benefits

States also provide military benefits to active-duty, veteran and even dependents of service members. Check with your state's Department of Veterans' Affairs. Texas, for example, offers tuition waivers for veterans, which means if you were a Texas resident at the time you joined the military you may be exempt from having to pay tuition at public colleges and universities after you are discharged. A good resource is Military.com, which offers a summary of state benefits at http://www.military.com/benefits/veteran-state-benefits/state-veterans-benefits-directory.html.

716.

Military Academies

The military runs its own higher-education academies that provide both a general college-level education with specialized military training. If you are accepted into a military academy you receive a full four-year scholarship that covers tuition, books, a monthly stipend and a computer. You also get free room and board.

To be accepted at a military academy you must be an unmarried U.S. citizen between the ages of 17 and 22. Selection is based on academic performance, skills, talents and achievements. Some academies require nomination by a member of Congress. Graduates are commissioned as officers and must serve for a specific number of years. Generally, military academy students intend to make the military a career.

U.S. Military Academy at West Point
West Point, NY 10996
845-938-4041
http://www.usma.edu

U.S. Naval Academy
Candidate Guidance Office
121 Blake Road
Annapolis, MD 21402-1300
410-293-1858
http://www.usna.edu

U.S. Air Force Academy
HQ USAFA/RRS
2304 Cadet Drive, Suite 2300
USAF Academy, CO 80840
800-443-9266
http://www.usafa.af.mil

U.S. Coast Guard Academy
31 Mohegan Avenue
New London, CT 06320
800-883-USCG
http://www.cga.edu

U.S. Merchant Marine Academy
300 Steamboat Road
Kings Point, NY 11024
516-726-5644
http://www.usmma.edu

717.

Enroll in a Servicemembers Opportunity College (SOC)

Being in the military can pose several challenges to getting your degree. You often have no control over your relocation from one base to another. You might get an assignment on a ship or at a base in a foreign country. You may receive specialized training that is not always recognized by colleges. To help you earn a degree, SOC was created and today is a consortium of more than 1,700 colleges and universities that provide educational opportunities for service members and their families.

By enrolling in an SOC-approved program, you can start or continue your education at military installations worldwide and SOC member colleges accept each other's credits as transfer credits should you need to relocate and switch schools. If you are in an isolated location you can also take or continue your education through distance learning courses. Get more information at http://www.soc.aascu.org.

How many years will I owe the military if I accept a military scholarship?

It depends on the program. In most cases it's a one-to-one trade. If the military pays for all four years of your education, then you owe at least four years of service. Sometimes you can serve in the Reserves instead of in active duty. However, if you are able to do this you will usually owe more time such as six years in the Reserves instead of four years in active duty.

718.

Take all the free tests you can

You can earn college credit by passing special exams. While civilians must pay for each exam, as an active military serviceperson (or veteran) you can take these exams for free. Some of the free exams that you can take are the undergraduate-level Excelsior College Examinations, College Level Examination Program (CLEP) and the DANTES Subject Standardized Test (DSST). Contact your education officer or test control officer for more information. The DANTES (Defense Activity for Non-Traditional Education Support) program administers examinations at more than 560 military installations to about 150,000 military personnel per year. Depending on your college, you can use your scores on DANTES tests to get credit. To learn more about the DANTES test program, visit http://www.dantes.doded.mil.

719.

Earn credit for your military training

Many colleges automatically give you course credit for your military service. Joliet Junior College in Illinois, for example, gives credit for physical education and biology to all members of the armed services. You may also be able to get additional credit for specialized training and education that you receive while in the military. For example, any College Level General or Subject Matter Tests taken at the United States Armed Forces Institute (USAFI) may count for credit.

To get credit for your military training, you need to provide documentation. Often this will come from one of the following sources:

720. Joint Services Transcript

One of the problems with earning credit for your military training is determining if it is equivalent to a college-level course and if so which one. To help sort things out the JST program was designed to evaluate the experience of service members for the purpose of granting college credit. While the individual college will decide whether or not to accept the JST recommendation for credit, the program has been widely adopted and is very helpful in allowing you to get credit for your military work. Website: https://jst.doded.mil

721. Select a program that maximizes credits

Colleges typically require that you take 25 percent of your courses at their institution. However, different institutions have different policies for transfer credit. It's important to understand the requirements so you can select a program that will allow you to maximize credits from the JST program.

722. Community College of the Air Force (CCAF)

http://www.au.af.mil/au/ccaf/

The Air Force has taken a different approach to the education of its service members. It has established the Community College of the Air Force, which is made up of over 125 military schools and affiliated civilian institutions. The CCAF keeps a transcript for all students, and those who take enough courses and meet all requirements can earn an associate degree in one of more than 66 areas in applied science. CCAF is open to all Air Force active duty, Air National Guard and Air Force Reserve Command personnel. The CCAF is a fully accredited college, and coursework along with degrees are accepted at most civilian colleges and universities. Since granting its first degree in 1977, the CCAF has given more than 237,000 associate degrees.

723. Save yourself a big headache by getting a copy of your VMET (Verification of Military Experience and Training) documents within 12 months of separation

Documentation of your military training can earn you college credits and save you money on tuition. Be sure to obtain your VMET documents within 12 months of your separation or 24 months of your retirement from the military. You can get your VMET papers at your transition support office.

724.

Apply for military and veteran scholarships

Many veteran organizations provide scholarships to veterans, their spouses and dependents. Contact these organizations to see if they offer scholarships that apply to you, and also get in touch with your local and state military and veteran organizations. You can find a good list of veteran associations, many of which offer scholarships, at the Department of Veterans Affairs website at http://www.va.gov.

Here are a few of the larger awards to get you started:

725. Air Force Sergeants Association Scholarship

http://www.hqafsa.org

Applicants must be an unmarried child, adopted child or step-child of an active duty, retired or veteran member of the U.S. Air Force, Air National Guard or Air Force Reserve Command and under the age of 23 by August 31 of the year in which the scholarship is received. Applicants must also be enrolled in or accepted to a college or university.

726. Air Force Aid Society

http://www.afas.org

The *General Henry H. Arnold Education Grant* helps Air Force members and their families realize their academic goals. You must be dependent sons and daughters of Air Force members, spouses of active duty members or surviving spouses of Air Force members who died while on active duty or in retired status.

727. American Veterans

http://www.amvets.org

The American Veterans provide scholarships to veterans and high school seniors who are both members of JROTC programs as well as those who are not. Veterans must be members of the

Can I go to college at the same time I am serving in the military?

One of the best ways to earn a degree while serving in the military is by looking online. Some programs require as few as a couple hours a day, and you can earn a bachelor's or master's degree online. It's important to check if you can use the GI Bill or Military Tuition Assistance at the college.

American Veterans, and high school seniors of either variety must be the child or grandchild of an American Veterans member or a deceased person who would have qualified as an American Veterans member. The high school senior and veteran's scholarships are $4,000 over four years, and the JROTC high school senior scholarship is a one-time $1,000 scholarship.

728. Anchor Scholarship
http://www.anchorscholarship.com
This award supports the dependents of current and former members of the Naval Surface Forces, Atlantic and Naval Surface Forces, Pacific.

729. Armed Forces Communications and Electronics Association
http://www.afcea.org/education/scholarships/
This association offers several scholarships. The *AFCEA General Emmett Paige Scholarship* is for active-duty personnel in the uniformed military services, honorably discharged veterans or their spouses or dependents who are full-time students in an accredited four-year U.S. college or university. Applicants must major in electrical, computer, chemical or aerospace engineering, computer science, physics or mathematics. *The AFCEA ROTC Scholarship* is for students majoring in electrical or aerospace engineering, electronics, computer science, computer engineering, physics or mathematics. Applicants must also be enrolled full-time as college sophomores or juniors and

be enrolled in an ROTC program. *The AFCEA Sgt. Jeannette L. Winters, USMC Memorial Scholarship* supports active-duty Marine Corps members or veterans. Applicants must be on active duty in the U.S. Marine Corps or honorably discharged and current undergraduates who are majoring in electrical, aerospace or computer engineering, computer science, physics or mathematics.

730. Army Emergency Relief (AER)
http://www.aerhq.org
The *MG James Ursano Scholarship Fund* helps the children of Army families with their undergraduate education, vocational training and service academy education. Applicants must be dependent children of Army soldiers, unmarried, under the age of 22, have a minimum 2.0 GPA and be enrolled, accepted or pending acceptance as full-time students in a post-secondary educational institution. Awards are based primarily on financial need.

731. Blinded Veterans Association
http://www.bluestarmothers.org
The *Kathern F. Gruber Scholarship Program* offers financial aid to the spouses and dependent children of blinded veterans. The veteran need not be a member of the Blinded Veterans Association but must be legally blind (either service-connected or not). Applicants must be accepted to or already be enrolled in a university or business, secretarial or vocational training school. There are eight scholarships worth $2,000 and eight scholarships worth $1,000.

732. Coast Guard Foundation Scholarships
http://www.uscg.mil
The foundation offers awards of up to $5,000 for Coast Guard dependents who are high school seniors or college students. Students must be the sons or daughters of enlisted men and women of the U.S. Coast Guard on active duty, retired or deceased or the children of enlisted personnel in the Coast Guard Reserve currently on extended active duty 180 days or more. The awards are based on academic promise, motivation, character, leadership and citizenship, and the deadline is April 1.

733. Daughters of the Cincinnati
http://www.daughters1894.org
The *Daughters of the Cincinnati Scholarship* helps to support daughters of United States Army and Navy officers. You must be the high school senior daughter of a career officer in the United States Army, Navy, Air Force, Coast Guard or Marine Corps (active, retired or deceased).

734. Disabled American Veterans
http://www.dav.org
The *National Commander's Youth Volunteer Scholarships* support active members of the Department of Veterans' Affairs Voluntary Service programs. You must be 21 years of age or younger and have volunteered a minimum of 100 hours in the last calendar year. Three one-time scholarships are available, valued at $10,000, $5,000 and $3,000.

735. Dolphin Scholarship Foundation
http://www.dolphinscholarship.org
The *Dolphin Scholarship* assists the children of Navy submariners or members. Applicants must be the unmarried children or stepchildren of Navy submariners or Navy members who have served in submarine support activities and must be under 24 years old at time of application deadline. Applicants' parents must have been part of the Submarine Force for at least eight years, have served in submarine activities for at least 10 years or died on active duty while in the Submarine Force.

736. 1st Marine Division Association Scholarship
http://www.1stmarinedivisionassociation.org
This program supports dependents of deceased or 100 percent permanently disabled veterans of service with the 1st Marine Division. Awards are up to $1,500 per year for full-time undergraduate students for up to four years.

737. Fleet Reserve Association
http://www.fra.org
The Fleet Reserve Association provides scholarships to FRA members, honorary members and their dependents, spouses and grandchildren.

738. Foundation of the First Cavalry Division Association

http://www.1cda.org

The *First Cavalry Division Association Scholarship* is for the children of 1st Cavalry Division troopers who have died or become totally disabled while serving in the division. Active duty members of the division, their spouses and children are also eligible.

739. Jewish War Veterans of the USA

http://www.jwv.org

The *Jewish War Veterans National Scholarship Program* offers scholarships to the direct descendants of members of the Jewish War Veterans of the USA who are either in good standing or deceased. You must be a high school senior who has been accepted by an accredited four-year college or university or a three-year hospital school of nursing.

740. Marine Corps Scholarship Foundation

http://www.marine-scholars.org

This foundation offers the *Marine Corps Scholarship Foundation Scholarship* to assist children of U.S. Marines or former Marines in pursuit of higher education.

741. Military Chaplains Association of the United States of America

http://www.mca-usa.org

The Military Chaplains Association provides scholarships to seminary students who plan to become military chaplains. You must be a full-time student in an accredited seminary and currently approved as and serving as a chaplain candidate in one of the Armed Forces.

742. Military Officers Association of America (MOAA)

http://www.troa.org

The *TROA Scholarship* is awarded to the children of military families. Applicants must be under the age of 24 and be the children of a member of the uniformed services. Children of enlisted personnel are also eligible for the scholarship. Recipients are selected on the basis of scholastic ability, potential, character, leadership and financial need.

743. Military Order of the Purple Heart

http://www.purpleheart.org

The *Military Order of the Purple Heart Scholarship* is for the children or grandchildren of a Purple Heart recipient or of a member in good standing with the organization.

744. Navy-Marine Corps Relief Society

http://www.nmcrs.org

The *Admiral Mike Boorda Scholarship Program* helps eligible Navy and Marine Corps members pay for their postsecondary, technical or vocational education. Applicants must be active duty service members accepted to the Enlisted Commissioning Program, the Marine Enlisted Commissioning Education Program or the Medical Enlisted Commissioning Program. *The VADM E. P. Travers Scholarship and Loan Program* helps the unmarried dependent sons or daughters of active duty or retired Navy or Marine Corps service members or spouses of active duty Navy or Marine Corps service members.

745. Navy Supply Corps Foundation

http://www.usnscf.com

The foundation offers the *Navy Supply Corps Foundation Scholarship* to aid family members of foundation members and enlisted Navy personnel, including reservists and retirees. You must be a family member of a member of the Navy Supply Corps Foundation or an enlisted member, meaning active duty, reservist or retired.

746. Non-Commissioned Officers Association

http://www.ncoausa.org

The Non-Commissioned Officers Association offers scholarships to the spouses and children of its members. You must be under 25 years of age if you are the child of a member in order to be eligible and must be enrolled at an accredited college or university. There are 16 scholarships; nine worth $900 for children of members, four worth $900 for spouses and three worth $1,000 for the best essay on Americanism and the highest high school academic record.

Do all military scholarships require that I join the Army?

No. There are some scholarships that are for the children and even grandchildren of service members. Even if you have no intention of joining the armed forces you can apply for these scholarships if one of your relatives has served.

747. Paralyzed Veterans of America

http://www.pva.org

The *PVA Educational Scholarship Program* offers scholarships to active life members of the Paralyzed Veterans Association and their immediate families for postsecondary education.

748. Seabee Memorial Scholarship Association

http://www.seabee.org

The *Seabee Memorial Scholarship* provides scholarships to the children and grandchildren of Seabees, both past and present, active, reserve or retired. You must be the child, stepchild or grandchild of regular, reserve, retired or deceased officers or enlisted members who have served or are now serving with the Naval Construction Force or Naval Civil Engineer Corps, or who have served but have been honorably discharged. Scholarships are for four-year bachelor's degrees.

749. Tailhook Association

http://www.tailhook.org

The *Tailhook Educational Foundation Scholarship* assists the members of and the children of the members of the U.S. Navy carrier aviation. Applicants must be high school graduates who are accepted at an undergraduate institution and are the natural or adopted children of current or former naval aviators, naval flight officers or naval aircrewmen. Applicants may also be individuals or children of individuals who are serving or have served on board a U.S. Navy aircraft carrier in the ship's company or the air wing.

750. The Retired Enlisted Association
http://www.trea.org
TREA offers *The Retired Enlisted Association National Scholarship* to dependents who are the children or grandchildren of members in good standing of TREA or TREA's National Auxiliary.

751. Third Marine Division Association
http://www.caltrap.com
The *Memorial Scholarship Fund* provides tuition assistance to dependents of division members who died as a result of combat service in Vietnam or to dependents of division as well as association members.

752. United Daughters of the Confederacy
http://www.hqudc.org
The *United Daughters of the Confederacy Scholarship* supports lineal descendants of Confederate soldiers.

753. Veterans of Foreign Wars of the United States
http://www.vfw.org
The VFW offers a variety of scholarships to students of varying ages. *The Voice of Democracy Scholarship* is a $25,000 award available to students in grades 9 to 12. *The Patriot's Pen* is an award for seventh and eighth graders with 28 national winners, who receive from $1,000 to $10,000 scholarships. There is also a *National Scout* award for a scout worth $5,000 and *National Recognition Awards* for varying accomplishments.

754. Women's Army Corps Veterans' Association
http://www.armywomen.org
The *Women's Army Corps Veterans' Association Scholarship* offers financial support to the relatives of Army Corps women who have demonstrated academic achievement and leadership skills. The scholarship is a one-time award of $1,500. Applicants must be U.S. citizens and high school seniors. Applicants must also be planning to enroll in or be enrolled in an accredited institution for postsecondary education and be the child, grandchild, niece or nephew of an Army Corps woman.

Save Money While In College

Save The Money You Already Have

As a college student, you probably find that your pockets are more often empty than full. So when you do have some pocket change, you want to do everything you can to make it stretch. This is no easy task. There are, after all, so many interesting and fun things to spend your money on. Nightly pizza breaks add up quickly.

To save money, you need to get serious about how you spend your money. This begins by being honest with yourself about how you spend. Download an app to track all of your expenses for the entire month. Every dime should be accounted for in this app. After the first month review your expenses and figure out how much you spent on necessities versus non-essential items. Most students are surprised to see what they actually spend their money on. Small habits such as a daily frappuccino add up to a surprising amount of dough.

You need to have an accurate idea of where your money is going before you can implement any savings strategies. Once you have identified your weaknesses in spending, you can work to address them by finding cheaper alternatives.

As you begin to save, continue to keep track of your budget until you are confident that you are in control and meeting your monthly savings goals. If you ever find yourself falling back into bad habits, re-open the app and start recording your expenses again.

Once you have your budget, you'll find many ways to save. Here are a few ideas to get started:

755.

Put yourself on the envelope budget

One highly effective way to control your spending is to use what is called the envelope budget. Get several envelopes and label them with the main categories of your monthly budget. For example you might have "food," "entertainment" and "basic living" envelopes. Put in the money that you have allotted for each activity based on your monthly budget. During the month take money from the appropriate envelope, but once your envelope is empty, you must stop buying. If you run out of your "entertainment" funds mid-month, you'd better start looking for some free options to have fun.

This simple strategy has helped thousands of students save money and develop good spending habits. For effect of using the envelope budget is that it trains you to pace your spending and to live within your monthly budget. Since you can carry any extra money over to the next month it forces you to save (what a concept!) for special purchases such as a spring break vacation.

756.

Use your credit cards responsibly—or not at all

If you're a college student then you've already been bombarded with credit card offers. Sometimes they arrive in the mail while other times they are in a booth on campus enticing you with a free t-shirt or gift certificate. As a college student you know how easy it is to obtain a credit card. While credit cards are virtually a necessity in our society, they can also lead to a lot of trouble if used irresponsibly. Anyone with a credit card can be tempted to spend indiscriminately, but putting it on the plastic means you have to face the consequences 30 days later when the bill is due. If you don't pay your balances in full at the end of each month, you subject yourself to interest payments and late fees that can potentially destroy your budget.

For example, let's say you charged $2,000 on your card and only paid the monthly minimum (about 2 percent) each month. On a card with an 18 percent APR, it would take you 19 years to pay off the purchase, and your total cost would be more than $5,800! Credit cards require a lot of self-restraint to be used responsibly. If you cannot keep your credit card spending under control, consider getting rid of the cards altogether.

757.

Cash is king

Credit cards are great, but you risk spending beyond your means and paying exorbitantly high interest rates. Avoid the trouble by paying for everything in cash or (preferably non-bouncing) check. One student who got into trouble with his credit cards instituted a 100 percent cash system. He discovered that he became acutely aware of how small impulse purchases could drain his stash. In fact, he became so cost conscious that he ended up saving money each month. By the end of the year he had a pile of extra cash in the bank.

758.

Swap your credit card for a debit card

If you simply can't control your credit card spending but don't want to give up the convenience of paying by plastic then consider changing your credit card to a debit card. A debit card offers all of the convenience of a credit card (including all of the protections against fraud) except that the money is deducted from your bank account when you use it. This way you are not able to spend more than you have.

759.

Save your pennies

Remember the penny jar or piggy bank you had as a child? There is no reason you can't do this now as an adult. Find a jar, cut a small slit in the cover and tape it shut. Every time you have change in your pocket, drop it into the jar. At the end of the semester you'll be surprised at how much you've accumulated. Better yet roll those pennies into a bank account that pays interest and let your coins grow.

760.

Never buy a new textbook

How often does this happen? On the first day of class your professor hands out a reading list of books. You spend a small fortune and a considerable amount of time to buy these books. But as the semester progresses, you realize you only read a few chapters in each book—or maybe you never get around to reading the assignment at all.

Rather than buy new or even used books that you'll only read a small portion of, use the library's copies or borrow them from your friends. Professors seldom assign entire books to read. Through some strategic borrowing you should be able to complete all the assignments without buying a single book.

If you do need to own a copy of the book then definitely buy it used. Some of the better sources for used textbooks (don't forget your local used bookstore) include:

- http://www.amazon.com
- http://www.chegg.com
- http://www.half.com
- http://www.efollett.com
- http://www.barnesandnoble.com/textbooks/

761.

Shop like a senior—senior citizen that is

Senior citizens who are on a fixed income rarely shop without that valuable money saver: coupons. But if you think poring over the Sunday paper with a pair of scissors is too much work, you can find coupons with a click of your mouse. Online coupons are much easier to find and use. Here are a few sites:

- http://www.mycoupons.com

- http://www.fatwallet.com
- http://www.thecouponclippers.com
- http://www.dealzconnection.com
- http://www.currentcodes.com
- http://www.techbargains.com
- http://www.dealcatcher.com

While the amount you save depends on how much you spend, students who are diligent in their coupon clipping ways can save about $45 per month.

762.

Cut your cell phone bill
Heading off to college is a good time to re-evaluate your cell phone plan. The one thing you want to test before buying a cell phone is whether or not you have reception in your dorm. Some providers are better than others on campus so you might want to wait until you get to college before picking a cell phone service. Once you figure out which services are strong on campus, shop around to find the best plan. Many carriers have unlimited plans, especially for families. Your college may also offer a student discount on cell phone plans.

763.

Use VOIP
To save money, use Voice over Internet Protocol (VOIP), or calling using the Internet. With a service like Skype, you can make free calls—even video calls—to other people who have the program. Or if you need to call people who don't have Skype, long distance calls cost as little as about 2 cents per minute.

764.

Start packing your own lunch

Instead of buying the overpriced pizza at the student center, why not pack your lunch? For when you're in a rush, get friendly with Cup-O-Noodles and other instant entrees. For dinner learn some basic recipes. The key to making eating at home work is variety. Don't stick to a single recipe that you'll burn out on. The usual suspects: frozen pizza and pasta. If you don't have a full kitchen in your dorm room, make use of that ubiquitous machine that makes great popcorn: your microwave. There are hundreds of dishes that can be made easily and quickly in the microwave. For some ideas take a look at the money-saving recipes in *Recipes and Tips for Healthy, Thrifty Meals* that is available for free at http://www.pueblo.gsa.gov.

765.

Master your microwave

Your largest expense besides rent is probably food. Eating out is particularly hard on your budget, as the typical meal purchased at a restaurant will cost you three times more than a comparable meal made at home. But who wants to slave over a hot stove and wash pots and pans? Well lucky for you that you live in the 21st century where the microwave is now a standard kitchen (and dorm room) appliance. You can make almost any dish in the microwave and for a fraction of the cost of eating out. If you need some recipes, take a look at http://www.recipesource.com.

766.

Don't go crazy with the meal plan

Before you get to college it sounds sensible to sign up for three meals a day through the college meal plan. The reality is very few students wake up in time for breakfast. Add to that the occasional eating out for lunch or dinner and suddenly you are paying for meals that you don't eat. When selecting a meal plan, it is usually better to start with fewer meals than you think. You can always increase your meal plan next semester or year. Plus, we've never heard of a college student going hungry.

767.

Buy dorm furnishings used

When it comes to futons, chairs, refrigerators and sofas, it is much better to buy used than new. Look on Craigslist, on kiosks and in library bulletin boards for used essentials. As the year comes to an end, befriend some seniors who are graduating and ask what they plan to do with their stuff. Make an offer and save a ton of money for things that you'll probably just sell when you graduate anyway.

768.

Get your technology at the bookstore

Schools often have some amazing deals for their students on computers and software. Before you buy a computer or software at a retail store, check out the deals at your bookstore. Often you'll find that you can save a ton of money. The same may also be true for cell phone plans and even gym membership.

769.

Take advantage of every free service your school offers

Your college campus is really a mini-city that offers all kinds of perks. Most schools have fitness centers and pools that you can use for free just by flashing your student ID. Many offer free or low-cost tutoring and remedial education programs, and some even have day care if you have a child.

770.

Get free food at campus events

You know where the free food is on campus? At campus events! Whether it's an Earth Day celebration or a concert sponsored by one of the dorms, there is always free food and drinks. Make it a habit to look for posters and flyers announcing these events to get your free grub.

771.

Make your campus your center of entertainment

While you could go off campus to watch a movie or to a club to boogie, you can get the same entertainment by watching movies on campus (usually at a discount) and going to campus-sponsored dances. Campus plays and performances are often a great deal for cheap entertainment. Explore what your campus offers in terms of entertainment before you head off campus.

I know that I can save a lot of money by living at home, but won't I miss out on all the fun?

Going to college is not only about going to classes. It's also about eating pizza with friends at 3 a.m., cheering your team on at the Homecoming game and playing video games when you should be at the library. Knowing this, what kind of lifestyle do you want and will that choice be possible both on or off campus?

If you're strictly considering studying, you probably would do better off campus living without roommates. Roommates and dormmates can be distracting.

On a practical level, you would probably have fewer distractions and more focused studying time off campus. But on a personal level, would you have the full college experience? Would you make an effort to get involved with activities and maintain relationships with friends? Plus, you have to remember that some distractions can be good since college is about more than studying.

So while we would definitely consider the money-saving aspects of living off-campus we encourage you to also think about what you are giving up and if you are willing to make the extra effort to be involved with the campus even if you don't live there.

772.

Buy in bulk and share

When you buy in bulk you save money. You've probably been with your parents to one of the giant warehouse stores. But the problem is that such large amounts are usually too much for one or even two people. However, if you get a bunch of people together you can split the membership fee for one of the warehouse stores and buy everything from detergent to peanut butter to socks in bulk and share.

773.

Get a coffee maker

Instead of spending a few dollars for your daily caffeine fix, invest in a decent coffee maker. Or go in on one with your roommates. Skipping the daily coffee shop run can save hundreds of dollars.

774.

Take fruit and cereal from the cafeteria

If you have a meal plan that gives you unlimited access to the cafeteria, take some fruit or cereal back to your dorm as a late-night snack. Kept in a refrigerator, fruit and cereal (put it in a Ziploc if it's not in one of those individual size boxes) will last a long time and save you money from making trips to the convenience store for a snack.

775.

Use Christmas and your birthday strategically

If you really want a new iPad or mountain bike, don't waste your money on it, but exercise some patience and request it for your birthday or Christmas. Your parents are probably wondering what you can use in college so why not tell them. If it's a really pricey gift, suggest that the family (including grandparents) pool their money together. If you plan strategically you'll never have to purchase the things you really want. Plus, you'll avoid getting clothes you hate or books you'll never read.

776.

Commute to college

Living at home has its down sides such as the fact that you may still have a curfew and can't throw unsupervised parties. But living at home and commuting to school has its benefits as well. Perhaps, most importantly, your parents and you will save on room and board costs, which can be from $5,000 to $10,000 per year. In addition, don't discount the home-cooked meals, laundry facilities and companionship of mom and dad.

777.

Buy a tuxedo

You might not be James Bond, but if you add up the number of black tie formals and dances that you will attend over the four years of college, you'll realize that spending $300 to $400 on a tuxedo will more than pay for itself. Remember, each time you rent you'll pay $50 to $100. Plus, you have to wake up early the next day to return the thing.

778.

Shop around for airfare

Whether you're going home for winter break or heading for a beach mecca during spring break, it pays to shop around to get you from point A to point B. STA Travel (http://www.statravel.com) specializes in travel discounts for students, and you can also get low airline fares and vacation packages at Expedia (http://www.expedia.com), Orbitz

(http://www.orbitz.com) and Travelocity (http://www.travelocity.com.)
If you have some flexibility with which airline and times that you fly,
you can save a lot at Priceline (http://www.priceline.com), the website
where you name your own prices.

779.

Spare the air by taking public transportation or biking

By going carless, you save money on gas, car insurance and parking.
Plus, you help the environment. Check out options for biking and public transportation. If you ride the bus or train investigate getting a pass.

780.

Trim your rent

The easiest way to save on rent short of moving is to get a roommate.
Turn an extra room or an extra large apartment into extra cash. Be
aware, however, that some apartments have legal occupancy limits
and your apartment manager may want to raise the rent. So before
you do anything, run it by the manager and see if adding an extra
person will save you money.

If you add a roommate, you'll probably have to sign a new lease with
both of your names on it. This is important because it will legally
obligate your new roommate to pay the rent and any damages to the
apartment. You'll also want to sign the renters' equivalent of a pre-
nuptial. Spell out everything that might be the source of a problem
such as who takes out the garbage, the frequency of having house
parties and what the policy is on guests staying over. (Roommates'
significant others have been known to bunk rent-free for months at a
time.) If things don't work out and you want to part ways with your
roommate, you'll have something written to back up your claims.

While each state has different laws that protect renters, do some basic
research about how adding a roommate will affect you legally.

781.

Live in a co-op

If you're willing to put in a little bit of cleaning, cooking or other household-type work, you can save money by living in a co-op. For students in Ann Arbor, Michigan, the Inter-Cooperative Council (ICC) has 18 houses and one apartment house in which students pay lower prices for room and board. Prices are lower because the co-ops are owned and run by the student members rather than landlords or the university, and student members contribute a few hours of work per week to take care of cooking, cleaning and other household duties. Check with your college to see if co-ops are available.
Website: http://www.icc.coop

782.

Try life without cable

Trust us, you'll probably live even if you miss a few episodes of your favorite cable TV show. Plus, most dorms and student unions have public areas with cable TV where you can watch sporting events and other popular shows. Or, watch TV online. Try going for a semester without cable. We bet that you won't miss it as much as you think. Plus, having an extra $40 in your pocket can go a long way.

783.

Get free room and board by being an RA

If you're good at doling out advice and not concerned about living with students who may be younger than you are, then you can get free room and board at many colleges by being a Residential Assistant (RA).

784.

Work for your rent

Residents who live near campus may have an extra room or cottage that they are willing to let you live in for free in exchange for doing a certain amount of work, such as housecleaning, yard work, errands and child care. Visit the housing office at your college to learn what kind of unique work for rent opportunities exist in your area.

785.

Avoid student activity fees of all types

Besides tuition and room and board, there are a host of other fees that range from activities fees to athletic coupon books. Avoid every fee that you don't think you'll use, especially if you can pay the fee later if you decide you want the service.

786.

Use your parents' health insurance until the very end

Most colleges automatically enroll you in their health care plan unless you opt out by showing that you already have insurance. Most employer-provided insurance will cover children up to the age of 21. Have your parents find out the details of their insurance plans. Chances are they can continue to cover you while you are in college and save you money for insurance that you don't need.

354 • 1001 Ways to Pay for College

787.

Ask for student discounts everywhere

Take advantage of student discounts. They're offered by many attractions such as movie theatres, ski lodges and amusement parks. There are several student discount cards including from Student Advantage (http://www.studentadvantage.com). You can also get discount entertainment coupon books from http://www.entertainment.com.

CHAPTER SIXTEEN

Make Your College Cheaper

Cheapen Your College, Not Your Education

With colleges, one of the surest ways to lower the price is to pick a cheaper college. To get the best education, you don't need to attend the most expensive school. In fact, the priciest school may not be the best fit for you. Think about buying a car. What's the real difference between a Mercedes and a Honda? Mostly it's the image that each car conveys. Putting aside the bragging rights, wouldn't both serve you well? With either, you'd get from point A to point B (which is the primary function of a car), and with one, you'd have a whole lot of cash left over.

Besides choosing colleges that cost less, you can also cut costs with strategies like getting credit by exam or graduating in 3 1/2 years instead of four. You could even choose to attend a tuition-free college. Yes, they do exist!

In this chapter we look at ways that you can make your total college costs cheaper without compromising the quality of your education. You can get a great education without going broke.

788.

Get started at a less expensive school and then transfer to graduate from a more expensive school

As you already know tuition prices vary widely. Yet, most colleges offer similar courses and credits that are transferable from one school to another. With careful planning you can start at a less expensive school such as a community college and after two years transfer into a more expensive college while still graduating on time.

A lot of students overlook their local community colleges. Yet, it's a great way to complete two years of your education for less than half the price of a four-year college. (Some four-year colleges even offer automatic admission or scholarships to community college students who transfer into their schools.) The reality is that when it comes time to get a job, potential employers are only interested in where you graduated from, not the path you took to get there.

The key to making this work is to choose a community college, or similarly cheap school, where your credits will transfer smoothly. Look for articulation agreements, special agreements that colleges set up with one another that specify which classes are equivalent and what credits will transfer. They also outline what it takes to actually transfer in terms of grades and other requirements. Make sure that you are transferring into a college that will count all (or at least enough) of the credits you have already earned to allow you to graduate on time. If your credits don't count and you have to repeat courses, you may take longer to graduate and lose any potential cost savings.

789.

Go to your state school

You may not realize it but your state college or university is already a good bargain. Compare tuition at your state college to a private college and you'll see just how much cheaper it is. Nationally, a public university costs an average of almost $25,000 less than a private university. The reality is that your state tax dollars are used to subsidize the price of in-state tuition. Simply choosing to attend your state university is like getting an automatic discount.

790.

Become the newest resident of the state

In the past you could sometimes just spend a year in a state, claim residency and then pay in-state tuition. However, most states are cracking down on students who claim to be residents but are only there to get discounted educations. All states make a distinction between being a resident of the state for taxation purposes and being a resident for tuition purposes. In fact, many states leave it up to the public university system to set the rules governing who can pay in-state tuition.

In general most states require that you meet the following requirements before you can claim residency for in-state tuition:

- Durational requirement. Most states require that you have lived in the state for at least 12 months before claiming residency.
- Intent to remain a resident. Most states require that you show your intention of remaining in the state even after you graduate from college.
- Independence. Many states require that you be financially independent from your parents before you can claim residency.

There are some exceptions to residency requirements including if you are from a military family or if your entire family has recently moved. Some states also make exceptions for students who live near the borders of the state. You can find a detailed description of each state's residency requirements at the College Board website at http://professionals.collegeboard.com/testing/international/state. However, once you become a resident you will enjoy a significant reduction in your tuition.

791.

Save money with a reciprocity agreement

Some state university systems have buddied up with neighboring state university systems to grant in-state tuition at each other's schools. These are known as reciprocity agreements and can save you a ton of money. Reciprocity usually exists with neighboring states. Contact the office of admission at the colleges you want to attend to see if there are any discounts including reciprocal in-state tuition rates.

What's the difference between a public college and a private college?

Keep in mind that there are always exceptions, but in general, private schools are more expensive than public schools. Most public schools are larger than private colleges. Depending on what you are looking for and the kind of student you are, this can be an advantage or disadvantage. Private schools tend to offer more guaranteed housing on campus than public schools. You are also more likely to get into the courses you want at most private schools than public schools.

These are the easy observations. The most controversial issue is quality. Many private schools are thought to have stronger academic reputations than public schools. However, there are many public schools that offer top-notch educations. More often than not it is the student who determines how strong of an education he or she gets.

The reality is that you can get an excellent education at almost any school. It mostly depends on how committed you are to taking advantage of the opportunity.

792.

Go to a less expensive undergraduate college so you can blow your money on an expensive graduate school

If you are planning to get a graduate or professional degree, then consider going to a cheap college and save your money for graduate school. For example, let's say that you want to be a doctor. You're not going to learn much about brain surgery during your undergraduate years. So why go to an expensive undergraduate college when you can go to a cheaper alternative? Then, if you want to attend the most elite (and expensive) medical school, you will have saved yourself a few clams.

793.

Consider the blue light special bargain schools

There are some schools that have a reputation for being bargain colleges. This distinction has no relationship to the quality of the education. *Kiplinger's Personal Finance Magazine* (http://www.kiplinger.com) publishes an annual list of bargain colleges. *U.S. News & World Report* (http://www.usnews.com) also publishes an annual list of Best Value colleges. You can find the list for free on the websites of these magazines.

794.

Work and learn through cooperative education programs

Would you like to make college more affordable while gaining valuable work experience? Cooperative education programs, known as co-op, allow you to work and go to school at the same time. Plus, cooperative education gives you the benefits of having work experience before you graduate and earning a paycheck without missing out on the college experience.

Co-op works because companies, governments and non-profit organizations agree to offer real jobs to students. Job assignments are managed by the college, and students are matched with jobs that fit their major or are in career areas that they wish to explore. Each year more than 50,000 employers hire college co-op students in nearly every field of work.

The best way to learn more about co-op is to speak to the cooperative education office at the college you are attending or plan to attend. Also visit the website of the National Commission for Cooperative Education at http://www.co-op.edu to learn more about co-op education. At the library, look for the *Directory of College Cooperative Education Programs*, which lists the more than 460 colleges that offer co-op programs. With cooperative education you can work while attending college and even graduate with a year or more of actual work experience on your resume.

795.

Attend a tuition-free college

You don't have to worry about tuition if there isn't any. A few colleges offer free tuition for all admitted students. Some of the schools also require that students agree to work on campus. Here are just a few colleges that offer a tuition-free option.

796. Military Academies

There are five military academies that offer free tuition: the U.S. Military Academy, U.S. Naval Academy, U.S. Coast Guard Academy, U.S. Merchant Marine Academy and U.S. Air Force Academy. They require service in the military for a number of years, but the commitment may be worth the free tuition.

797. Deep Springs College in California

http://www.deepsprings.edu
Every student is awarded a full scholarship that covers tuition and room and board. Incidental expenses such as books and travel are not covered and are estimated to be about $2,800 per year.

798. College of the Ozarks in Missouri

http://www.cofo.edu
The college guarantees that every student's cost of attendance will be met through a combination of its endowment, financial aid and its mandatory student work program.

799. Webb Institute of Naval Architecture in New York

http://www.webb.edu
This school only offers one undergraduate major in naval architecture and marine engineering. However, if this is what you want to major in then you'll be happy to know that tuition

is free. Room and board and other miscellaneous expenses are estimated at about $10,690 per year.

800. Curtis Institute of Music in Pennsylvania

http://www.curtis.edu

Since 1928 this college has awarded full-tuition scholarships to every student regardless of financial situation. Room and board and other expenses (including instrument maintenance and supplies) are estimated by the college to be $19,385 per year.

801. Berea College in Kentucky

http://www.berea.edu

Offering 26 majors, 18 minors and four pre-professional programs, Berea College also provides every student with a full-tuition scholarship. Room and board and other expenses are still your responsibility and you can use a combination of financial aid, scholarships and (of course) your own money to pay for them.

802. Alice Lloyd College in Kentucky

http://www.alc.edu

Through a combination of grants, scholarships, financial aid and on campus work programs, ALC is able to guarantee that every student will be able to pay for tuition.

Earn College Credit To Graduate Early

803.

Take an accelerated degree program

If you can't increase the amount of money you have, then the only way to decrease your college costs is to lower the price. One way to do this is to finish early. If you can graduate a semester sooner, that's one less semester that you'll have to pay for. Check if your college or the colleges you are applying to offer an accelerated degree program. Look for one that allows you to graduate in three years instead of

four. For example, through Mississippi College's Accelerated Degree Program, you can earn 30 or more hours a year toward your major in business administration, accounting or marketing by attending eight-week sessions that meet twice per week. This shaves off time and therefore money from the cost of your degree.
Website: http://www.mc.edu/accelerated/

804.

Use those AP tests scores to gain advanced standing

You may have wondered why you'd ever want to voluntarily subject yourself to more exams than you are required to take. The reason is that college prices are usually based on semesters. Since you typically spend four years (or eight semesters) to get your bachelor's degree, if you can cut the time it takes to graduate you can save a bundle. One way to shorten the time you are in college is to enter already having earned some credits. If you have taken the Advanced Placement or International Baccalaureate exams and received passing scores, you may be eligible to start college as a sophomore instead of a freshman. The rules that govern advanced standing vary by college so contact your admission office to get the details. If you are planning on taking an AP or IB test, visit the websites of the test makers. For the AP tests visit http://www.collegeboard.com/student/testing/ap/about.html and for the International Baccalaureate tests visit http://www.ibo.org.

805.

Use the College Level Examination Program (CLEP) to skip classes

In addition to AP or IB courses that give you advanced standing, your college may also let you take CLEP exams to receive college credit. There are currently 2,900 colleges that give credit or advanced standing to students who pass CLEP exams.

There are two types of CLEP exams. One is a general subject exam that covers math, English, humanities, natural science and social science and history. The other is a subject exam that covers a specific course. A passing score in this exam will usually give you credit for that specific course. There are currently 30 subject exams.

A CLEP exam costs $80 to take but could save you thousands of dollars in tuition. Plus, you don't want to take a course in an area in which you are already proficient. To learn more about CLEP and read examples from actual exams, visit http://clep.collegeboard.org.

806.

Take a DSST exam
Originally designed for the military, the DANTES Subject Standardized Tests (DSST) can now be taken by anyone. More than 80,000 people take the DSST each year to receive college credit. By passing the DSST exam you can earn credit for what you already know and thus save money. Learn more about the tests and find a test center at http://www.getcollegecredit.com.

807.

Earn credit with Excelsior College Examinations
There are 40 undergraduate-level Excelsior College Examinations that are accepted at nearly 900 colleges and universities. The undergraduate-level Excelsior College Examinations (as well as the DSST and CLEP exams) are free to military personal. You can preview the test material online, get a free study guide and find a testing location at http://www.excelsior.edu.

808.

Take the Graduate Record Exam as an undergraduate

While the GRE is usually for graduate school admission, some colleges allow undergraduates to earn credits with GRE scores. Check with your department to see if GRE scores can be used to satisfy specific course requirements. You can learn more about the GRE at http://www.ets.org/gre/.

809.

Job Ready Assessment tests can count for credit

There are 75 Job Ready Assessment tests that you can take to get credit in vocational or technical fields. Exams include tests in accounting, computer programming, construction, drafting, plumbing, welding and more. Visit the National Occupational Competency Testing Institute at http://www.nocti.org.

810.

Get college credit for life experience

If you are an adult or even graduate school student you might be able to get college credit for your professional and life experiences. Most schools recognize that you can gain college-level knowledge through your own life experiences. If your experiences are general and not related to a specific course, you might obtain General Studies credit. Or, you may get credit for specific courses if you have had related experiences or training.

In the book *College Degrees by Mail* there are examples of ways that colleges may recognize life experiences. For example:

- Work can demonstrate such skills as typing, filing, inventory control, accounting, computer programming, welding, editing and sales.

- Homemaking can show your proficiency in home maintenance, household planning and budgeting, childcare, meal planning and nutrition and child psychology.

- Volunteer work can show experience with community services, political campaigns, church activities and service organizations.

The first thing you should do is contact your department or admission office to see what experiences qualify and what kind of substantiation you need to provide.

811.

Get credit through a learning portfolio evaluation

In order to judge whether or not you should receive college credit for your experiences or previous studies, colleges want proof. You can provide this with a learning portfolio. In the portfolio you give a self-assessment, detailing the type of learning or training you have received outside of the classroom. Usually you will write a main essay and provide supporting documents. You want to make a case for how this learning is comparable to college-level learning and prove to the college that you possess the knowledge within this field. A typical portfolio may include:

- Your work history along with any volunteer experiences
- Formal educational experiences and special training
- Specific recognition for your knowledge including any licenses
- Hobbies and interests
- Meaningful life experiences
- Specific knowledge and skills gained

The key is to not make a laundry list of everything that you have done but instead to explain what you have learned and how it applies to your field of study. Be analytical about what you have gained from the experience, and demonstrate that this learning is equivalent to what you would learn in college. Look at the course catalog and match your knowledge to specific courses. You also need to show that you understand the theories behind your knowledge. In other words, just because you can drive a boat does not mean you understand the theory behind hydrodynamics. It will help if you speak to a member of your department to get the specific details on what your portfolio should look like.

812.

Earn credit by credential evaluation

Credit by evaluation is when a college looks at any education or training that you have received outside of a traditional institution and determines if it is equal to a course offered by the college. This can include course work and training while in the military, while working or in schools that are not accredited or in organizations that are not primarily educational institutions. Speak to your department to request credit by evaluation. Most schools use the *National Guide to Educational Credit for Training Programs*, the *Guide to Educational Credit by Examination* and the *Guide to the Evaluation of Educational Experiences in the Armed Services* published by the American Council on Education (http://www.acenet.edu) to determine how your experience is equivalent to college courses.

813.

Earn credit by taking a proficiency or challenge exam

Some colleges let you take a proficiency exam in a specific course to prove that you have the knowledge or experience necessary to pass the exam. Speak to your professor or department head to see if an exam is an option at your school.

814.

Graduate early with summer school

Summer school is often used to get a head start on a class or to make up for less than stellar grades. However, another use for summer school is to build credits that will let you graduate early. Summer school courses are shorter since you often meet every day and cheaper. Another advantage is you can take summer classes near your home and even schedule them around your summer job. Check with your college to make sure that the summer course credits will transfer without any problems.

815.

Take the maximum number of credits you can

If your school charges a set price for the semester you might be able to load up on credits by taking more than the recommended number to help you graduate early. The danger is that you overload yourself, and your grades suffer. However, if you can fit in one or two extra classes each semester you could graduate a semester or even a year early.

816.

Combine a BA with an MA or MD

If you know that you are going to obtain a graduate degree you might be able to shave a year off of your education (and therefore one year's less tuition payment) by combining your undergraduate degree with a graduate degree. This not only saves you money but may also give you an advantage when job seeking because you'll have an advanced degree.

For example, you can earn a bachelor's and master's degree in five years at the University at Buffalo (http://www.grad.buffalo.edu), which has more than 30 combined degree programs in areas including accounting, engineering and social work.

817.

To graduate on time choose your major early

The number one cause of students taking extra time to graduate is switching majors. Whenever you switch you run the risk of having to make up required courses. This takes time and can add an extra semester or even year. Start thinking about your major even before you go to college. During your first year, explore a bunch of different majors and classes. While you don't want to lock yourself into something too early, you what to explore your options and then declare your major in your second year.

Give Yourself A Tuition Break

818.

Get a two-for-one tuition deal

Imagine getting two educations for the price of one. This may be possible if you have a twin, or even a sibling, and you both attend the same college. Some schools understand that it is much more difficult for a family to support two students at the same time and have come up with some interesting two-for-one deals. If you have a twin and you want to go to the same school, then take a look at programs like the *Twin Award Program* at Sterling College in Kansas and the *Twin Scholarship* at Northeastern Oklahoma A&M College. At Sterling you can get free tuition for one student while at Oklahoma A&M you get free room for one student. Lake Erie College in Ohio makes their two-for-one deal open to siblings who are close in age. If you have a sibling or twin and you both want to attend the same college it won't hurt to send an email to the admission office and inquire if they have any discounts for both of you to attend.

819.

Take advantage of tuition remission, if you can

If you are an employee or the child of an employee or alumnus of a college you may get a break in your tuition. At Loyola University in Chicago, for example, one of the employee benefits is the Faculty and Staff Children Exchange Program (FACHEX). This gives the children of employees free tuition at Loyola and 25 other Jesuit colleges and universities.

At Oberlin College in Ohio the children of employees are eligible to receive a 100 percent rebate on their tuition if they are accepted. Oberlin also has a full-tuition exchange with other schools that belong to the Great Lakes College Association (GLCA).

To a lesser extent some colleges also give tuition breaks for the children of alums. At Mississippi State University, for example, students who are the sons or daughters of alumni who must pay out-of-state tuition for graduate school can earn a 50 percent reduction in tuition as long as they maintain a 3.0 GPA. So if you or your parents have any connection to a college, check for a tuition remission program.

820.

If your parents work for a college–whether as a dean or custodian–check into Tuition Exchange

One benefit of employment by a college or university may be discounted tuition. This assumes that you want to attend the same college where mom or dad works, but what if you want to go somewhere else? You just might be in luck. Tuition Exchange is a non-profit group with over 530 member colleges and universities. Each of the schools has allocated money for *Tuition Exchange Scholarships*. A year before you begin applying for college, contact Tuition Exchange. Once you are certified as a child of an employee at an eligible institution, you apply normally and will be considered for a Tuition Exchange award. While the scholarships can be competitive, you have a good chance

of winning since the applicant pool is small–you might be the only one applying for a Tuition Exchange scholarship at your college. Visit the Tuition Exchange website to see if the college where your mom or dad works participates in the program.
Website: http://www.tuitionexchange.org

821.

Save some money with an alumni referral

Who says colleges don't know how to market themselves? Alumni of the College of St. Catherine in St. Paul and Minneapolis, Minnesota, get free referral cards that they may give to students. These referral cards grant students application fee waivers and one-time tuition discounts of between $300 and $600 if they enroll. If you know graduates of colleges that you want to apply to, ask them to contact their alumni offices about application fee waivers and tuition discounts for referrals.

822.

Pay for tuition monthly instead of in one lump sum

Depending on your cash flow it might be easier to pay for tuition in small amounts each month instead of in one big lump sum at the start of each semester. Some schools allow you to spread your payments over the year instead of paying once or twice a year. Check with the college to see if they offer this type of payment. If your school participates in the TuitionPay monthly payment program, you can pay a small fee to have your tuition divided into payments, with no interest. Currently more than 1,500 schools participate in this plan. To see if your school participates in TuitionPay, visit http://www.tuitionpay.com.

823.

Pay your tuition with livestock

Cash cows really do exist! For the past five years Lindenwood University in St. Charles, Missouri, has allowed students to substitute livestock for cash when paying for tuition. The university uses the livestock to feed its 2,500 students. Is your school willing to accept an alternative form of payment? The only way to find out is to ask.

CHAPTER SEVENTEEN

Be A Dorm Room Entrepreneur

Launch Your Dorm Room Empire

To make extra money as college students, we always had part-time jobs. These included some truly odd jobs including watching dozens of hours of boring video as part of a paid psychological experiment, cleaning homes in spite of an allergy to dust and flipping burgers on Friday nights. But the extra cash that we earned from these occupations went a long way in making our college experience more enjoyable–after all it's hard to have a good time when you are broke.

Traditionally, students have used part-time jobs as a source of extra cash. Unfortunately, regular business hours don't always fit with a life of fluctuating workloads and unpredictable extracurricular activities. Employment is often characterized by endless battles with managers over schedules and last-minute scrambles to find co-workers willing to substitute shifts. At its worst, employment results in your sacrificing schoolwork and extracurricular activities.

In our entrepreneurial climate, however, students are increasingly shunning traditional part-time jobs and meeting their financial needs with a combination of resourcefulness and moxie. This does not mean that work has gotten easier. In fact, in some cases these imaginative entrepreneurial ventures are more difficult than traditional jobs. But the payoffs come in the flexibility to determine one's own schedule and not sacrifice the full benefits of the college experience. For many, it is also their first foray into entrepreneurship, a valuable business lesson. For a few, it even leads to a career.

The following ideas showcase some of the successful alternatives that students have used to fund their education. While these money-makers have the potential to generate substantial income, they are best used to fill the gaps in your finances.

Unlike most business ventures, the students we've met who shared their experiences were struggling to pay for college and could not invest more than a few dollars in an idea. They did not have the luxury of startup capital to build a business. Rather, they had to find ways to fill a need without having to spend money. It is inspiring to see how these students were able to transform what they already owned into a source of spendable cash. They are some of the purest examples of entrepreneurship in action.

Selling To Your Dorm

Living in a dorm or college apartment is a uniquely college experience. You see your hallmates at all hours of the day and night, share meals and even play football in the halls. Dorm life presents some unique selling opportunities that don't exist anywhere else.

824.

Recycle your way to riches

See that pile of cans in the corner of your room? Look closer. Besides being an ant haven, it's actually a pile of cash. If you live in a state with a redemption tax, you are sitting on potentially hundreds of dollars in cans and bottles. But since you personally can only drink so many six packs of Mountain Dew, you'll need to harness the collective consumption of your entire dorm to make recycling profitable.

Some students set up a box outside of their door and at parties. Others have even provided regular door to door pick up of cans and bottles. One student in California, which has a 5 cent redemption, makes $50 a month just from his dormmates.

825.

Organize an Ebay sell-a-thon

Everyone has stuff they don't use. With the limited storage space in a dorm room combined with the annual move, you have the perfect opportunity to help turn one person's junk into another person's treasure.

One student began by organizing a monthly Ebay sell-a-thon in his dorm. For the uninitiated, millions of people sell unwanted items on online auction sites like Ebay or Yahoo. For a 20 percent commission, he would write the description, take a digital photo, post the item for sale on the online auction site and ship the goods to the buyer. Students were glad to pay the commission to get rid of their unused belongings.

You can also do this offline by posting communal "For Sale" signs around campus. On one poster list everyone's items and your phone number as the primary contact. You handle all of the inquiries and negotiate the sales and you get a percentage of each sale while your friends get some money for their goods.

The end of semesters are the best times to sell. Target freshmen who are still collecting the basic necessities like futons, bikes and books. The two largest online auctions are Ebay (http://www.ebay.com) and Yahoo! (http://auctions.yahoo.com). For advice on getting started, read *Internet Auctions: A Guide For Buyers and Sellers* from the Federal Consumer Information Center (http://www.pueblo.gsa.gov).

826.

Bake your own bread

There are two things college students can never get enough of: sleep and food. While you can't help students get more sleep, if you have a knack for baking or candy making, you could start a small empire supplying late-night snacks and brain food.

Begin small and build a reputation. The best types of food are non-perishable snacks like cookies, brownies and candy. One student made lollipops using her mother's secret recipe. In fact, she was so successful that when she graduated she actually sold her recipe and supplies to an underclassman who gladly took over her business.

To get started with candy making, try http://www.getsuckered.com, which also offers a free newsletter.

827.

Be the games master

Most dorms have at least one foosball, pinball, pool or ping pong table–the perfect conditions for organizing a tournament. One dorm room entrepreneur organized a monthly foosball tournament by charging $5 per team and used 80 percent of the money as prizes.

Be aware that some types of tournaments with cash or prizes are considered an illegal form of gambling. Check with your local government or pool hall for what's acceptable. You will also probably have to hold the tournament offsite, but you should be able to find a local establishment with the right table game to sponsor your event.

828.

Turn your car into a money machine on wheels

Having a car on campus usually means that you are special–particularly in urban areas where student vehicles are rare and parking scarce. If you have a car, take advantage of your four-wheeled power by using it to transport goods that are difficult for students to get.

One student used his truck to bring in a whole cord of firewood to his Boston college. With the temperatures dropping, he unloaded all of the wood to dormmates by selling small bundles for a few dollars. He made a 500 percent profit that helped keep him warm that winter.

What else can you transport? How about mattresses, carpets or furniture? Find the stores that are just far enough away from campus to make carrying a futon difficult and poster the telephone poles with your offer to deliver.

Harness Your Brain Power

The mind is a terrible thing to waste–especially if you can use yours to turn a profit.

829.

Tutoring: Teaching for treasures

Tutoring is a great source of income if you are strong in a particular subject. For example if you have a knack for economics and got an "A" in Economics 101, poster the lecture hall the following year offering to tutor anyone who is having trouble. A more brazen approach would be to arrive at the lecture early and make an announcement before the class starts. (Get the professor's permission first.)

Another lucrative area is tutoring high school students in the usual subjects as well as for the SAT, ACT or other standardized tests. Just be sure you still remember how to prove those algebra theorems! Make an appointment with the guidance counselor of the nearest high school and ask for help informing students that you are available for tutoring.

Pricing for tutoring is usually by the hour and ranges between $25 and $35. However, consider giving a discount to students who are willing to sign up for regular sessions. For example, you might charge $200 for 10 one-hour sessions to practice for the SAT.

830.

Edit your way to riches

If you are a good writer and careful editor you can start an essay and resume editing service right from your dorm room. Potential customers are international students who need help polishing their English, science majors who are forced to take humanities courses and job-seeking seniors.

Set your rate based on word count. For example, $25 to edit a 1,000-word essay, $40 for a 2,000-word essay and $55 for a 3,000-word essay. The key is to make sure that you are earning a fair amount per hour. If it takes you an hour and a half to read and edit a 1,000-word essay and you charge $25 then you are making $17 per hour. Pretty good. If it takes longer, then either accept less per hour or charge more for your services.

One student at Harvard started an admission essay editing service on the web from his dorm room. It got so big that after he graduated he raised venture capital to turn it into a full-time business.

Two editing must-haves are *The Chicago Manual of Style* and *The Elements of Style* by William Strunk and E.B. White. You can also get the government's free publication, *Resumes, Applications, and Cover Letters* at http://www.pueblo.gsa.gov.

831.

Get paid to talk

With almost half a million international students in the U.S., most colleges have a sizable international population, especially during summers. Many of these students are struggling to refine their English skills. You would think that being in the U.S. would make this easy, but for many international students it is difficult to find students with the patience to help them practice conversational English.

Teaching conversational English is not difficult–you need to be able to explain concepts and have patience. International students find it especially difficult to learn idioms and slang. Advertise where international students live and near the classes they take. You can do one-on-one private lessons or organize a group. Rates for private lessons are usually between $20 and $25 per hour and for group lessons you might charge only a third of that per student.

832.

Be a computer guru

While most people know how to use a computer, not everyone knows how to use specialized software like Photoshop or Indesign. These programs are popular with clubs and organizations that publish newsletters, magazines, newspapers and flyers. Even the administration uses this software to produce campus publications.

The problem is that while a few of the club members may know how to use the software, there are many more members anxious to help but who are totally unknowledgeable. That's where you come in. Offer a refresher or beginners course on using the software for a flat fee. The club will be happy to pay since it will make their members more productive. You could probably even use the school's computer lab to conduct your training.

Aim for campus groups that produce a lot of newsletters or magazines and contact the administration as well. A good price is probably between $150 and $250 for a two-hour hands-on course.

Turn School Work Into School Green

Most of the work you do for classes is purely directed at getting good grades. However, there are some cases in which you can use your work and scholastic skills to earn money.

How can I learn more about becoming an entrepreneur and starting my own business?

Perhaps it's because they're the Davids trying to compete with the Goliaths, but entrepreneurs have a strong sense of sharing and helping. Fellow entrepreneurs will be one of your best sources of advice and support. You can find them in your community through organizations like the Rotary Club. You can even find them online at websites such as:

http://www.inc.com
http://www.businessownersideacafe.com

In addition, the Small Business Administration (http://www.sba.gov) offers a lot of articles on starting a small business, including a list of offices in your area. The SCORE Association (Service Corps of Retired Executives) will even match you with retired executive volunteers to provide counseling.

833.

Recycle your essays into contest winners

In college you will probably write more essays than you will at any other time in your life. What can be done with the prose over which you slave late into the night? Often with a few edits you can recycle these essays into contest entries. Have you read and written about *Atlas Shrugged* by Ayn Rand? If so, you can enter it into the essay contest sponsored by the Ayn Rand Institute. The first prize is $20,000!

There are hundreds of essay contests held each year. Check with your English or literature department, which often maintains a list of essay contests. Also be sure to ask all of your professors since they are usually the first to know about a contest in their department or field. Learn more about the Ayn Rand essay contest at http://www. aynrand.org and about the Elie Wiesel Prize in Ethics Essay Contest at http://www.eliewieselfoundation.org. Also look at Chapter 3 to find more contests you can win.

834.

Be your professor's sidekick

Do you have a favorite course? Ask the professor if you can be a research assistant. Usually this means going to the library and researching topics about which the professor is writing. Be sure you like the subject your professor is working on!

Often professors have grant money to help them with their research and this includes money for research assistants. You will prob-ably compete with graduate students so you must demonstrate your abilities. You'll usually have to accept the rate the professor is offering, but remember that you will also be learning more about your field and getting to know the professor.

Monetize Your Hobbies And Passions

Making money off of something you would do for free is the ultimate joy. Not surprisingly students often find that their hobbies and interests can be turned into cold, hard cash.

835.

Turn your fan site into green

If you have a website that receives decent traffic, you can sell advertising banners on it and join affiliate programs to sell other companies' products. Your site can be on anything that attracts visitors. For example, if you have a site dedicated to the USC Trojan football team, you can join the Amazon.com affiliate program to sell books like sports almanacs directly on your site.

The main caveat is that you cannot use free web hosting accounts or your school account to make money. Consider building your site first on a free account and then when you have the traffic move it to a low cost commercial Internet Service Provider and start adding banners and affiliate offers. To turn your site into cash, try these services: http://www.google.com/adsense, http://www.cj.com, http://www.linkshare.com and http://www.burstmedia.com.

836.

Organize an outing

If you like to snowboard, hike, scuba dive or do any other popular activity, you can turn this passion into a paid money-maker. Here's how: Get a group of people together who share your passion and organize a trip. You make arrangements for transportation, lodging and maybe even food. Make sure you research carefully and know the costs. Then set a price for each person including a fee for your efforts.

Try to keep things as cheap as possible. If you need to stay overnight, check motels or even cabins. Look into renting a van to transport everyone. For your first trip keep the group small before moving up to larger groups. You will learn a lot on your first trip and it's better to work out the kinks. If you keep the prices low and earn a reputation for a great trip, you'll have people begging you to do it again.

837.

Throw a party

If you are a real party animal, why not put your talent to work? To do this cheaply and safely you will need to partner with a local club or bar. Speak with the owner and make the following proposal. You want to use the establishment for a private party and will guarantee that a certain number of people will attend. The club or bar keeps the profits from the liquor sales. Plus it will be an excellent marketing opportunity since you'll bring a lot of new customers. You sell tickets to the party and keep the profits from ticket sales. (Depending on the owner you may have to help them defer some costs for security, DJ and other expenses.) The advantage of working with a club or bar is that they already have the licenses, staff and insurance to cover an event.

What you need to do is sell the tickets. Get a buzz started about the event. The party should have an interesting theme and you might re-cruit the help of some popular partiers on campus who will encourage others to attend. The first event will be the most difficult, but if you pull it off you will earn a reputation as a great party host and getting people to come to your next event will be much easier.

838.

Pass on your passion

College is all about learning, and there are a lot of things students want to learn beyond what your school provides. Almost any hobby or interest that you have whether it's photography, knitting or ball-room dancing is a commodity. Find a place and set aside time once a week for lessons. With the right price you will soon find others who are willing to pay for your expertise.

Hock Your Youth

Your youth is a valuable commodity. It won't last forever so you better cash in on it now. Here are some ways you can turn your youth into cash:

839.

Become a focus group regular

Companies know that your age group is a fickle crowd and are constantly testing new products and ideas on college students. There are specialized marketing firms that help companies do this by organizing focus groups. A focus group is where 10 to 15 students are assembled around a conference table and a moderator leads them through a discussion designed to get their opinions on various product ideas. They may even have the group test a product. This whole session is videotaped and observed by people from the company whose product is being tested. The responses from a series of these groups are used to help the company decide which products to make and how to market them.

The best thing about being in a focus group is that you just need to be yourself and give your honest opinion about whether or not you like the product. You get paid for your time and the conference room is usually stocked with free food and snacks. To be a part of a focus group, find the marketing companies that organize them. Look online for "Marketing," "Consulting" and "Market Research." Call the companies and ask if they hold focus groups and if you can sign up to be on a panel. You'll have to give them some personal information and then wait until they get a client who is trying to find out more about people like you.

840.

Be a psych experiment

Psychology departments are forever conducting experiments on students. While the pay may not be much, it usually requires little effort on your part. You may be asked to take a written exam, watch videos or be interviewed. Often you won't know the objective of the experiment until after it's over. The best way to find out who needs students is to check the bulletin boards in the psychology department and ask all your psych major friends to let you know if they hear of an experiment.

841.

Be a street marketer

Companies and local businesses all want to reach the students on your campus. You and your peers are big consumers, and they want to get their message in front of you. You can help them. Use the free kiosks on campus to post flyers. Distribute coupons or even product samples directly to dorm rooms. It's hard work, but the pay is great.

The best way to get started is to create a professional-looking flyer explaining what you do and how much you charge. Keep it simple. For $80 you'll hang 250 flyers. For $200 you'll drop coupons throughout the freshman dorms. Hand out these flyers to local business owners. You will also want to offer photographs of you actually performing the promotion as proof that you did the work. This is a common practice among even large promotion companies. If you want to see how a big company does it, take a look at http://www.marketsource.com. You might get some good ideas.

Selling To Mom And Dad

While students usually don't have a lot of extra money, their parents might.

842.

Create and deliver custom care packages

Care packages are a welcome gift to any student, but it's not always easy for parents to assemble and send these packages on a regular basis. This is where you come in. You can build an awesome care package with unique items everyone needs—i.e., chemical hand warmers for winter, Post-it notes or the newest junk food that is sweeping your campus. Create some flyers for your classmates to send to their parents. Develop a web page for your friends to pass around.

Only buy the ingredients to make the care package when you receive an order. Plus, you can hand deliver it to the recipient so there are no postage costs for your customers. This should allow you to easily undercut the competition. Be sure to set up a regular schedule where you mail your past customers reminding them that it's that time again to send a care package. Right before or right after mid-terms and finals are great times to encourage parents to send care packages. Check out http://www.carepackages.com for some great ideas.

843.

Hidden graduation gold

Every parent and relative who comes to commencement wants to give the graduate something special. One great gift idea is a diploma holder. These usually sell for over $100 at the bookstore but are nothing more than a simple frame with matting cut to fit the size of the diploma.

If you invest in an inexpensive mat cutter, you can easily make one of these holders. You can even add some embellishments like a photo of the school mounted above the diploma. The best way to get started is to go to the bookstore and see what they are selling. Craft your own and price it competitively. You can pass out flyers and let your graduating friends know that you are selling your own frames for much less than what the bookstore is charging. A picture or sample of your frame will usually close the deal.

Cash In On Your Talents And Skills

Everyone has skills that are marketable although few people think about selling something that they enjoy doing.

844.

Build your own Dell

Have you read the Michael Dell story? He is the founder of Dell computers and started by making PCs in his dorm room at the University of Texas. If you can build computers from components you too can start your own cottage computer factory.

To stay competitive with the ever lower prices of computers you might want to offer to pre-install all of the popular software and hardware recommended by your school. For a competitive edge, you can also include helping your customer set everything up and get connected to the school network.

To get started, check out Microsoft's reseller program at http://www.microsoft.com/OEM/ where you can get discounts if you are a systems builder. You'll also want to find cheap components. Get product reviews and great building tips at http://www.tomshardware.com. Finally check out the pricing of your competition as well as be inspired by Michael Dell at http://www.dell.com.

845.

Be crafty

Craft fairs can be serious business. For a few dollars you can purchase a table and sell your creations. While anything can sell, the most

popular items are priced between $5 and $20 and make good gifts.

Before you make a thousand widgets and purchase a table, attend a local craft fair and confirm that it is well attended and the clientele are people who would buy your goods. What kind of things have students sold successfully? Handbags, painted glass, woodwork, jewelry and original photography to name a few items. Check your local papers for listings of craft fairs as well as http://www.craftfair.com or http://www.etsy.com.

846.

Music for hire

If you are musically talented you can rent yourself out to various parties and events. Colleges hold hundreds of events from reunions to faculty dinners to visiting dignitaries that require live music. Plus, there are many off campus events like weddings and parties where music is needed. No matter what instrument you play, if you can play it well and you own a tuxedo or gown (required for many events) you can find a gig. Recently we spied a flyer on the Stanford campus for a bagpipe player—nearly all of the tearoffs at the bottom of the flyer were gone! (Yes, a bagpipe.)

847.

Singing telegrams

If you have a decent voice and are not easily embarrassed, offer singing telegrams. It might sound a little silly, but at $10 a song (and a song lasts about a minute) this can add up quickly. Singing telegrams are great for birthdays or any special event. Advertise with posters and flyers and since you obviously aren't easily embarrassed why not give the largest class on campus a free sample of your services before the lecture begins? We think you'd look good in a gorilla suit.

848.

Massage therapy

It's not just high-powered business executives who get massages. A treatment for some injuries and stress relief, massage therapy is in demand among students. Prices can range from $15 to $30 for a 20-minute session. However, you need to be certified in many states. To learn which states require certification and how to get certified, check with the National Certification Board for Therapeutic Massage and Bodywork at http://www.ncbtmb.com.

849.

Green thumbs equal greenbacks

If you are able to grow house plants (and it's not as easy as it seems) you can turn your dorm into a greenhouse and sell your plants to others who want to add a little color to their rooms.

Planting bulbs is probably the quickest and easiest way to get started. Growing from seeds is more difficult and takes longer but can make you a larger profit. Visit a local nursery to see what kind of plants grow in your area. Look for wholesalers who sell bulbs. One longtime mail order supplier of bulbs and seeds is Burpee (http://www.burpee.com). The website http://www.bhg.com/gardening/ also has good tips for growing many types of plants.

Serve Your Professors

Do something to help your professor and your pocketbook at the same time.

Is it really possible to make money from a business that I start in college?

You may have heard the legend of how Michael Dell started his business in his college dorm room in 1984 with $1,000 and the idea to sell custom-built computers directly to consumers. Today Dell employs 40,000 people, with revenues of over $10 billion per quarter.

But the reality is you're not trying to start the next Dell. You just need to earn enough to put a dent in your tuition bills. It's helpful to get tips and advice on a business that is similar to yours.

For example, if you want to start a pet sitting business, check out Pet Sitters International at http://www. petsit.com. This is an organization for professional pet sitters and offers answers to frequently asked questions about pet sitting, including what you need to do to open a pet sitting business, whether you need a license and advice for contracts with clients. Similarly the Dartmouth College Composition Center at http://www.dartmouth.edu/~writing/materials/tutor/ offers a lot of great advice for tutoring students in writing, including advice on how to get started in a session and how to give feedback.

These resources will help you get your business started and put you on the road to earning a profit. Of course, there is always the possibility that your business could become the next Dell, and if it does, just remember the two authors who gave you the idea. Our address is in the back of the book!

850.

Become a Ph.D. in house-sitting

Professors do a lot of traveling, often taking entire semesters and summers off to do research. There is a great need for pet watching and house sitting while they are away. Most professors would rather have a student they know and trust watch their house instead of a stranger. Plus, your cut rate student prices represent a huge advantage over commercial services.

Make sure all of your professors know that you are available for such jobs and give them a way to contact you. If you have done such services before, include a list of references.

If You Have The Gear Use It

Some money-makers require a fairly substantial capital investment. However, the following make use of expensive but relatively common equipment that can be found on campus. So if you have it you might as well use it.

851.

DJ for dollars

Great parties are defined by great music. There is a real demand for DJs who have the equipment, songs and talent to provide good music. If you have the equipment (or can borrow it from someone) you can turn a tidy profit by offering your services. Approach your student government, which is always looking for cheap DJs. Once you get your first break, word of mouth will get you more gigs. Rates run from $150 for a small party to over $800 for providing music to a large event.

852.

Be a shutterbug

If you are a talented photographer with the appropriate equipment, your services will be welcome at formals, graduation and other events. Advertise your services to the people who make the hiring decision. Once you get in you'll be called on over and over again. Your biggest advantage and selling point over an outside photographer is that you are a student and are cheaper. Keep your prices low to begin

with, and raise them as you become more established. Consider letting your clients view and order your pictures online through Shutterfly at http://www.shutterfly.com.

Give The Community What It Wants

Your college is an integral part of the community in which it is located. Take advantage of the fact that your neighbors are familiar with students and support your education.

853.

Digging for gold

Gardening and dog walking are great part-time jobs that you can get by flyering the neighborhood. Plus, it doesn't take much skill to mow a lawn or walk a dog–assuming that you are comfortable with animals. Charge by the hour and try to get a regular gig. Plus, once you get a job, ask the owner for recommendations of others who might need your services. One student took this to the extreme and ended up with an entire block of clients!

854.

Changing diapers and entertaining the young

If you are good with kids, babysitting is a great way to make money. With rates at $10 to $20 an hour this has become a big money maker for many students. Of course, you have to deal with some brats. Besides the obvious places to look for work such as with professors who have kids and people in the community, make sure you hit the graduate students. Quite a few have young children, and if they live on campus you won't have far to go to work!

855.

Earn dollars behind the wheel

If you have a car and are 21 years or older, you can drive for Uber or Lyft. An advantage of driving for one of these companies is that you can set your own hours and schedule. This flexibility works well so that you have plenty of time for classes and homework. Earnings typically range between $10 to $20 an hour.

856.

Piggy back on local events

Chances are there are a few really big events near your campus. At Harvard, for example, there is the Head of the Charles Regatta, a boat race and street fair that attracts tens of thousands of spectators. You can cater to people's excitement at these events by selling the one thing everyone wants: t-shirts. The key is to have a good design and an army of students willing to pound the pavement selling out of their backpacks. Be aware that there might be local laws restricting these kinds of sales and/or trademark issues with the event.

CHAPTER EIGHTEEN

Internships and Part-Time Jobs

Working For Your Education

Getting a job usually means committing to regular hours. The problem is that as a college student nothing in your life is regular. Rather than sacrifice school or extracurricular activities, you need to find a job that is as flexible as your life, or at least one that is compatible with it.

One of the most flexible jobs is an internship. While some internships offer only college credit, others pay actual monetary compensation. Companies that offer internships are usually familiar with the lifestyle needs of college students. They often provide flexible schedules. Another bonus is that if you do a good job as an intern it could lead to a full-time position after you graduate.

So how do you find the best part-time jobs and internships that will give you the best work experience and a little something for your wallet as well? Some of the best places to look are at your campus career center, in student publications and on the Internet.

Your campus career center is one of the first places that companies think of when they are looking for part-time employees and interns. Let the career center specialists know what kind of experience you have and also that you are interested only in paid jobs or internships. They can help you locate positions that are available or give you advice on which companies to contact. Student publications such as your school newspaper also have advertisements for part-time jobs and internships. Of course, the mother of all job listings is the Internet where you will find an endless supply of jobs.

The only problem with the above methods is that everyone else is doing the same thing. That means that you'll be competing with a lot of other students for the same positions. While you need to get in the game, you should also keep an eye open for creating your own job.

For example, you might notice that a local company always advertises for full-time sales associates. That probably means that they have a need for salespeople but can't find enough help. While they would probably rather hire a full-time worker they may also consider a part-time worker. Approach the business with your resume and make them an offer to hire you on as a part-timer or intern.

Another common source of work is at your own school. Imagine that you are doing well in a class, and you learn that your professor is working on a new book. You can politely ask her to keep you in mind if she needs a research assistant. The people and places that are not advertising but need help are perfect places for you to approach. Being the first, you won't have to beat out a ton of competition and you will have a greater say in the nature of the work.

Let's take a look at some of the best places to find jobs and internships. While you want to look for unadvertised job opportunities you also need to get into the mix of sending your resume out and applying the traditional way.

Internships And Jobs On The Net

Fire up your computer and head over to these job sites that are specifically for college students or have special sections for college job seekers.

857. College Recruiter
http://www.collegerecruiter.com

858. Craig's List
http://www.craigslist.org

859. HotJobs.com
http://www.hotjobs.com

860. InternJobs.com
http://www.internjobs.com

861. Internsearch.com
http://www.internsearch.com

862. Internships.com
http://www.internships.com

863. monsterTRAK
http://www.monstertrak.com

864. Rising Star Internships
http://www.rsinternships.com

865. TrueCareers
http://www.truecareers.com

The Best Internships And Part-Time Jobs

The following are some of the more interesting internships and jobs that are open to students. An ideal job not only pays you for your work but also gives you work experience that can prepare you for your future career. Remember that these are just a sampling of the jobs and internships open to you. Start exploring your school and community to find more.

866. Academy of Television Arts & Sciences
http://www.emmys.org
If you've always dreamed of attending the Emmys, continue to dream. But you can get experience in one of 27 categories of telecommunication as a part of the Academy's Summer Internship Program. The program is an eight-week summer internship with most opportunities in Los Angeles. Applicants should be full-time undergraduate or graduate students versed in professional television production, techniques and practices. Interns receive $4,000.

867. AFL-CIO
http://www.aflcio.org
The Union Summer program is a five-week internship to help students gain experience in union organizing skills. College juniors and seniors may apply. Work may include interviewing workers, organizing picket lines, marches or demonstrations

and educating about workers' right issues. Students receive a stipend and housing and are placed nationwide.

868. American Association of Advertising Agencies
http://www.aaaa.org
You may think that you could have created the talking Chihuahua Taco Bell campaign. Here is the chance to prove that you would make a gifted advertising executive. The Multicultural Advertising Internship Program (MAIP) offers African American, Asian American, Hispanic American and Native American college students experience in advertising.

869. American Conservatory Theater (A.C.T.)
http://www.act-sf.org
You can get behind the theater curtains. The A.C.T. in San Francisco offers college students and graduates advanced training in theater production and administration, including roundtables with guest speakers and brown bag lunches with guest artists. Interns may receive a stipend.

870. Association of Psychology Postdoctoral and Internship Centers (APPIC)
http://www.natmatch.com/psychint/
There are plenty of matchmaking websites for dates, but APPIC sponsors the Internship Matching Program through which psychology students can be matched with one of more than 1,000 participating internship programs in the U.S. and Canada. You can submit your resume for review on the website.

871. Black Data Processing Associates (BDPA)
http://www.bdpa.org
This national organization sponsors an online database in which computer science and computer engineering students can submit resumes for corporations to review and consider for internships. Previous corporations participating include Abbott Laboratories, Allstate Insurance Company, GE Aircraft Engines, Hewitt Associates, Household International, IBM Global Services, Kraft Foods, Lucent Technologies, Motorola, Procter & Gamble, Sears, Tellabs and United Stationers.

872. Calvary Women's Services

http://www.calvaryservices.org

This is a non-profit agency that provides housing and support to homeless women in Washington, D.C. You can work as a summer intern coordinating the volunteer database, producing materials for volunteers, helping with recruitment and assisting with running the shelter. Applicants should be rising college juniors and seniors, and interns receive a $2,000 stipend.

873. Emily's List

http://www.emilyslist.org

Start your trek toward the White House with Emily's List, a Washington, D.C.-based political action committee that assists progressive Democratic politicians. The organization offers internships in its political, development, research and communications departments. Applicants must have strong written and verbal communication skills. Interns are paid a $500 per month stipend and a $30 per month Metro card.

874. Environmental Careers Organization (ECO)

http://www.eco.org

Attention nature lovers! This organization places about 750 students in paid internships each year. Interns study environmental law issues, do environmental field research, give tours at national parks and develop environmental marketing campaigns. The website has listings that you can search by sponsor or location. Most internships begin in the summer. The fields that are most highly desired include botany, chemical engineering, chemistry, civil engineering, computer science, earth science, energy, environmental engineering, environmental health, environmental science, environmental studies, fisheries, forestry, geography, GIS (geographic information systems), geology, hazardous waste management, health and safety, hydrology and hydrogeology, landscape architecture, natural resource management, parks/recreation management, policy/public administration, range management, regional planning, solid waste management, surveying, toxicology, urban planning and wildlife science/management.

875. Fermi National Accelerator Laboratory

http://sist.fnal.gov

Based in Batavia, Illinois, the laboratory offers paid internships for college undergraduates in physics, electrical engineering, computer programming and mechanical engineering. The program focuses on minorities that have been historically underrepresented in science. Students conduct laboratory research.

876. Hershey's Intern Professionals Program (HIPP)

http://www.hersheysjobs.com/students.html

For chocoholics, this is the internship of all internships. The national chocolate manufacturer offers internships of up to three months and co-op opportunities of three months or longer for students to gain work experience. Jobs are located in Hershey, Pennsylvania, near Harrisburg. The company is looking for all majors and all levels of education including graduate students. Hershey's pays for a housing search trip, moving expenses for students and enough chocolate to last a lifetime.

877. Hispanic Association of Colleges and Universities (HACU)

http://www.hacu.net

What do the CIA and Ronald McDonald have in common? You could be employed by either through this organization's National Internship Program (HNIP). The program has placed thousands of college students in paid internships, which are 10 or 15 weeks in length and are in Washington, D.C., and in other areas of the country. Previous employers have included the Central Intelligence Agency, Price Waterhouse Coopers LLP, Department of Health and Human Services, Federal Deposit Insurance Corporation, Federal Reserve Board, State Farm Insurance, Department of Defense, Goldman, Sachs & Co., Target Corporation, McDonald's Corporation, Department of Labor, Department of State, Department of Transportation and Environmental Protection Agency.

878. Johnson Space Center Cooperative Education Program

http://pathways.jsc.nasa.gov/

You may have stopped dressing up as an astronaut for Halloween, but you can still fulfill your dream of working at NASA. Undergraduate and graduate students across the country alternate semesters at school with semesters at JSC in paid, full-time positions to get hands-on experience in areas including aerospace engineering, mechanical engineering, electrical engineering, math, physics, biology and even business and accounting. The program allows you to work in the space program that creates spacecraft, trains astronauts and controls space missions.

879. Kate Spade

http://www.katespadeandcompany.com

The Kate Spade & Company Summer Internship Program gives students experience in merchandising, design, sales, finance, marketing and product management. The ten-week program features a weekly speaker series to introduce students to various departments.

880. L&T Health and Fitness

http://www.ltwell.com

Get paid to work out. L&T Health and Fitness provides health and fitness programs to companies and state and federal government agencies. As an intern, you will gain training in fitness assessments and consultation, equipment maintenance, health promotion, customer service, special event planning, risk management and group exercise class instruction. Interns work 20 to 40 hours for 8 to 12 weeks for a stipend. Internships are available in: Arizona, Connecticut, District of Columbia, Georgia, Illinois, Maine, Maryland, New Jersey, North Carolina, Ohio, Pennsylvania and Virginia.

881. Lockheed Martin

http://www.lockheedmartinjobs.com

Get your feet wet in the aircraft and technology industry. Based in Manassas, Virginia, the Naval Electronics & Surveillance Systems-Undersea Systems (NE&SS-Undersea Systems) offers co-op and internship programs for college students to gain experience in areas including systems engineering, computer science and software engineering. In the co-op program, students typically alternate work and school over two or three semesters, and in the internship program, students work full-time for about 12 weeks in the summer. Students should be pursuing their bachelor's, master's or Ph.D. in electrical engineering, mechanical engineering, computer science, computer information systems, computer engineering, material science, management information systems, chemical engineering or industrial engineering or be undergraduate or graduate business students. Students receive salaries, overtime, holidays, sickness days and relocation assistance.

882. Marriott
http://www.marriott.com
If you'd like to work in the hotel industry, the international hotel chain offers paid internships in accounting and finance, banquets/catering, culinary, front office, housekeeping, human resources, restaurants and sales at lodging proprieties across the country and its corporate office. The internships are generally at least 10 or 12 weeks, and most properties prefer that they last six months. Some offer housing assistance.

883. National Association of Professional Surplus Lines Offices
http://www.napslo.org
The association provides paid, nine-week summer internships to college students who plan to pursue careers in the surplus lines insurance industry, which specializes in unique or hard to place risks. College juniors and seniors are preferred, and graduate students may also apply. Insurance majors are preferred and finance or business majors may also apply. Interns gain experience in underwriting risks, claims, accounting, marketing and regulation and receive a salary, stipend, travel expenses and housing expenses and also compete for an additional internship in London.

How do I put together a resume for a job or internship?

If you think of your life as a book, then your resume should be the table of contents. In other words, it gives potential employers a quick snapshot of your experience and background.

The general areas that you should cover in a resume are:

Name and contact information: At the top of your resume, put your name, address, telephone number and email address. You want employers to be able to easily contact you.

Goal: What kind of position are you seeking? This can usually be done in a single sentence.

Work experience: What jobs have you had, especially any that demonstrate skills you will use in the position you are applying for?

Education: Include your high school, college and, if applicable, graduate school. Include the year that you graduated and if you graduated with honors. For college or graduate school, you can state your graduation date as "expected," and also list your major.

Leadership and extracurricular activities: Since you may not have a lot of work experience yet, your extracurricular activities can demonstrate some of the skills that you will need for the position.

As you are completing your resume, keep the following tips in mind:

Aim for a specific position. In other words, don't send the same resume to every potential employer. Write about your skills and background as they apply to the particular position you are seeking.

Use active verbs. Whenever possible, make your resume come alive with words like, "managed," "led," "coordinated" and "directed."

Focus on accomplishments. Instead of just giving a job description, explain what you achieved in a role. What results did you produce? Were you responsible for managing other employees or a particular project?

Aim for perfection. Remember that this single document may be the only impression you get to make with a potential employer. It needs to be flawless.

One last tip, and this is probably the hardest to follow: keep your resume to a single page. You are not going to be able to include everything from your life, but by keeping it to one page it forces you to include only the most relevant information. Also, most employers won't read past the first page anyway.

884. National Cancer Institute

http://www.cancer.gov/researchandfunding/cancertraining/atnci

Students who are completing their master's degree or Ph.D. can apply for six-month paid internships in health communications and science writing. Students should have backgrounds in public health, health education, science, biostatistics, epidemiology, communications, marketing, public relations, news writing or science writing. Interns receive monthly stipends of up to approximately $2,600, paid holidays, flexible work schedules and health insurance. The National Cancer Institute is located in suburban Washington, D.C., in Bethesda, Maryland, and Rockville, Maryland.

885. National Capital Planning Commission (NCPC)

http://www.ncpc.gov

In 1,000 years the Capital will probably look much the way that it does now. That's thanks to the NCPC, the federal government's planning agency responsible for preserving the beauty and urban design of the Capital. Located in Washington, D.C., the agency offers paid and unpaid internships in architecture, business management, community planning, computer-aided design (CAD), economics, environmental science, geography, geographic information systems (GIS), landscape architecture, historic preservation, law and urban design.

886. National Gallery of Art

http://www.nga.gov/education/

Attention future curators! In Washington, D.C., the National Gallery of Art offers paid internships to college graduates and graduate students in professional museum training. Through the Graduate Curatorial Internships, graduate students and recent postdoctoral graduates work with curators on collection or exhibition projects. Through Internships in the Museum Profession, interns work closely with the design and installation department. Recent undergraduate graduates may apply, but graduate students are preferred.

887. National Institutes of Health (NIH)

https://www.training.nih.gov/programs/sip

The NIH offers approximately 1,000 paid internships in a number of its institutes and centers. The program is for eight weeks during the summer and provides monthly stipends of up to $1,500 for high school students, $1,800 for college students and $2,700 for graduate students. Most work is in research laboratories and applicants should have taken courses in biology and chemistry. Laboratories are in Bethesda, Maryland; Baltimore, Maryland; Frederick, Maryland; Research Triangle Park (Raleigh/Durham), North Carolina; Hamilton, Montana and Phoenix, Arizona.

888. National Wildlife Federation (NWF)

http://www.nwf.org

Give lawyers a good rap. Law students who have completed at least two semesters of law school can work in paid summer internships through the Legal Internship Program of NWF, the national conservation education and advocacy organization located in Washington, D.C. Interns assist attorneys in work involving endangered habitat, wetlands, water quality, land stewardship and sustainable communities. They work on litigation and national policy initiatives. Unpaid spring and fall internships are also offered for school credit.

889. Nike

http://www.nikebiz.com

Imagine working alongside Michael Jordan and LeBron James. Okay, you won't actually work alongside the basketball superstars, but you can work for the same company as they do and even help design the shoes that they may hawk. Nike offers a nine-week Adrenaline internship program during summers to give students experience in areas including sports marketing and logistics, product development and information technology. While there are some positions in other major U.S. cities, most are located in Beaverton, Oregon.

890. Pacific Northwest National Laboratory

http://www.pnl.gov

The National Security Internship Program is for undergraduate and graduate students in areas such as nuclear science, electrical engineering, computer science, physics or chemistry. Internships typically start in the summer for 8 to 12 weeks and may continue through part-time work during the school year. Interns receive a salary or stipend and tuition reimbursement for committing to work as full-time employees after graduation. The company is based in Richland, Washington.

891. San Diego Zoo

http://www.sandiegozoo.org/zoo/education/zoo_internquest

If you never thought you were close enough to the animals at the zoo, here's an opportunity to get even closer. The zoo offers internships for both high school and college students. For high school students, the InternQuest program is a seven-week program that allows students who wish to pursue careers in the life sciences (biology, zoology, human or veterinary medicine, wildlife management, botany, etc.) to learn from zoo experts. The Education Department offers paid internships for both high school and college students to assist with the Safari Sleepovers and Summer Camps. Undergraduate and graduate students who plan careers in health and science professions may also apply for research fellowships at the Center for Reproduction of Endangered Species (CRES).

892. Sandia National Laboratories (SNL)

http://www.sandia.gov (Albuquerque)

http://www.sandia.gov/locations/livermore_california.html (California)

The Science & Technology Outreach (S&TO) Student Internship Program (SIP) provides paid internships for undergraduate and graduate students majoring in science, math, engineering, technology, computer science and MIS. Students work in the Albuquerque, New Mexico, and Sandia, California, areas. The program actively recruits students from historically underrepresented groups. Interns receive a salary and round trip airfare or mileage and can participate in a mentor program.

893. Smithsonian National Zoo

http://nationalzoo.si.edu

The Smithsonian National Zoo's Conservation & Research Center (SNZP-CRC) in Washington, D.C., offers internships in conservation biology (behavior, ecology and GIS, genetics and nutrition), reproductive sciences (gamete biology and endocrinology) and science education and training through its Research Internship Program. Some of the internships offer stipends and/or housing.

894. The National Academies

http://www.nationalacademies.org/internship/

Through the Christine Mirzayan Science & Technology Policy Internship Program, graduate students in science, engineering, medical, veterinary, business and law analyze science and technology policy. The program is for 10 or 12 weeks and provides a stipend for expenses.

895. U.S. Department of Energy (DOE)

http://www.dep.anl.gov

Through the DOE's Science Undergraduate Laboratory Internships (SULI) and Student Research Participation Programs, college sophomores, juniors and seniors conduct research at the Argonne National Laboratory and other laboratories in physical and life sciences, mathematics, computer science, engineering, coal, conservation, environmental impact and technology, fission and fusion technology. The program is for 15 weeks and provides a stipend, housing allowances and transportation.

896. U.S. Geological Survey (USGS)

http://education.usgs.gov/careers.html

Undergraduate and graduate students gain field, laboratory and research experience through the State Water Resources Research Institute Program. Interns are employees of participating universities and colleges, and applicants can get more information from their state USGS representative or institute director.

897. U.S. Tennis Association

http://www.usta.com

Here's your opportunity to meet the Williams sisters (or at least to increase your chances of meeting them). The national governing body of tennis offers internships, some that provide stipends. Recent openings have been for communications students to work on public relations tasks, mechanical engineering students to develop methods for court surface testing, net tightness and lighting and sports management/psychology graduate students to perform fitness evaluations.

898. Walt Disney World College Program

http://www.wdwcollegeprogram.com

It takes a lot of work to create the magic of Disney, and you can help. Through this program, you can gain experience in costuming, culinary arts, custodial, entertainment as character performers or character greeters, food and beverage service, guest services, hospitality, front desk operations, housekeeping, life guarding, merchandise, operations, attractions, recreation, transportation and vacation planning. Advanced internships are available in accounting/finance (revenue and currency control, work force planning), communications and journalism (editorial assistant, communications coordinator), education, business (cast activities, guest relations, labor maintenance analyst, merchandise operations), horticulture, human resources, marketing and sales, recreation and the sciences (animal behavior, nutrition research, reproductive biology, plant science, aquaculture). Internships are generally a minimum of five months.

899. Warner Music Group

http://www.wmg.com

This could be your big break in the music industry. Or at the very least give you some work experience at an international music conglomerate. The company offers unpaid internships for college credit only during the spring and winter and paid internships for high school and college students during the summer in Los Angeles and New York. You can get more information in the frequently asked questions area of the company's website. Your internship may consist of a lot of grunt work, but you have to remember that this is the way that most everyone gets started in the business.

CHAPTER NINETEEN

Be A Part-Time Student

Working And Studying

What makes going to school so expensive? Besides the price of tuition, it's the fact that to be a student you also have to be unemployed. Aside from part-time jobs, most students cannot hold a full-time job and go to college. With zero income and tuition to pay, it's no wonder that the student life is synonymous with the poor life.

But why can't you work and go to school? The biggest problem is that class time and work time are usually both between 9 and 5. Plus, there is the all important sleep time. Yet this has not stopped millions of students from working and getting their degree. It can take longer to complete your degree if you opt to work and go to school since you usually take a reduced class load. The upside is that you can work and earn money to pay for your education.

There are several options for combining work with school. Some students begin with night programs to get their basic courses out of the way, then move to a weekend course and even finish their last year as full-time students. There is no single "correct" way that you can combine work and school and the only rule is to do whatever fits your specific situation.

Let's take a look at some of the options that let you work while still earning your degree.

900.

Night school isn't just to get your high school diploma

You might think of night schools just as high schools where adults can complete their GED. However, night programs have exploded to encompass everything from single skill courses such as learning computer skills to getting your entire bachelor's or master's degree.

Colleges with night programs usually offer classes that meet one or two nights a week. You may be able to sign up for as many as four courses per week. Most schools don't offer courses on Friday or the weekend. These programs allow you to continue working while also working toward learning a new skill or a degree.

Don't deceive yourself to think this will be easy. Most night students report that life takes on a whole new level of chaos as they juggle family time, work, classes and homework. But the flexibility of night programs can't be matched, and they are usually one of the most economical ways for you to get more education without having to quit your job.

901.

Adult education is often a bargain

If you need vocational or technical training or basic educational skills, adult education may be a great choice for you. State and federally funded adult education centers are usually run out of high schools, community centers, community colleges and public universities. Their primary mission is to provide low- or no-cost training for students who need to acquire new skills due to a forced career change.

Most adult education classes can be taken while working, and in fact your employer may even pay for your schooling. Some programs also give discounts to students over the age of 55, and many states designate certain types of classes as eligible for receiving state subsidies, which greatly reduce costs.

To find programs available in your area, start with your state's office of adult education or simply look in the phone book for your nearest adult school. Most are held at high schools or colleges, although some also have dedicated campuses. You can also visit the Department of Education's Office of Career, Technical and Adult Education which can point you in the right direction at http://www.ed.gov/about/offices/list/ovae.

902.

Use your evenings and weekends to get a graduate degree

Professional schools are getting into the action of helping full-time workers get their advanced degree. The U.C. Berkeley part-time MBA program is a good example. While a traditional MBA requires that you be a full-time student for two years, the part-time program allows you to work full-time and attend either evening or weekend classes. If you choose the evening schedule you'll meet twice a week for 3 1/2 hours per session. If you go the weekend route you'll meet on Saturdays from 9 a.m. to 6 p.m. You take the same courses as full-time business school students and earn the same degree, but since you are meeting for less time it will take you three years to graduate.

Part-time programs are growing in popularity as an advanced degree becomes more of a career essential and as more adult students find that they cannot afford to give up their jobs to go back to school. Since you won't be giving up your day job you'll need to select a program at a school near you. Call your local colleges and ask about their evening or weekend programs.

903.

Extension programs let you work and study

Most colleges offer continuing education or extension programs. These are typically held in the evening and are usually open enrollment, which means that you don't need to go through a selective admission process to get into the program. Best of all you can earn complete degrees and graduate certificates without having to become a full-time student.

The Harvard Extension School, for example, enrolls more than 13,000 students each year. Unlike the college, the Extension School accepts students on an open enrollment basis. Students can take just a few courses to improve their job skills or they can get an entire undergradu-

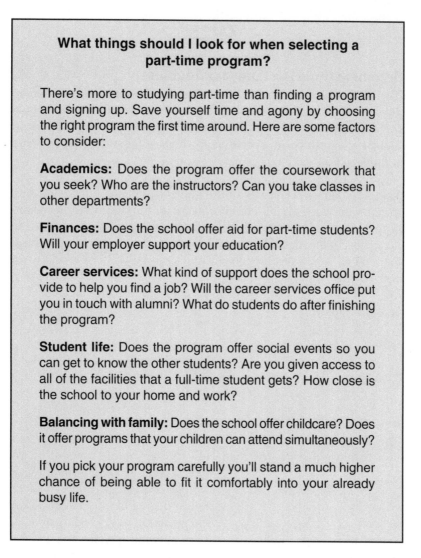

What things should I look for when selecting a part-time program?

There's more to studying part-time than finding a program and signing up. Save yourself time and agony by choosing the right program the first time around. Here are some factors to consider:

Academics: Does the program offer the coursework that you seek? Who are the instructors? Can you take classes in other departments?

Finances: Does the school offer aid for part-time students? Will your employer support your education?

Career services: What kind of support does the school provide to help you find a job? Will the career services office put you in touch with alumni? What do students do after finishing the program?

Student life: Does the program offer social events so you can get to know the other students? Are you given access to all of the facilities that a full-time student gets? How close is the school to your home and work?

Balancing with family: Does the school offer childcare? Does it offer programs that your children can attend simultaneously?

If you pick your program carefully you'll stand a much higher chance of being able to fit it comfortably into your already busy life.

ate or graduate degree. The school offers more than 550 courses in 50 fields of study. Many of the instructors are the same faculty who teach during the day at Harvard College.

Contact your local colleges to see if they offer an extension or continuing education programs. This may be an excellent way for you to get a degree without being a full-time student.

904.

Summer school isn't only for flunkies

You might think summer school is just for the students who flunked algebra, but most colleges offer summer sessions that allow you to take the same classes that are offered during the school year. If you are lucky enough to be in a profession where you get summers off then summer school may be the perfect option for you.

Summer courses are usually more intensive since you have less time to cover the same amount of information as during the regular school term. However, summer school is usually cheaper than the same class taken during the regular term, and you learn the same material. Credit that you earn in a summer course can almost always be used toward your degree or transferred later to a full-time program. Contact your local college to get the details on their summer session and see if it's an option for you.

905.

Explore distance learning options

The Internet has brought a whole new life to distance learning, which used to take place via snail mail. Now through online courses you can

take classes at your convenience. Online courses also offer a much higher degree of interaction and let you get closer to the feeling of being there without actually being there. As an added benefit, they are often cheaper than in-person courses.

Your local college or university usually offers distance learning courses. Rutgers University School of Business in New Jersey, for example, offers an online management certificate in everything from marketing to information technology. The program combines online animated instruction and seminars with two one-day, in-person training sessions.

To find a distance learning program, visit www.collegeispower.com to search for a program that fits you.

906.

Explore hybrid courses

Hybrid, or blended, courses combine online learning with in-classroom learning. These courses are generally defined as having more than 20 percent of the class taught online. Many part-time students prefer hybrid classes because they allow some scheduling flexibility with the online component but still incorporate valuable face-to-face time with professors and fellow students.

907.

Don't get a degree when a certificate will do

Less expensive than degree programs, certificate programs are offered part-time, in the summer or through adult education programs and do not require you to take as many courses as you would to earn a degree. While not as highly regarded as an actual degree, depending on your reasons for going back to school, they might be just what you need and at a fraction of the cost. Certificates generally signify proficiency in a specific area, which for career advancement may be all you need to jump to the next level or make a career switch.

908.

Combine part-time with full-time study

What's great about being a part-time student is that you can build up credits while still maintaining your job to be able to afford your education. After you have built up enough credits through summer, night or weekend programs you may find that you want to finish off your degree in one or two years of full-time study. This might be especially useful if you are looking to change jobs anyway.

By combining part-time with full-time study, you fund your part-time education through work and then you use your savings, borrow or win scholarships to pay for your last year or two of full-time education. You will graduate with a degree from a four-year college and have saved yourself many years of tuition payments.

Opportunities For Adult Students

Special Resources For Adult Students

Congratulations on your decision to go back to school. You are part of a growing number of adults who are going back to college and are willing to invest in your education for both professional and personal reasons.

But while education is known to free the mind, education itself is anything but free. And unlike a student fresh out of high school, adults don't have parental support, counselors and an easy to reach network of scholarship and financial aid programs. Plus, with families to support, mortgages to pay and a host of other obligations, it is not as easy as taking out a student loan figuring that you'll pay it back later. Unlike an 18-year-old, you know about loans and debt and want to do whatever you can to avoid adding more.

If you're an adult student and you turned to this chapter first you're missing out on a lot of money-saving ways to pay for college. Almost everything in this book works for adult or non-traditional students. However, there are a few specific options that are only available to adult students. So if you are part of the growing number of adults returning to college, then in addition to the ideas in the previous chapters add these to your arsenal.

Before we get into the specific options just for adult students, here is a recap of a few of the ways to pay for college that appear in previous chapters that are also very useful to you:

Find a scholarship in Chapter 2. Remember many scholarships don't have age limits.

Win a guaranteed scholarship in Chapter 4. Adult students certainly qualify for the various guaranteed scholarships offered by colleges.

Reward programs for students in Chapter 5. You can name yourself the beneficiary in many of these programs. Get friends and relatives to participate to accelerate your earnings.

Savings strategies in Chapter 6. There are many ways for you to save and invest for college. Even if you plan to go back to school in a year you should start saving now.

Tax breaks in Chapter 7. Save your tax dollars and put more money back in your pocket to pay for school.

Apply for financial aid in Chapter 8. Each year over $238 billion in financial aid is awarded. You should lay your claim to what you deserve.

Get state resources to pay for college in Chapter 11. Your state has a lot of resources and even scholarships for students of all ages.

The best way to borrow money in Chapter 12. Borrowing money may be unavoidable. Learn where to borrow and how to borrow intelligently.

Loan forgiveness programs in Chapter 13. Imagine not having to repay your student loan. Ever! These programs can make that a reality.

Save money while in college in Chapter 15. There is a lot that you can do to save the money you already have.

Make college cheaper in Chapter 16. Why pay full price? Use these strategies to make your college less expensive.

Be a part-time student in Chapter 19. There is nothing wrong with working and going to school. Take a look at these options.

Now let's take a look at more special options just for adult students.

**I haven't studied or taken a test in 10 years.
How do I get back into that way of life?**

Like riding a bike, being a student will come back naturally. It may take a few weeks to acclimate to your new lifestyle but don't worry: You'll adapt. To help with your transition consider these tips:

Create a good study space. Sitting on the couch in front of the TV is not the best study space. Find a quiet area with comfortable seating and good lighting.

Schedule time to study. You need a block of uninterrupted time to study. This might mean exiling yourself to the public library just to get away from the chaos of home.

Study at the best time of the day for you. You know whether you are a morning or night person. Take advantage of your natural times of high energy.

Join a study group. Working with a group helps you learn the material better by discussing it with others and introduces new ideas.

Get tutoring help. Most schools offer tutoring help, or find a teaching assistant or star fellow student to give you some help.

Get extra help from your professors. Take advantage of your professors' office hours.

Keep a list of questions about the material. This will help direct your conversations with your professors.

Take notes. Both in lectures and while reading, take notes to help you remember the material better.

Review your notes. What good are all those notes if you don't use them? Reviewing your notes will help you recall the information in class and on exams.

909.

Low-cost childcare

If you have a family, then finding affordable child care may be the difference between you being able to attend college or not. The Office of Postsecondary Education, which is a part of the U.S. Department of Education, has created the Child Care Access Means Parents in School Program. Schools can apply for grant money to create low cost or no cost childcare options for low-income students. Contact your school to see if they participate in this program and if you qualify to take advantage of it.

Scholarships Just For Adult Students

Like any student looking for a scholarship you should check out Chapter 2 for tips on where to find a scholarship. It's important to know that most scholarships are not based on age. A scholarship will usually specify its target recipient such as an undergraduate student or students majoring in accounting. It usually doesn't matter if you are a 17-year-old high school student or a 79-year-old adult student. So don't think that you can't apply for scholarships that are not specially marked for adult students.

That being said there are a few scholarship programs that are just for adult students. Remember you will find many of these awards in your own backyard or community, but here are some places to start:

Your college. Your school is the first place you should look for awards. Given that adult students make up a large percentage of a college's total enrollment, many schools are establishing scholarships just for adult students. Some are even using these awards as incentives to get adults to apply. The University of Toledo in Ohio, for example, has established an Adult Scholarship Committee within the Office of Undergraduate Admission to review applications for scholarships from half-time and full-time adult student applicants. Iowa State University offers four scholarship programs for adults. The *Adult Student Scholarship Fund* provides money to cover all textbooks and related expenses while the *Adult Student Scholarships* give up to $2,000 to pay for tuition.

Your employer. As a benefit for working at your company, your employer may support your education. Ask your human resources department.

Agencies and associations dedicated to adult education. There are many agencies and associations for adult learners. In addition to providing information and resources, some also provide scholarships. Search your community and state for these awards. Begin by visiting your nearest adult education center or school. From there do your detective work to uncover the various agencies and associations that support adult education.

Charitable foundations. Education is a cause that foundations often support. While their efforts may be geared toward helping high school students, some also direct funds toward helping adult students.

Businesses. Some businesses support students with scholarships. Besides those listed in Chapter 2, check with businesses in your community.

Now let's take a look at some scholarships specifically designed for adult students:

910. A. Harry Passow Classroom Teacher Scholarship
http://www.nagc.org
This award sponsored by the National Association for Gifted Children is given to NAGC members who wish to continue their education. You must be a teacher of gifted students of grades K-12.

911. Adult Students In Scholastic Transition (ASIST)
http://www.ewiconnect.com
Executive Women International offers this award to assist adults who face major life transitions. Applicants may be single parents, individuals just entering the workforce or displaced workers.

912. ASL Adult Education Foundation Scholarship
http://www.alphasigmalambda.org
Each year the national chapter of Alpha Sigma Lambda Honor Society awards eight scholarships to adult student members.

Scholarship applications are sent to all national councilors in early spring, and you should check with your chapter.

913. Business and Professional Women's Foundation Career Advancement Scholarship
http://www.bpwfoundation.org
Sponsored by the BPW Foundation, this award helps disadvantaged women who want to further their education. Each year the foundation awards more than $120,000 to women over the age of 25.

914. Career Development Grants For Women
http://www.aauw.org/fga/
The American Association of University Women offers financial support for women who hold a bachelor's degree and are preparing to advance their careers, change careers or re-enter the work force. The AAUW also offers academic grants, which help women pay for master's degrees, second bachelor's degrees or specialized training.

915. Career Transition for Dancers
http://www.careertransition.org
The award is for dancers who are seeking second careers. You must have had a performing dance career of seven or more years and have 100 weeks or more of paid employment within seven years or longer.

916. Chips Quinn Scholarships
http://www.chipsquinn.org
If you are a Chips Quinn alumnus you can apply for a scholarship to attend journalism and newsroom-management seminars. You must have been working at least three years in newspaper newsrooms and have the endorsement of your current newspaper's editor to apply.

How can I possibly balance school and other commitments?

Think about how busy you are. Now, imagine how busy you would be if you had three to five less hours in a day. That will be your life as an adult student, balancing school with family, other commitments and maybe even work. How can you manage? Here are some tips to help you keep your sanity:

Set realistic goals. Before you tackle any new task, it's always a good idea to set goals. That way you'll know exactly what you are trying to accomplish. In this case, are you trying to earn a degree? Take courses to enhance your existing career? Change careers? Whatever your goals are, make sure that they are realistic and fit within your life as a whole. Be honest about how long it will take to accomplish your goal. If not, you'll only set yourself up for failure.

Set a schedule. If you're working around your family, a job or other commitments, it's important that you figure out how you will fit everything into a day. Get a calendar so you can see your schedule visually.

Communicate with your family. Make sure that you're all on the same page about what your goals are and how going back to school will affect everyone. It may be time to assign some additional responsibilities to other members of your household.

Communicate with your professors. You don't want to ask your professors for special treatment, but if you let them know what your situation is, they will probably be more understanding if you ask for changes in your schedule or even extensions on assignments.

Communicate with your employer. If you are working while going to school, let your employer know as well so that your schedule can be accommodated.

Prioritize. Figure out what really matters in life and what is a "nice to have." Limit your other commitments, and don't be afraid to say "no."

Share responsibilities with your family. Ask family members to help out with tasks that you would normally do. Explain that your going to school will benefit everyone so you can use some extra help.

Overload yourself as little as possible. By virtue of balancing school with your other responsibilities, you will overload yourself. But as much as possible, shed what is not vital.

917. Continuing Education Awards

http://www.mlanet.org/p/cm/ld/fid=43
The Medical Library Association helps MLA members develop their knowledge of librarianship through continuing education programs. You must already hold a graduate degree in library science and be a practicing health science librarian.

918. Continuing Education Grant/Loan Program

http://www.pcusa.org/financialaid/scholarships.htm
This program aids Presbyterian Church (U.S.A.) members pursuing post graduate educations. Applicants must be PCUSA church members enrolled in a Ph.D. or equivalent postgraduate program in religious studies.

919. Datatel Returning Student Scholarship

http://www.datatel.com
Applicants must be returning to school in the upcoming year after an absence of at least five years and either attend a Datatel Client college or university or work at a Datatel non-education site and attend any college or university.

920. Educational Foundation for Women in Accounting

http://www.efwa.org
The *Women in Transition Scholarships* and *Women in Need Scholarships* both provide financial assistance to female students who are pursuing degrees in accounting. Trying to get a Ph.D. in accounting? You might just be interested in the *Laurel Fund.*

921. Elizabeth Greenshields Foundation Grants
http://www.elizabethgreenshieldsfoundation.org
This award promotes an appreciation of painting, drawing, sculpture and the graphic arts through supporting art students, artists or sculptors. To apply you must have already started or completed training at an established school of art or have demonstrated through past work and future plans that you will make art a lifetime career.

922. Executive Women International (EWI)
http://www.ewiconnect.com
Single parents and individuals just entering the workforce or displaced workers can apply for an *Adult Students In Scholastic Transition* (ASIST) award.

923. Frank G. Brewer Civil Air Patrol Memorial Aerospace Award
http://ae.capmembers.com/programs/awards/
This award is for applicants who have made noteworthy aerospace achievements over a number of years.

924. Golden Key GEICO Life Scholarship
http://www.goldenkey.org
If you are a member of the Golden Key Society and are an adult student you can apply for this award. You must have already completed at least 12 undergraduate credit hours in the previous year before you apply.

925. Insurance Professional Scholarships
http://www.inssfa.org
The National Association of Insurance Women (NAIW) Education Foundation offers scholarships to help you advance your career in insurance. To apply you must be employed in the insurance industry for at least two years.

926. Jeannette Rankin Foundation
http://www.rankinfoundation.org
This group raises money to help women 35 years of age and older who want to better themselves through education. You

---

What kind of support can I expect from my college as an adult student?

Because you have different needs than 18-year-old high school seniors, you will find that many colleges have special departments or services for adult students. Typical services include assistance with the admission and financial aid process, study skills courses and tutoring.

The Adult Student Services department at Kansas State University even offers help with housing referrals, childcare, public school enrollment and community family programs. The Center for Returning Adult Student Development at Iona College in New York provides meeting and workspace with computers, social events and a monthly newsletter for adult students.

Ask your college what services it offers for adult students, and take advantage of them. It's a great opportunity to make the transition from work to school and to meet other students with similar backgrounds as you.

---

can apply for an award if you are a woman over 35 years old who plans to obtain an undergraduate or vocational education.

927. Rita Levine Memorial Scholarship

http://www.mensafoundation.org/scholarships
Sponsored by the MENSA Education and Research Foundation, this essay-based award is for women who are returning to school after having had to interrupt their educations.

928. Western Union Foundation Scholarship Program

https://foundation.westernunion.com/education_programs.html
This program is designed specifically for non-traditional students who have overcome personal challenges, exemplify initiative, exhibit a commitment to learning and working hard, and demonstrate financial need. Special consideration is given to applicants who show academic promise and a strong desire for advancing their educational and career goals.

929. Women's Opportunity Awards

http://www.soroptimist.org

Sponsored by Soroptimist International this award helps women who are heads of their households and are entering or re-entering the workforce to obtain education and skills training. Applicants must also be attending or have been accepted to a vocational/skills training program or an undergraduate degree program. Apply first at the community level through your local Soroptimist club.

CHAPTER TWENTY-ONE

Opportunities For Graduate Students

Special Opportunities For Graduate School

Most graduate students are prepared for the academic rigors of dissertations, oral exams, board exams and research galore. What most grad students are not ready for is the life of near poverty. This is especially true for graduate students who also have families to support. Still, the financial sacrifices can be worthwhile. Whether you are trying to get your master's, MBA, JD, MD or Ph.D., a graduate degree can be a huge boost to your career. For some professions it is even a prerequisite.

Fortunately, there is money out there for graduate students. Everything that we have discussed so far in this book is applicable to you. Don't skip the previous chapters on scholarships, financial aid, loans and loan repayment programs. In fact, let's recap a few of the strategies listed in previous chapters that are fully applicable to helping you pay for graduate school.

Find a scholarship in Chapter 2. Most scholarships today don't have age limits. You'll find that some awards are open to both undergraduate and graduate students, especially when it comes to awards from professional associations.

How to win a guaranteed scholarship in Chapter 4. Take advantage of the various guaranteed scholarships including getting in-state tuition even though you are an out-of-state student.

Reward programs for students in Chapter 5. You can name yourself the beneficiary in many of these programs. If you get friends and relatives to participate, you can accelerate your earnings.

Savings strategies in Chapter 6. There are many ways for you to save and invest for graduate school, especially if you are a year or more away from starting.

Loan forgiveness programs in Chapter 13. Imagine not having to repay your student loan. These programs can make that a reality.

Save money while in college in Chapter 15. There is a lot that you can do to save the money you already have.

Make college cheaper in Chapter 16. Why pay full price? Use these strategies to make your college less expensive.

Be a part-time student in Chapter 19. There is nothing wrong with working and going to school. Many graduate schools offer the options listed in this chapter.

When funding your education you need to take advantage of the various financial aid programs, low-cost student loans, tax advantages and, if possible, loan repayment options. Remember one advantage (or disadvantage depending on how you look at it) is that as a graduate student your financial need will usually be assessed based only on your income (and your spouse's if you have one), which means your parents are totally out of the picture. These programs are all detailed in previous chapters of this book. Here's a quick cheat sheet.

Tax breaks in Chapter 7. Save your tax dollars and put more money back in your pocket to pay for school.

Maximize your financial aid in Chapter 8. Each year over $238 billion in financial aid is awarded. You should lay your claim to what you deserve.

Get state resources to pay for school in Chapter 11. Your state has a lot of resources and even scholarships for students of all ages.

The best way to borrow money in Chapter 12. Borrowing money may be unavoidable. Learn where to borrow and how to borrow intelligently.

While financial aid and loans are important, there is no substitute for free money. When you were an undergraduate you looked for scholarships. As a graduate student, you will similarly look for fellowships. One major difference in finding money for graduate work is the importance of academics and research. A lot of your money may come from organizations that want to support your studies on a specific subject. They won't care about your involvement in extracurricular activities, leadership or community service like many of the scholarships for undergraduates. Instead, they will look at your commitment to the field of study, the topic of your research and what future impact you can make on our body of knowledge.

When you apply for fellowships, scholarships and grants as a graduate student, focus on demonstrating your long-term commitment to academics and research. Or if you are in a professional program such as business school or law school, show your commitment and future leadership potential within those communities. Your judges are no longer casual members of clubs or volunteers. They are the small circle of leaders in your future career field—professors, deans and industry leaders. To win their support, show them the intensity of your passion for your field and your ability to contribute to its advancement. Here are some tips for getting started with fellowships:

930.

Your school is your best source of fellowship aid

Your graduate school is the best source of money. Depending on your school and program there may be money for fellowships, which cover tuition and can even cover part of your living expenses. Most of these fellowships are merit-based rather than need-based. It's important to research these options before you apply.

In general most of this money is available for Ph.D. students who will be in the program for five to six years. Shorter programs like law school, business school and master's programs that are between two and three years offer much less funding, and awards are usually given to the most highly qualified applicants.

931.

Outside fellowships

Most fellowships are given by your department, which is why it is important to start your search for money at your school. However, there are fellowships awards by governmental and private organizations that support graduate and postgraduate study, research or work placement. They typically fund study in a specific area. The best part about fellowships is that they do not have to be repaid. Where do you find these awards? Take a look at these places:

Department and professional publications. Read newsletters distributed by your department, check the department bulletin board and look at professional publications in your area.

Your peers. There's probably a small circle of people who study your field. Ask fellow students about awards they know of or that they have won themselves.

Professors. Communicate your goals for the future so that if your professors come across an appropriate program or award they will think of you. Share ideas for research and employment. Your professors may be able to help you develop proposals to fund your ideas.

There are also fellowships that are national in scope that do not require you to study at a specific school. The following list is not meant to be comprehensive but to give you a starting point for fellowships.

932. AAUW Educational Foundation
http://www.aauw.org/fga/fellowships_grants/american.cfm
The *American Association of University Women American Fellowships* are for female doctoral degree candidates completing their dissertations or female scholars seeking funds for postdoctoral research leave from accredited institutions. Applicants must be U.S. citizens or permanent residents and are evaluated on the basis of academic accomplishment, teaching experience and active commitment to helping women and girls through service in their communities, professions or fields of research. There are 20 postdoctoral research leave fellowships that offer

one year of financial support. Fifty-one dissertation fellowships are available, as well as six publication grants for short-term/summer research.

933. AFCEA Ralph W. Shrader Scholarship, AFCEA Fellowship and Milton E. Cooper/Young AFCEAN Graduate School Scholarship
http://www.afcea.org
The Armed Forces Communications and Electronics Association offers several graduate student awards for electrical, computer, chemical or aerospace engineering, mathematics, physics, computer science, computer technology, electronics, communications technology, communications engineering or information management. You do not need to be affiliated with the U.S. military.

934. Alice W. Rooke Scholarship and Irene and Daisy MacGregor Memorial Scholarship
http://www.dar.org
If you are in medical school studying to become a doctor you can apply for these two scholarships sponsored by the National Society Daughters of the American Revolution. The *Daisy MacGregor Memorial Scholarship* is specifically for students studying psychiatric nursing at the graduate level.

935. American Astronautical Society Scholarships to the International Space University
http://astronautical.org/awards/scholarships
If you are interested in going to the International Space University summer session, you can attend for free with this award sponsored by the American Astronautical Society.

936. American Bar Association Law Student Division
http://www.abanet.org/lsd/
The website of the national organization of lawyers offers a clearinghouse of law school-related scholarships and competitions.

937. Andrew W. Mellon Fellowships in Humanistic Studies
http://www.mellon.org
The Woodrow Wilson National Scholarship Foundation sponsors this fellowship, which is for college seniors or graduates

How do I win a research grant?

When applying for grants, keep these points in mind:

How will your research benefit the field? Awarding grants is not a selfless task. The committee wants the bragging rights for backing research that advances the field. To fulfill this need, explain the potential significance of your research on the field. Show why your research is meaningful. Include specific applications of your research if they are not immediately apparent.

Your plan of action. It's important to convey that you have goals for your research, but it's equally important to explain how you're going to get there. An essential component of a grant proposal is an outline of your plan of action. Include measurable objectives, a timeline and budget. Make it clear that you have an organized plan for accomplishing your objectives.

Fit with the future you. The selection committee realizes that few people do research for philanthropic reasons. They want to know what's in it for you, your reasons for being interested in the research and how it fits with your future career plans. Explain how you hope to use what you learn in the future and what your future plans are.

Offer specifics. Be as specific as possible to show the seriousness of your efforts. For example, don't just offer your hypothesis. Describe the line of reasoning that you have taken to reach it. Offer an excerpt of the sources you plan to use. Giving them a taste of what you have found so far is a great way to demonstrate your commitment to the project.

who intend to pursue a career of teaching or scholarship in the humanities. Applicants must be applying to graduate school for a Ph.D. program in the humanities and must be U.S. citizens or legal permanent residents. Each year approximately 85 scholarships are available; each one covers full graduate tuition and fees for the first year of graduate school and includes a $17,500 stipend.

938. ANS Graduate Scholarship

http://www.ans.org/honors/scholarships/

The American Nuclear Society offers assistance to full-time graduate students who are pursuing advanced degrees in a nuclear-related field.

939. APF/COGDOP Graduate Research Scholarships

http://www.apa.org/apf/

The American Psychological Foundation gives this award to graduate students in psychology.

940. Association for Women in Science Graduate Awards

http://www.awis.org

This award is for female students enrolled in a behavioral, life, physical or social science or engineering program leading to a Ph.D. degree. Awards are given based on academic achievement, the importance of the research question addressed, the quality of the research and the applicant's potential for future contributions to science or engineering.

941. Bruce J. Heim Foundation Scholarship

http://www.asme.org

The American Society of Mechanical Engineers provides an award for member graduate students whose career goal is to further the exploration of space.

942. Compton Foundation, Inc.

http://www.comptonfoundation.org

The Compton Foundation's *Environmental and Sustainable Development Program* provides financial support to master's and doctoral degree candidates from Mexico, Central America and Sub-Saharan Africa who intend to focus their research and careers on the environmental issues of developing countries. To be eligible for a fellowship, master's degree students must be advanced or second-year students from programs that require graduates to complete a thesis or engage in an internship or other practical experience. For doctoral degree student fellowships, students must have an approved research proposal for work based in a developing country and must be seeking support for field research that will lead to their dissertation. The Environmental and Sustainable Development Program is funded in three-year cycles with $750,000 allotted to each cycle, but depending on the number of grants given out, individual scholarships may vary.

943. Consortium for Graduate Study in Management
http://www.cgsm.org
The *Consortium for Graduate Study in Management Fellowship* is for MBA study at a CGSM member school. Applicants must be U.S. citizens and members of one of the following minority groups: African American, Hispanic American or Native American. The fellowship covers full tuition and fees for two years of full-time study.

944. Dental Student and Minority Dental Student Scholarship
http://www.ada.org
If you are entering your second year in an accredited dental program you can apply for this award sponsored by the American Dental Association. It is designed to help minority and non-minority students with need pursue careers in dentistry.

945. Dr. James Watson Fellowship Program
http://www.gcsaa.org
If you are studying turfgrass science or a related field, the Golf Course Superintendents Association of America Foundation has an award for you.

946. Doctoral Scholars Forgivable Loan Program
http://students.sae.org/awdscholar/loans/doctoral/
The Society of Automotive Engineers assists promising engineering graduate students to pursue careers in teaching at the college level. Selection is based on scholastic achievement, desire to teach, interest in mobility technology and support of the SAE Collegiate Chapter Faculty advisor.

947. Doctoral Study Grants
http://www.abc-usa.org
The American Baptist Churches support Baptist students pursuing educational opportunities who plan to teach in a college or seminary in a field of study directly related to becoming ministerial leaders.

948. Fannie and John Hertz Foundation

http://www.hertzfndn.org

The Fannie and John Hertz Foundation provides approximately 24 graduate fellowships each year to students working towards a Ph.D. in the physical sciences. To be eligible, applicants must be students of the applied physical sciences, U.S. citizens or legal permanent residents and must be willing to morally commit to making their skills available to the United States in time of national emergency. Applicants may either be undergraduate seniors or ongoing graduate students.

949. Film and Fiction Scholarships

http://www.theihs.org

The Institute for Humane Studies supports filmmakers and writers who are pursuing a master of fine arts (MFA) degree in filmmaking, fiction writing or playwriting. Applicants must also have a demonstrated interest in classical liberal ideas.

950. FLAS Fellowships

http://www.ed.gov/programs/iegpsflasf/index.html

In an effort to encourage the study of languages that are considered of strategic importance to the country, the U.S. Department of Education has created the *FLAS Fellowship* to provide tuition and stipends to students undergoing advanced training in designated foreign languages. You don't have to major in the language but must study it in combination with another program. In fact, FLAS awards may go to students in a wide variety of humanities and social science graduate degree programs, as well as professional fields. Apply for the FLAS through your graduate program.

951. Foreign Affairs Fellowship Program

http://www.woodrow.org

The *Thomas R. Pickering Graduate Foreign Affairs Fellowship* is presented to students who are interested in joining the U.S. Department of State to pursue a career in foreign service. Applicants must be U.S. citizens who are seeking admission to a U.S. graduate school for the following academic year and who intend to enroll in a two-year full-time master's degree program related to foreign service (public policy, international affairs, public administration or academic fields such as business, economics, political science, sociology or foreign languages). Applicants must have an undergraduate GPA of 3.2 on a scale of 4.0 and must maintain a 3.2 GPA throughout participation in the program. The fellowship covers tuition, room, board and mandatory fees for the first two years of graduate study with reimbursement for books and one round-trip travel.

952. Fund for Justice and Education
http://www.abanet.org/fje/losfpage.html
The *American Bar Association Legal Opportunity Fund* was established to provide financial aid to minority law students. Applicants must be entering, first-year law students for the year that they apply, and they must have a minimum cumulative undergraduate GPA of 2.5 at the time of graduation or as of the last completed semester at time of application. Applicants must be U.S. citizens or permanent legal residents and must present proof of enrollment and plans to enroll in an ABA-accredited law school. The scholarship fund awards each recipient a one-time scholarship of $5,000, but the scholarship may be renewed for two more years provided recipients maintain satisfactory academic standards.

953. Golden Key Graduate Scholar Awards
http://goldenkey.org
If you are a member of the Golden Key Honor Society you can apply for one of twelve $10,000 scholarships for postbaccalaureate or professional study. You must plan to enroll in graduate school in the fall in which you receive the scholarship.

954. Graduate Assistance in Areas of National Need (GAANN)
This program provides fellowships to assist graduate students with financial need who plan to pursue the highest degree available in a field designated as an area of national need. Currently, these areas include: biology, chemistry, computer and information science, engineering, geological science, mathematics and physics. Contact your department for application information.

How do I write a winning fellowship essay?

In your essay focus on the progress you have made in your field. The best essay is one that gets the selection committee excited about your work and makes them want to fund your education so you can complete it. Tempt them with what you have done, reveal some early results even if they are only preliminary or describe the plans for your research. Give the selection committee a tantalizing view into what you are learning. Take advantage of knowing who is on the committee and what their interests are.

Give them something they can't get anywhere else. Don't just restate what's in your application or curriculum vitae. If you do this, you will simply waste space. Essays should provide information and insight about you that is not included in the applications.

Finally, don't be afraid to get personal. Reveal something about yourself. What motivated you to choose this area of study? What do you feel is the most exciting thing about the field? Who has been a mentor for you? What do you hope to accomplish after you get your degree? Answering a question like one of these will give the selection committee insight into your thoughts and help to distinguish you beyond your achievements.

955. Graduate Fellowship in the Field of Concrete

http://www.concrete.org

The American Concrete Institute gives this award to graduate students who are studying the field of concrete. You must have been accepted for graduate study in engineering, architectural or materials science.

956. Grant Programs for Medical Studies

http://www.pcusa.org/financialaid/

To aid Presbyterian Church members pursuing a postgraduate education in a medical profession, PCUSA sponsors this need-based grant. Applicants must be PCUSA church members who are in good academic standing and have financial need.

957. Henry Hecaen and Manfred Meier Neuropsychology Scholarships

http://www.apa.org/apf/

The American Psychological Foundation gives this award to graduate students who demonstrate need and have a promising career in the field of neuropsychology.

958. Henry Luce Foundation

http://www.hluce.org

The *Luce Scholars Program* provides stipends and internships for 18 young Americans to live and work in Asia to increase awareness of Asia among future leaders in American society. Applicants must be U.S. citizens with at least a bachelor's degree who are no more than 29 years old on September 1 of the year they would enter the program. Applicants cannot have had significant exposure to Asian culture or Asian studies. Applicants are nominated by 65 colleges and universities and should have a record of high achievement, outstanding leadership ability and a clearly defined career interest with evidence of potential for professional accomplishment.

959. Hispanic Scholarship Fund/National Society of Hispanic MBAs

http://www.nshmba.org

The *National Society of Hispanic MBAs/Hispanic Scholarship Fund Scholarships* provide financial aid to Latino graduate students working towards a master's degree in management/business. Scholarships are one-time awards and range from $2,500 to $15,000, but applications for renewal can be made every year. Applicants must be of Hispanic background (one parent Hispanic or both parents half Hispanic), must be U.S. citizens or legal permanent residents and must be accepted into a graduate management/business major at an accredited college or university for the term of application. Scholarships are awarded upon evaluation of academic achievement, contribution to the community, financial need, letters of recommendation and an essay.

960. Jacob K. Javits Fellowship Program

http://www.ed.gov/programs/jacobjavits/index.html

This program provides financial assistance to students who have demonstrated superior academic achievement, exceptional promise and financial need for graduate study leading to a doctoral or master's degree. The U.S. Department of Education awards fellowships in selected fields of study of the arts, humanities and social sciences.

961. Japanese American Citizens League Graduate Awards
http://www.jacl.org
The JACL offers scholarships to national JACL members who are attending graduate school. A personal statement, letter of recommendation, academic performance, work experience and community involvement are considered.

962. Japanese American Citizens League Law Scholarships
http://www.jacl.org
If you are a national JACL member and are studying law you can apply for this award.

963. Jeanne S. Chall Research Fellowship
https://www.literacyworldwide.org/about-us/awards-grants/ila-jeanne-s-chall-research-fellowship
The International Literacy Association supports member graduate students planning or beginning their dissertation on the field of reading.

964. Johnson F. Hammond, MD Memorial Scholarship
http://www.ama-assn.org
This scholarship is offered to medical students pursuing a career in medical journalism. The scholarship is a one-time award of $3,000. The *Jerry L. Pettis Memorial Scholarship* is offered to third- and fourth-year medical students who demonstrate interest and involvement in the field of science communications. The scholarship is a single award of $2,500. For both of these scholarships, applicants must be nominated by the dean of an AMA-approved medical school in order to be eligible. Financial need is not a consideration.

965. Medtronic Physio-Control Advanced Nursing Practice Scholarship
http://www.ena.org/foundation/grants/
The Emergency Nurses Association gives this award to promote

research and education in emergency care. Applicants must be nurses pursuing advanced clinical practice degrees to become clinical nurse specialists or nurse practitioners. Preference is given to applicants focusing on cardiac nursing.

966. Mexican American Legal Defense and Educational Fund

http://www.maldef.org/leadership/scholarships
The *Law School Scholarship Fund* is for students in their first, second or third year of law school. Applicants must have demonstrated involvement in and commitment to serve the Latino community through the legal profession, academic and financial achievement and financial need.

967. MLA Scholarship

http://www.mlanet.org/p/cm/ld/fid=303
This award sponsored by the Medical Library Association aids graduate students who are studying health sciences librarianship.

968. National Potato Council Scholarship

http://nationalpotatocouncil.org/events-and-programs/scholarship-program/
If you are in a graduate program studying a potato-related area, you can apply for this award sponsored by the National Potato Council.

969. Paul and Daisy Soros Fellows Program

http://www.pdsoros.org
The *Paul and Daisy Soros Fellowships* are two-year graduate fellowships for study in the U.S. for new Americans. Each fellowship is $20,000, paid in two installments. Applicants must be resident aliens, have been naturalized as U.S. citizens or must be the children of two naturalized citizens. Applicants must either have a bachelor's degree or be in their last year of undergraduate study. Applicants who have already obtained a bachelor's degree and are in the process of working on their graduate degree are also eligible for a fellowship unless they are in their third year or later of the same graduate program. Applicants must be under 30 years of age.

970. Philip Merrill College of Journalism

http://merrill.umd.edu/academics/masters-programs/fellow-ships-and-aid/

There are multiple fellowships available at the Philip Merrill College of Journalism as well as assistantships which offer both tuition remission and stipends.

971. Professional Engineers in Government (PEG)

http://www.nspe.org

The National Society of Professional Engineers offers this award to engineering students who are pursuing an MBA, master's degree in public administration or master's degree in engineering management and who are engineering interns or licensed professional engineers.

972. Rock Sleyster, MD Memorial Scholarship

http://www.ama-assn.org

Sponsored by the American Medical Association Foundation, this scholarship is a one-time, $2,500 scholarship offered to fourth-year medical students. Applicants must be U.S. citizens enrolled as students in U.S. or Canadian medical schools who aspire to specialize in psychiatry. Recipients are chosen on the basis of demonstrated interest in psychiatry, financial need and academic performance.

973. Ronald E. McNair Post Baccalaureate Achievement Program

http://www.ed.gov/programs/triomcnair/index.html

Created in 1996 to honor Dr. Ronald E. McNair, an astronaut and physicist who died in the Challenger explosion, this award helps students who are from similar backgrounds as Dr. McNair enroll in graduate study. McNair participants are generally from disadvantaged backgrounds and have demonstrated strong academic potential. You need to apply through your college.

974. Sidney M. Edelstein International Studentship

http://www.chemheritage.org

The Chemical Heritage Foundation offers this award to support the research of Ph.D. students in the chemical sciences. You must have filled all the requirements for your Ph.D. except for the dissertation.

975. Summer Graduate Research Fellowships

http://www.theihs.org

The Institute for Humane Studies supports graduate students who are interested in scholarly research in the classical liberal tradition. You must be a graduate student in an area related to the classical liberal tradition and should be focusing on a discrete writing project.

976. William F. Miller, MD Postgraduate Education Recognition Awards

http://www.arcfoundation.org/awards/postgraduate/miller.cfm

The American Association for Respiratory Care provides this award to respiratory therapists pursuing advanced degrees.

977.

Research Grants

There are various types of research grants for graduate students. Provided by the federal and state governments, graduate schools or private organizations, this form of aid does not need to be repaid. Grants are usually awarded based on a specific research proposal and pay for such things as travel, research-related materials including specialized equipment and miscellaneous expenses. Here are a few examples of research grants:

978. American Institute for Contemporary German Studies Grant

http://www.aicgs.org

If you are a Ph.D. candidate doing research in the cultural, political, historical, economic or social aspects of modern Germany you can apply for this research grant.

979. American Society of Safety Engineers

http://www.asse.org

If you are working on your advanced degree and have a research project that you need to get funded, take a look at the *Research Fellowship Program.*

980. American-Scandinavian Academic Fellowships and Grants

http://www.amscan.org

The American-Scandinavian Foundation gives grants to graduate students who want to conduct research in Scandinavia. Some language proficiency is required.

981. AMS Graduate Fellowship in the History of Science

http://www.ametsoc.org/amsstudentinfo/scholfeldocs/gradfellowshipprogram.html

The American Meteorological Society offers this fellowship to students writing dissertations on the history of the atmospheric or related oceanic or hydrologic sciences.

982. Fine Arts Grant, Painting

http://www.alphadeltakappa.org

Alpha Delta Kappa sponsors this grant for students pursuing a graduate degree program or other study course or extensive project. Applicants must submit, along with references and a completed application, 20 professional-quality color slides of 15 pieces of original work in painting media completed within the last two years.

983. Fine Arts Grant, Strings

http://www.alphadeltakappa.org

Alpha Delta Kappa aids string performers who want to continue their studies in graduate school. You must submit along with your application a tape or CD of your performance.

984. Gaige Fund Award and Raney Fund Award

http://www.asih.org

The American Society of Ichthyologists and Herpetologists supports graduate students who plan to become herpetologists. Applicants must be members of the ASIH, and the award may be used for museum or laboratory study, travel, fieldwork or other activities that will enhance their careers and their contributions to the science of herpetology.

What makes a good letter of recommendation when applying for a fellowship or grant?

Throughout your applications you have the opportunity to praise yourself and your accomplishments in glowing words of admiration. Recommendations offer professors and others the opportunity to do the same and to confirm that you are as great as you say you are. To get the most powerful recommendations possible, follow these strategies for selecting and preparing your recommenders:

Be strategic about whom you ask. The most important principle for selecting recommenders is how well they know you. You may have received the highest grade in class, but if your professor couldn't pick you out from a crowd, he or she is not the best person to ask.

Do the grunt work for your recommenders. To make writing recommendations easier, provide all of the background information and forms they need

Include a cover letter. Write a brief letter describing the awards you are applying for, their deadlines and helpful reminders of information they may want to include in the recommendations.

Don't forget your curriculum vitae. Like a resume this is a concise overview of your academic honors, course-work and achievements.

If you put some thought into whom you ask and make your recommender's job as easy as possible you'll be rewarded with a strong letter of recommendation.

985. Graduate and Postgraduate Study and Research in Poland

http://www.thekf.org

This award from the Kosciuszko Foundation helps fund graduate research at universities in Poland. If you are a graduate student and are able to conduct research in Polish you can apply for this research grant.

986. Harry S. Truman Dissertation Year Fellowships
http://www.trumanlibrary.org/grants/
The Harry S. Truman Library Institute for National and International Affairs offers graduate students who are writing their dissertations funds for study.

987. Harry S. Truman Research Grant
http://www.trumanlibrary.org/grants/
The Harry S. Truman Library Institute for National and International Affairs offers research funds for graduate and post-doctoral scholars.

988. International Research and Studies Program
http://www.ed.gov/programs/iegpsirs/applicant.html
This program supports surveys, studies and instructional materials developed to improve instruction in modern foreign languages, area studies and other international fields to provide full understanding of the places in which the foreign languages are commonly used. It is administered by colleges, which means you must check with your department for more information. This award is funded through the U.S. Department of Education.

989. Normand R. Dubois Memorial Scholarship
http://www.entsoc.org/about_esa/
The Entomological Society of America supports research by graduate students on the use of biologically based technologies to protect and preserve forests. Applicants must be pursuing a master's or doctorate at an accredited university and propose research to advance knowledge of the best way to preserve forests using biological materials.

990. NSF Graduate Research Fellowship Program
http://www.nsfgrfp.org
The *National Science Foundation Graduate Research Fellowships* are three-year fellowships for the fields of science, mathematics and engineering. Applicants must be U.S. citizens, nationals or permanent resident aliens. Applicants should be pursuing either their master's in mathematical, physical, biological, behavioral and social sciences; engineering, the history of science and the philosophy of science or a doctoral research-based degree in science education. There is a $27,500 stipend for 12-month tenures and a cost-of-education allowance of $10,500 per tenure year.

991. Research Fellowship Program

http://www.asse.org

The American Society of Safety Engineers awards this research fellowship to promote safety and health research. You must be a graduate student working toward a master's or Ph.D. Preference is given to applied safety-health projects that have broad appeal.

992.

Get paid to step into a classroom

When you were in college, you may have looked up to your knowledgeable teaching assistant, the person who bridged the gap between students and professors. For many graduate students, you will now have the chance to be that admired teaching assistant.

Many graduate schools supplement students' educations with employment opportunities to teach undergraduate classes. For some schools, such employment is a requirement to graduate or a part of the financial aid package.

Keep in mind that you don't have to only teach in the subject area that you are studying. The undergraduate college may be shorthanded in other areas where you have some specialization. For example, let's say that your undergraduate major was English and now you are getting your master's in economics. At your college they require that every incoming freshman undergraduate take a basic essay-writing class. You could legitimately be a teaching assistant for this course even though it has no relationship to your present study of economics. Take a look at the undergraduate classes where you have some background and approach the professors to see if they need teaching assistants. You can do the same at the continuing education school of your college and even at local private-tutoring academies.

993.

Become a paid researcher

As a graduate student you have had a lot of experience researching a subject. Your professors are both teachers and researchers, and most will be conducting long-term research projects. Approach a few of the professors that you find interesting and see if there is any need for a research assistant. Professors often receive grant money to help them with their research, and some of the money is usually used to hire graduate students to help with research.

994.

Enter an academic contest

The research that you are already doing and the papers that you are already writing can win you money through academic contests. These are similar to essay contests except that the topics are usually very specific to your area of study. Take a look at foundations and research organizations in your field. Flip through the professional journals and you'll find various contests where you can enter papers and research that you have done to win prizes. Here are some examples of academic contests:

995. American Marketing Association

http://www.marketingpower.com

The *Hans B. Thorelli Best Paper Award* and the *S. Tamer Cavusgil Best Paper Award* are for articles published in the *Journal of International Marketing*. The *Hans B. Thorelli Best Paper Award* consists of $1,000 and a plaque, presented to the author(s) of the article that is deemed to have most significantly contributed to international marketing theory or thought. The *S. Tamer Cavusgil Best Paper Award* is awarded to the author(s) whose article best advances the practice of international marketing management. Awards are presented by the editorial board of the *Journal of International Marketing*.

996. CEC Graduate Student Poster Contest

http://ceramics.org/acers-community/award-winners-resources
The American Ceramic Society is looking for posters on research performed in ceramic science. Graduate student winners are recognized at the annual meeting banquet of the society.

997. Essay Prize Contest

http://www.ptc.org
To promote the development and use of telecommunications in the Pacific Hemisphere, the Pacific Telecommunications Council sponsors this essay contest for graduate students and students who have graduated from graduate school within the past five years.

998. International Graduate Student Paper Contest

http://asmcommunity.asminternational.org
ASM International sponsors an annual paper contest that recognizes the best graduate student technical paper in the field of materials science or engineering.

999. SCS Dissertation Award

http://www.cmstudies.org
The Society for Cinema Studies offers a dissertation award with a cash prize of $1,000. You must be a member of SCS and have completed your dissertation.

1000.

Employer-paid education

In certain industries a professional degree is seen as a necessity. Companies in these areas may offer as a benefit of employment the option to go to graduate school on the company's tab. The catch: After you graduate you must work for the company for a minimum number of years—often the same amount of time that you were in school.

Consulting companies are perhaps the most well known for their support of employees who want to get their MBA. In exchange for working after graduation the company will pay for all or most of your educational expenses. It's a win-win for both the company and the employee. Check with your employer to see if they offer any benefits for getting an advanced degree. If your company is small you might even be able to work out a deal with the owner. If you don't fulfill your end of the bargain by not working for the company after you graduate then you must pay back the amount of money that the company spent on your education.

Conclusion

Onward To Your Future

Congratulations! You've come a long way since starting this book. You now know 1000 ways to make college a reality including winning scholarships, maximizing financial aid, saving on taxes, cutting tuition prices and getting money from your state, the military and the government. We hope that whether you started this book with a comfortable college nest egg or empty pockets that you now feel more confident about finding your own path to pay for college.

Now that you know all of the ways that you can pay for college, it is time to actually put some of these methods to work. You may need to tweak some of the strategies to fit your own situation, and of course, you should try to combine strategies in order to reach your goal.

We want to conclude this book by sharing with you the one thousand and first way to pay for college, which is:

1001.

Be creative

Creativity is what enables any student to find the money to pay for school. It fact, it is creativity that is the source of many of the strategies in this book. It is also creativity that will help you implement some of these solutions in your own life. Who knows? You may even develop a brand new way to pay for college. (If you do please send us a note so we can include it in our next edition!) Remember, there is no cookie cutter way to pay for college. There is no "right" way to go about finding the money you need. If you can add creativity to the knowledge that you have gained from this book, we believe that you will find your own path to making college possible.

We would like to leave you with a story about a student. When we first met her, her situation looked bleak. She was an average student, and it was clear that she couldn't count on an academic scholarship. Her father had recently lost his job, and the family was struggling on her mother's income to pay the bills and feed her brothers and sisters. Yet, when she applied for financial aid, she was awarded only loans and a small grant. She was accepted to several private colleges that all cost more than $35,000 per year, which was far more than her family could afford even with the grant. Plus, the colleges were unable to offer more help.

This was her situation when we met. We asked her what her dream was for the future. It turned out she wanted to go to college to become a doctor. It was her lifelong dream that now seemed impossible. We gave her some suggestions and offered her encouragement. That was the last we heard from her until recently, when she wrote us a letter. She explained what had happened since we met.

She had accepted our advice to go to a community college for the first two years. That saved her family a huge amount of money and allowed her to work, save and fulfill her basic education requirements. During those two years she worked two jobs. One was as an assistant to a professor. She created this job by approaching her professor and asking if he needed a research assistant. She did everything from researching information for the professor's new book to returning his books to the library. It was perfect since she could work between classes. Her other job was as a waitress, which was not a job she necessarily enjoyed, but the money she earned in tips made it worth it.

She invested all of her money into certificate of deposits and mutual funds. After two years, she saved enough money to transfer into her state college. She earned an automatic transfer scholarship, which she had researched before applying. She also applied for several university and private scholarships and won a few. With her family still struggling and her father still out of work, she continued to work during college. One job that she found particularly rewarding was starting her own English conversation tutoring business. There were many international students on campus who were trying to learn English. She ran small classes at a nearby coffeeshop. She also decided to borrow some money in student loans.

Two years later she graduated on time with a degree in biology. She spent the next year working in a hospital, which only confirmed her love of medicine. This year she was accepted into medical school, and while she knows it won't be easy, she no longer worries about how she'll pay for it. The fact that she was able to pay for all four years of college has given her the confidence that she can always find a way to pay for her education.

We love getting letters like this, but this was extra special to us since we had seen the "before" picture. When we met she had no clue how to pay for college and doubted whether she would even be able to go. While it was by no means an easy route, it was clear that she found an inner drive and resilience. She used her resources and made the best of it. She was creative in her approach and never once wavered in her focus on obtaining her education.

And the medical school that she will attend in the fall is none other than our old alma mater, Harvard.

Learn from this student's example. She is just one of thousands of students who are successfully paying their way through college. Don't be afraid to take your future into your own hands, and remember that there is no better investment that you can make than in your education.

We wish you the best!

Index

B

D

H

I

J

K

L